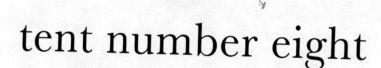

tent number eight

Gloyd

McCoy

2011

GLOYD MCCOY

tent number eight

An Investigation of the Girl Scout Murders

& the Trial of Gene Leroy Hart

TATE PUBLISHING *& Enterprises*

Published by Tate Publishing & Enterprises, LLC
127 E. Trade Center Terrace | Mustang, Oklahoma 73064 USA
1.888.361.9473 | www.tatepublishing.com

Tate Publishing is committed to excellence in the publishing industry. The company reflects the philosophy established by the founders, based on Psalm 68:11,
"The Lord gave the word and great was the company of those who published it."

Published in the United States of America

ISBN: 978-1-61777-632-8
History, United States, State & Local, Southwest (AZ, NM, OK, TX)
11.06.14

dedication

For Penny, Cody, Gabriela, and Jazmin

acknowledgments

The author wishes to acknowledge the role of his parents, Causine and Leota McCoy, in making the publication of this book possible. He thanks his wife and children for their support. This book is for them.

The newspaper reporters from across Oklahoma who left a printed record of this case are Oklahoma heroes. The participants and observers of this case who provided information to the author are also thanked. The staff at the State of Oklahoma Historical Library are thanked for their help. Tate Publishing Company, especially editor Briana Johnson, is thanked for their help and advice.

table of contents

the story to come

On June 12, 1977, three Oklahoma girl scouts, Lori Lee Farmer, age eight; Doris Denise Milner, age ten; and Michele Heather Guse, age nine, left their homes in the Tulsa, Oklahoma area for the final time. The girls did not know they would never return home.

The girls traveled by bus to Camp Scott in northeastern Oklahoma to participate in the American tradition of summer camp. Upon arrival, the girls, who had never met before, were assigned to share tent number eight, the tent at the farthest outpost of the camp. Sometime during their first night there, Lori, Denise, and Michele were murdered. They were murdered in a manner so horrific it defied any concept of human dignity. It was a terrible way to end three young lives.

It was the beginning of a new age in Oklahoma. Brian Barber of the Tulsa World wrote:

> [T]here lives weren't the only things stolen that [night]. A sense of innocence was ripped from every man and woman by the beginning and then they were denied a conclusion ending the Oklahoma horror story.[1]

Denise Milner died of strangulation. She was sexually molested. Michele Guse was killed by blows to her head. She had been sexually assaulted. Lori Farmer died from blows to the brain. She too had been sexually assaulted. Hollywood could not come up with anything as horrifying as what occurred in and around tent number eight that fateful night.

On the morning the girls went to camp, they had no idea of the danger to come. They had no reason to fear for their safety. They were where they were supposed to be. There would be adults there to protect them. Never in the history of the Girl Scouts had there been multiple violent deaths at a Girl Scout camp. No one, especially the girls, anticipated that horror was about to take place.

At a later civil trial concerning the deaths of the three girls, Francis Hesselbein of the National Girl Scout Organization testified the three girls were the only victims of violence in the seventy-three years history of the Girl Scouts.[2] Over thirty million girls had participated in camping activities. Such was a remarkable safety record.

Ms. Hesselbein did not mention one prior victim. A Girl Scout counselor was murdered in 1963. Margaret "Peggy" Beck, age sixteen, was sexually assaulted and strangled until she died at the Flying G Girl Scout Camp near Golden, Colorado. On a Saturday night her tent mate had checked into the camp's infirmary due to illness. Peggy was sleeping alone. The next tent was seventy-five yards away from everyone else.

When Peggy was found dead in her tent the next morning, the camp staff believed she had died of natural causes. Her tent was cleaned, and her personal items were packed to be sent home. Authorities were not called until eight hours after her body was discovered.

An autopsy was conducted. When the results were announced, scout officials were shocked. Peggy had been sexually assaulted and strangled. Over 300 people were questioned, but the crime remains unsolved today.

Peggy Beck's murder was mentioned as a possible link to be checked early in the Oklahoma investigation. Robert B. Allen of *The Oklahoma City Times* wrote, "The sex slayings of the Tulsa area girls bore some of the similarities of an unsolved assault murder of a Denver girl while she was on an outing."[3]

Oklahoma officials checked out the Beck murder but were told the chief suspect was deceased.[4] The Beck case is still open and listed on various unsolved crimes lists.

Although her death was not at a Girl Scout camp, another young Girl Scout's death received substantial notoriety. In 1975, Marcia Trimble, age nine, was abducted, sexually assaulted, and murdered in Nashville, Tennessee. Her body was not found until Easter Sunday over a month after her disappearance. She was found in a neighbor's garage, a place that had been previously searched. At the time of her disappearance, she was delivering Girl Scout cookies. Marcia Trimble's death was called the end of an age of innocence for Nashville.[5]

For decades, Marcia Trimble's murder was unsolved and haunted her family and the entire city of Nashville.[6] However, there was an ending to that story. DNA evidence helped solve the crime over thirty years later. In July 2009, a jury convicted Jerome Barrett of the crime.

Although the Tennessee prosecutors presented evidence that Barrett had made some incriminating statements to other jail inmates, the prosecutor's only real evidentiary link of Barrett to Marcia Trimble was the fact that sperm found on her blouse contained his DNA. It is hard to justify a man's sperm on the blouse of a dead nine-year-old girl. Defense counsel could not explain or even offer an innocent explanation of this evidence.

Barrett, a black man who had led a life whose primary purpose appeared to be committing the crime of rape, had not been a suspect at the time of the murder. The crime occurred in a white middle-class section of Nashville. Barrett would have stood out, so they said. None of the persons who gave information about Marcia's whereabouts ever mentioned a black man.

The police and prosecutor had long assumed that Marcia had been killed by someone in the neighborhood. One neighborhood boy was arrested, but no charges were filed. Many of the original investigators scoffed at the idea that Barrett committed the crime. Barrett did not fit the evidence they had found.

In Tennessee, forensic analysis and DNA evidence solved the crime. Although there were still many questions as to how Barrett abducted Marcia Trimble and why he killed her, the identity of the perpetrator was resolved. In Oklahoma, the murders of Lori, Denise, and Michele remain unsolved.

There will never be a dramatic DNA finding regarding the Oklahoma case. No samples are available for any future DNA testing. Oklahoma officials did not take care of any of the other evidence. Law enforcement was sloppy with what evidence they found. For years the evidence of the case was kept in an old dusty jail cell. It is highly doubtful that the State of Oklahoma could put together a trial on the case unless they had an outright confession.

The murder of Lori, Denise, and Michele and the events thereafter is the dysfunctional event in Oklahoma history. The story can never be left behind, and the painful memories cannot be put to rest. There is no final explanation to close the matter. The so-called Oklahoma Girl Scout Murder Case will never be solved.

Gene Leroy Hart, a Cherokee Indian with prior felony convictions, was charged with committing the murders. Hart had several burglary convictions. He had also pled guilty to two rape charges. He had escaped from jail and had been on the lam for four years when Lori, Denise, and Michelle were murdered. He was the logical suspect. A jury acquitted him.

Law enforcement and prosecutorial personnel were convinced then and remain convinced today that the jury had found a killer not guilty. Compounding the mysterious nature of the case, weeks after his acquittal, Gene Leroy Hart died of a heart attack. Justice was served some said. He was poisoned others said.

This book will tell the story of the events that began in 1977. This book, however, cannot provide the ultimate answer to the question that has begged to be answered since that night: "Who killed the Girl Scouts?"

"There's a growing lore to the Girl Scout murders," said S. M. "Buddy" Fallis, the prosecutor in the case.[7] Former Mayes County district attorney, Gene Haynes, was quoted in 2008 saying:

> The families of the victims certainly deserve an ending to the case. This is one of the most infamous cases in state history. Over thirty years later my office still receives inquires about the case, as well as

letters and calls from people claiming to know who committed the murders.[8]

Hopefully, the reader will be able to see why things turned out the way they did in the 1979 trial and gain insight into this important part of Oklahoma history. Who killed the Girl Scouts? No one will ever be able to answer that question with certainty.

the murder site

Lori, Denise, and Michele were killed at Camp Scott located in Mayes County. Camp Scott had been operated by the Magic Empire Council of Girl Scouts since 1928. The Magic Empire Council covered a six-county area of Oklahoma (Craig, Mayes, Osage, Payne, Rogers, and Tulsa).

Generations of girls had attended camp at the location. David Gustafson from *The Paper*, a Pryor, Oklahoma, newspaper, wrote, "At the height of its popularity, Camp Scott was the home to thousands of girls from northeast Oklahoma who frolicked in the wilderness, learning arts and crafts and the Girl Scout way of life."[9]

Camp Scott was located near the town of Locust Grove, Oklahoma. The land was hilly and covered with trees. It was a wilderness area covering 410 acres.

The camp was only a few miles from a highway on which hundreds, sometimes thousands, of cars traveled every day. Despite that fact, campers had the feeling they were in the middle of nowhere. The remoteness of the area makes it apparent why a crime such as occurred in 1977 could happen.

Camp Scott was named in honor of H. J. "Scotty" and Florence Scott, long-time supporters of the boy and girl scout organizations. The couple donated the land that became a gruesome murder site. The land was acquired in 1928 and had remained unchanged except for the few buildings of the campground.

Locust Grove is approximately thirty-four miles east of Tulsa, twenty-three miles from Tahlequah, Oklahoma, and forty-one miles from the Arkansas border. The town was named for the locust tree that grows in the area.

An area near what later became the town of Locust Grove was the site of a Civil War battle on July 3, 1862. Approximately 250 Union troops surprised and defeated a similarly-sized battery of Confederate soldiers. Many of the Confederate soldiers were Cherokee Indians. The Cherokee Nation sided with the Confederacy during the Civil War due to their unfair treatment by the United States of America, most notably the Trail of Tears.

Many of the Cherokee soldiers from the Battle of Locust Grove escaped to Tahlequah and told their tribe what had occurred. The Battle of Locust Grove led to much disillusion among the Cherokees about the Confederate cause.

In 1977 there was much disillusion among the Cherokee people regarding the charging of one of their own with the dastardly crimes described in this book. Cherokee people helped hide Gene Leroy Hart from law enforcement. The Cherokee Nation donated money to defend him in court.[10]

Many have said it was the "Indian influence" that caused Hart's acquittal. However, no Indian was on the jury. The reason Gene Leroy Hart, the accused perpetrator of one of the cruelest crimes in Oklahoma history, was acquitted was the prosecutors did not prove him guilty beyond a reasonable doubt. The story is that simple. The acquittal of Hart was not based on any "influence" but the lack of evidence.

Gloyd McCoy

their last day ever

Lori, Denise, and Michele arrived at Camp Scott on Sunday June 12, 1977, along with 140 other campers at approximately 2:30 p.m. The girls were scheduled to stay at camp for two weeks. Earlier that morning, the three girls and their parents joined the rest of the campers in front of the Magic Empire Headquarters in Tulsa. After good-byes, the three girls got on the bus.

The girls did not know each other. There was no interchange between the girls or their families at the time of departure. The thought they would be forever linked was not a consideration. The departure was uneventful.

After an hour or so journey, the bus caravan left the main highway and went down a narrow road known as "the Cookie Trail." The name of the road was in honor of the cookie sales, which supported the Girl Scout Organization. After a short drive down the trail, the girls arrived at Camp Scott.

The girls met on the bus. When they arrived at camp, they became tent mates.

The girls were assigned to tent number eight. The tent and the area around it would be their place of doom.

Investigators would later surmise that the perpetrator chose tent number eight due to its location. Tent number eight was the most remote tent and closest to the edge of camp.

A fourth girl was supposed to be in tent number eight. However, a mix-up in camp registration forms had incorrectly placed her in the wrong unit. She was going to be moved and assigned to tent number eight. Because of an approaching thunderstorm, camp officials decided to wait until the next day to make the switch. The decision to wait saved the girl's life.

The girl's name was never mentioned in any of the media reports. There was discussion she was never told of her close brush with infamy.

Strange events had occurred at Camp Scott in the months preceding the murders. In April 1977, a weekend camp was cut short when someone ransacked a cabin. Over the summer, personal items had begun to disappear from the camp. A note was found inside an empty donut box that said, "We are on a mission to kill three girls in tent one." That note was disregarded because it also contained statements about Martians. A fake body was also found hanging in effigy.

One might speculate the parents of the girls and other girls' parents might have canceled summer camp if that information had been disclosed. Would the girls' stay at Camp Scott have been cancelled if their parents had known of the claimed events? One can only speculate. As in any such situation, there are "what ifs." Interestingly, none of these facts were ever linked to the man charged with the murders. The note on the "mission" even said, "We are on a mission."

The temperature that day was in the high 90s, hot and humid. A storm front was moving toward the camp, and it was expected the front would bring cooler weather as well as a thunderstorm.

Camp Scott was divided into several sections, each named after an Indian tribe. Twenty-seven girls, including the three future victims, were assigned to the Kiowa Unit, which included tent number eight.

Tent number eight was the farthest tent away from the main area. The tent was 150 yards from the nearest counselor. Because of the foliage, tent number eight could not be seen from the counselor's area.

The camping ground as well as the surrounding area was very dense with trees and plants. An Oklahoma State Bureau of Investigation agent, Harvey Pratt, who also happened to be American Indian, said of the area: "Those hills were so dark. The canopy of trees was so thick, and at night, you couldn't see where the trees ended and the sky began"[11]

Eventually, the expected thunderstorm came upon Camp Scott. When the storm hit the camp, at approximately 6:00 p.m., Lori, Denise, and Michele were at the dining tent eating.

The storm was not severe by Oklahoma standards. However, the rain was heavy, and there was thunder and lightning. There was no danger of tornado activity. Ironically, years later, when it was announced that a verdict had been reached in the trial, it began to rain.

Lori, Denise, and Michele waited at the dining tent until the storm subsided. They then went to tent number eight. They were tired.

They would need a good night's sleep as their next day was full of planned activities, so they thought. They did not know or anticipate that soon they would be dead.

What happened in the tent before the criminal event is unknown. Perhaps the girls talked about camp and got acquainted. Perhaps they giggled and told stories. Perhaps the girls were scared. For some reason never explained, the tent was a long way from the other campers. That fact and the darkness surrounding them could have raised the girls' anxiety level.

sounds in the night

The first evening of camp, a moaning, guttural sound was heard in the woods near the Kiowa area. The moaning was heard at approximately 1:30 a.m. Whether the three girls heard the sounds is not known. It is also not known if the sounds were made by the killer or killers. The report of sounds adds a spooky perception to the events. A counselor, Carla Wilhite, an Oklahoma State University coed, went out to investigate.

Standing at the intersection of a trail, 150 yards from tent number eight and the dirt road that led up to the main camp, Wilhite stood for a moment and listened. The moaning stopped. Wilhite turned to leave. The sound began again.

Wilhite swept the area with her flashlight. The moaning stopped again. Telling herself it was probably an animal, she returned to her tent. She did not seek help. The sound had stopped. She did not want to wake up another counselor. Besides, it was dark, and she would have to walk a ways. Whoever she asked to come with her would probably grumble. She didn't want anyone to think she was scared or that she couldn't handle her job.

She went to sleep. She would sleep peacefully.

Campers from four other areas of the camp later reported they heard moaning sounds during the night. A light shining in the woods was also reported.

Wilhite should have called the camp staff together for an investigation of the sounds and light. Another alternative would have been to call the county sheriff or the highway patrolman who lived just down the road. Nothing was done.

Carla Wilhite chose to go to bed despite the fact she was perplexed by the sounds. The best way to avoid sounds in the night is to go to sleep. She would regret her failure to call for help forever.

At the later trial, Wilhite would testify to the sounds. However, the prosecutors made no argument that the sounds were made by Gene Leroy Hart or told the jury what the sounds were and especially did not offer any criticism of the camp staff for failing to investigate the sounds. Neither did the prosecutors make any argument that the sounds were those of the victims. The only thing said at the trial was that sounds had been heard.

At around 2:00 a.m., the flap on tent number seven in the Kiowa Unit was pulled open, and someone looked inside. Three of the four scouts were asleep. One girl was not. She could see in the darkness a beam of light from a flashlight and the silhouette of a figure. The flap closed.

The "figure" moved toward tent number eight. The girl in tent number seven did not know what to do. So she did nothing. Why the girls in tent number seven were bypassed is one of the many mysteries of the case.

At approximately 3:00 a.m., a girl in the Cherokee section of the camp heard a scream. She sprang up on her cot. The scream came from the direction of the Kiowa Camp, which was approximately two city blocks away.

The girl checked her watch for the time. She then awoke one of her tent-mates. The two girls did not hear anything. They did not know what to do. So they did nothing.

Later Girl Scout officials discounted any reports of screams heard in the night. Robert B. Allen of the *Oklahoma City Times* reported, "There were reports that at least two of the girls [at the camp] had heard screams around 3:00 a.m. Monday but some camp authorities discounted them. One employee of the camp said, 'Girls often hear things and scream and giggle during their first night of encampment.'"[12] During the later investigation, Girl Scout officials made sure to present a version of what happened in such a way as to detour any fault on their parts.

Around the same time, a scout in the Quapaw Unit heard a girl scream. Someone was crying out, "Momma, Momma." The girl did not know what to do. So she did nothing. After hearing nothing else, the girl lay back down and went to sleep. She, unlike the girls in tent number eight, would wake up in the morning. "Momma, Momma," the ultimate cry of despair was never heard again.

In 1985, in a civil suit involving the murders at Camp Scout, a former scout told of the screams. Marilea Tennant, then sixteen, testified she reported screams at 3:00 a.m. A counselor told her to ignore them.[13]

In the hundreds of articles written about the murders of the three girls, not a single article was written criticizing Camp Scott officials or the Magic Empire Council for lack of security or failure to respond to obvious signs of danger. It was as if the Girl Scout hierarchy was granted immunity from criticism. The only critics of the scout organization were the parents of the three girls; the Girl Scout organization was effective in damage control.

the letters

Although it is not known what all took place in tent number eight prior to the murders, one thing is certain. Before they died, each of the three girls participated in one of the rituals of summer camp. They each wrote a letter. Little did they know that it would be the last letter they would ever write.

Michele Guse wrote her last letter to her Aunt Karen:

> Dear Aunt Karen
>
> How are you? I am fine. I am writing from camp. We can't go outside because it is storming. Me and my tentmates are in the last tent in our unit. My tentmates are Denise Milner and Lori Farmer. My room is shades of purple.
>
> Love
> Michele[14]

Michele's father, Richard, would say years later he believed his daughter may have had some type of premonition that she would not return home. When she left, his daughter hugged everyone for a longer time than she usually did. She also stressed to her mother to remember to water her African violets.

GeorgeAnn Guse said her daughter was an active and athletic young girl. "She was very excited [about going to camp], and she sat on my lap and told me that she was going to miss me."

Michele's father would go to Camp Scott to help search for clues. Near where tent number eight was located, he found a scrap of paper on which a letter had been started. He recognized his daughter's handwriting. Michele was starting another letter when something happened to stop her. The paper said simply, "Dear Momma and Daddy." As he read the words, Richard Guse began to sob.

Lori Farmer wrote her letter to her parents and siblings:

> Dear Mom and Dad and Misti and Jo and Chad and Kathy
>
> We're just getting ready to go to bed. It's 7:45.
>
> We're at the beginning of a storm and having a lot of fun.
>
> I've met two new friends, Michele Guse and Denise Milner. I'm sharing a tent with them.
>
> It started raining on the way back from dinner. We're sleeping on cots.
>
> I couldn't wait to write. We're all writing letters now cause there's hardly anything else to do.
>
> With Love
> Lori[15]

Lori Farmer's mother, Sheri, had a theory on her daughter's last moments. "Lori took two decks of cards with her to camp. One deck was found neat and in its case. The other deck had been strewn all over her sleeping bag. I imagine she was a bit nervous and excited by her first night at camp and probably couldn't sleep. She must have had her flashlight out and was playing solitaire when the killer came into the tent."[16]

Going to camp had been Lori's idea. Mrs. Farmer had picked the camp because it "sounded like a really fun place to go."

Mrs. Farmer was the one who took Lori to the bus. "And she never came back," she said. Mrs. Farmer remembers Lori leaving on the bus and thinking how young she looked. In fact, because she had been advanced a grade in school, Lori was the youngest camper at Camp Scott.[17]

Lori had been a Girl Scout for two years. One of the reasons it was decided to send her to Camp Scott's first summer session was because it featured photography as one of the crafts to be learned.[18]

Lori had expressed an interest in learning photography. She wanted to learn everything. She was going to have the opportunity to learn how to develop photographs using darkroom techniques.

Denise Milner wrote her letter to her mother:

Dear Mom

I don't like camp. It's awful.

The first day it rained.

I have three new friends named Glenda, Lori, and Michele.

Michele and Lori are my roommates.

Mom, I don't want to stay at camp for two weeks.

I want to come home and see Kassie and everybody.

Your loving child.
Denise Milner[19]

Days before leaving for camp, Denise Milner started to worry about going to Camp Scott and wanted to back out. She had never attended camp. She had planned to go with some of her friends. The friends, however, had backed out. The friends had waited until the last minute to let Denise know they were not going.

Denise was faced with the prospect of going to camp and not knowing anyone. Denise's mother convinced her to go ahead and go to camp. Mrs. Milner was proud of her daughter for selling enough cookies to earn the camping trip. There were many reasons to be proud of her daughter.

Denise was a straight A student and had been accepted to the prestigious Carver Middle School, a Tulsa magnet school for exceptional children. Denise was looking forward to going to the school. She was not, however, looking forward to going to camp.

At camp, a homesick Denise had asked a counselor if she could call her mother. The counselor suggested Denise go to sleep, and if she was still homesick in the morning she would be allowed to make the call. It was a call that would never be made.

Denise's father, Walter, a police officer, took her death especially hard. Years later he would remark he thought constantly about his little girl who called him "Da" because when she was small she could not pronounce *Dad*. She also could not pronounce *grandmother* or *grandfather*. She would call them "Meemo" and "Grandpo." Mr. Milner said, "I guess I was thinking about the sweet sixteen birthday party she would have had." He began to cry.[20]

"oh, my god!"

The sun began to rise over Camp Scott at approximately 6:00 a.m. on Monday, June 13, 1977. A counselor, Carla Wilhite, the same counselor who had heard the moans the night before, awoke early and left her tent to go take a shower.

The second day of camp seemed off to a promising start. The sun was shining brightly. Unfortunately, that day would be the last day anyone would camp there.[21] It would be a day of infamy. If the state of Oklahoma exists for ten thousand years, this day will always be on the list as one of the worst days ever.

Wilhite began jogging down the path. She reached the intersection of the trails where the night before she had heard the moaning sound. She noticed three sleeping bags under a tree.

She was puzzled.

Her first thought was that some luggage had been dropped off.

Wilhite's eyes then focused on a body.

Wilhite screamed. Unknown to her, it was the body of Denise Milner.

Wilhite ran and woke up other staff members. They all ran to the location of the body and the sleeping bags.

There would never be a worse day for those at Camp Scott than what they were about to experience. In all likelihood, in the back of every staffer's mind was the thought of whether or not they would be blamed for what had happened. There always has to be a scapegoat.

All who returned were sickened by what they saw.

Denise Milner was nude from the waist down. Her pajama top was pulled up underneath her arms. Her hands were tied behind her back with duct tape. She was beaten about her face. Around her neck a cord and an elastic bandage was visible. A round cylinder shaped object about four inches long made of terry cloth was attached to the cord. The elastic bandage had been used as a blindfold; the terry cloth object had been used as a gag.[22]

The camp staff was too terrified to open the other sleeping bags. Michele and Lori were inside those sleeping bags. Both bodies had been bound into a tight, compact fetal position. Michele and Lori's sleeping bags contained bloody sheets that had been used by the killer or killers to wipe down blood found on the wood floor of tent number eight.[23]

For those who actually viewed the bodies of all three slain girls, the image was haunting. Mayes County Sheriff Pete Weaver would say in 1985, "Even now…years later, I can still look over at that tree and see those little girls' bodies."[24]

A theory later developed that both Michele and Lori had died inside the tent—struck by a heavy blunt object at the back of their heads while they slept. Denise, it was theorized, had been led away from the tent while alive. She was then raped and killed. Denise's face had been beaten with such force that the object responsible had left behind its shape. Later, the official cause of death was said to be strangulation. Photographs of the dead girls would later horrify jurors and spectators.

Crime scene investigators believed small footprints leading from the cabin proved Denise Milner walked from the tent with the killer. Of course, there is no way of proving whose footprints they were or when they were made. The girls were obviously in and out of the cabin during the day.

The Camp Scott staff was so shocked upon discovering the crime scene they never looked in the sleeping bags. It was not until law enforcement officers came that the bags were checked. At that time, officials first learned there were three dead girls.

The Oklahoma Highway Patrol was the first law enforcement agency called. At the time, there was no 911 service. The Oklahoma Highway Patrol just happened to be the first agency on the list of emergency numbers at the main lodge. Barbara Day, the administrator of the camp, had been told by the chief of police of Locust Grove to not call the county sheriff in case of an emergency, implying that he would be of little help.

The first law enforcement officer to arrive at Camp Scott was Oklahoma Highway Patrol Trooper Harold Berry, an eight-year veteran. He also happened to live just down the road from the camp.

Berry "saw two sleeping bags and a partially uncovered girl. I felt something inside the sleeping bags, but I didn't open them...I made arrangements to secure and rope off the area, and I stayed with the bodies until Sheriff [Pete] Weaver and Doctor [Don] Collins arrived."[25]

A fleet of emergency vehicles soon arrived. The emergency vehicles were followed by a regiment of Mayes County officials.

Mayes County Sheriff Glen "Pete" Weaver was among the next law enforcement officers who descended upon the area. It would be the second time he had ever set foot upon the campgrounds.

Weaver was a tall, gangly, grizzled veteran Oklahoma lawman. He was rarely without his stereotypical sheriff-style straw cowboy hat. He wore wire-framed glasses. Weaver had business on the side. He ran "Pete's Drive-In," a burger joint in Pryor, Oklahoma, and raised cattle.

Weaver was born May 21, 1921, in Salina, Oklahoma. He served in the United States Army Air Corps in the Indochina Burma theater during World War II.

When the tragedy happened, Weaver became the man on the spot. He will be forever linked to the tragedy. At the time of his arrival, he did not know that the murders would eventually cost him reelection in 1980. He would never regain his job as sheriff. His reputation would be forever blemished because of accusations that he planted evidence to incriminate the primary suspect in the case. Weaver, due to certain comments to the press, would often come across as a bumbler.

Weaver had a colorful history. In 1970, he was the incumbent sheriff. He was charged with being a public drunk. He was charged in the Langley, Oklahoma, municipal court. A Langley waitress filed a complaint against the then forty-six-year-old sheriff. She alleged he was intoxicated at Frost's Drive-In and ran through the establishment waving his pistol and colliding with her. Weaver claimed someone may have dropped "a pill" in water or coffee he drank. He was acquitted. He would, however, lose the next election.[26] He would regain his position four years later.

In 1969, Weaver and then District Attorney Bob Vinzant got in a dispute over a state prisoner. Joe Dodson, a convicted rapist, had been released from custody to help in the investigation of the attempted bombing of Cherokee County Assistant District Attorney Bill Bliss of Tahlequah.

Weaver complained the inmate had never been returned to the prison following his assistance. For some reason, he blamed the district attorney despite the fact that all he had to do was load the guy up in a sheriff vehicle and tell the deputies to return him to his lawful place of incarceration.

Weaver became so upset over the matter he filed a petition asking for a grand jury investigation into his office and the district attorney. "I'm looking forward to it," Weaver said. The petition was not granted. Joe Dodson eventually escaped from the jail. Weaver would report he could not find him because he did not have a warrant.

One of Sheriff Weaver's responsibilities was to administer the county jail. His reputation would take a hit in that area. There had been escapes from the jail, most notably Gene Leroy Hart, the eventual accused in the Girl Scout case.

In June of 1976, a Mayes County jail inmate died while in custody. William Beene, age sixty-five, had been placed in jail on suspicion of driving while intoxicated. He had been involved in an auto accident near Langley. An autopsy showed he died of internal injuries apparently caused when he was thrown against the steering wheel of his pickup truck.[27]

Mayes County jailers, who were under the supervision of Sheriff Weaver, ignored repeated requests for medical attention for the man. One inmate said, "We hollered all night." District Attorney Sid Wise, the classic biased investigator, said there was no indication of negligence by Weaver or his staff. Remarkably, it appears no civil suit was ever filed.

In August of 1979, two of Weaver's deputies were suspended from duty due to the excessive use of force. The two deputies were Roy LeForce and Ray Teague. The judge ordered, "[T]hey are not to set foot in the Mayes County Jail."[28] The judge was William Whistler who would later be the judge in the trial of the one accused of killing Lori, Denise and Michele.

One prisoner said Deputy LeForce grabbed him by his hair, pulled him off his bunk, and then slammed his face into a wall. LeForce beat up the prisoner's two cellmates because LeForce believed the three men had cut their wrists in an attempt to be transferred out of the jail. None of the three had cut their wrists.

There was also testimony that Deputy Teague had told one of the inmates, "I will beat you until your hands fall off." LeForce told the clobbered inmates that if they told anyone, "I'll shoot you in the gut so you will lay in the hospital and suffer a long time, and if that doesn't work, I've got a Doberman at home that will tear you apart."

The Mayes County Bar Association issued a resolution asking for a complete investigation. Weaver said, "I'll see them all in hell before the bar association tells me how to run this jail."

Weaver later hired a female deputy, twenty-nine-year-old Francis Bump. He said he hired her primarily because of the complaints of police brutality. He said, "She's a very attractive young gal. We're an equal employment opportunity employer here—and besides that I don't think anybody will say she could beat a prisoner."[29] Weaver then said that the presence of perfume and the five-foot-two, 110-pound brunette might affect the behavior of the eighteen or so inmates. "It may create more problems than it solves—I don't know. Only time would tell." Miss Bump, who lived in Salina, was quoted saying she liked her work.

The Washington Post reported some Mayes County citizens thought Weaver was anti-Indian: "Weaver is criticized as being anti-Indian, someone from the plains and the more white-oriented area of Western Mayes County than those from the hilly and heavily Indian eastern part like Locust Grove."[30] The perception that Weaver was against Indians would grow when Gene Leroy Hart, a Cherokee, would be charged with killing the three Girl Scouts. Weaver would be a life-long advocate of the guilt of the accused, Gene Leroy Hart.

The pressure of the murder case and other duties would later cause Weaver to suffer a heart attack.[31] District Attorney Sid Wise said that Weaver also was concerned about a rock concert to be held in Mayes County and that the pressures of his job had contributed to his ailment.

Weaver was an advocate of putting prisoners in tents rather than prison. He said, "If tents were good enough for soldiers in World War II, Korea, and Vietnam, they ought to be good enough for prisoners."[32] Weaver was a staunch believer in incarceration. "Laws like burglary would have no clout if you can't send a prisoner to jail for breaking the law."

Weaver did accomplish some good things during his tenure as sheriff. In 1977, for example, he broke up a $100,000 drug operation. The drug in question was PCP.[33]

Also arriving at Camp Scott was ambulance driver David Parker, a part-time driver for the Jim Green Funeral Home of Pryor. At that time in Oklahoma, it was not unusual for local funeral homes to also operate an ambulance service. Parker "thought [he] was going to an automobile accident until [he] met Sheriff Weaver at the intersection of Highways Thirty-Three and Sixty-Two."[34]

Mayes County District Attorney Sid Wise was summoned to the camp. Accompanying him was a newcomer to his staff Royce Hobbs. Hobbs had only been a prosecutor for a few weeks. The day he arrived at Camp Scott and the horror of what he saw was not the ideal way to break into the prosecutor business.

"I was there when they opened the sleeping bags," Hobbs said over thirty years later. That statement was all that was needed to be said to express his thoughts of the events. Many others over the years would express similar feelings based on the fact "[t]hey were there when they opened the sleeping bags."

Sid Wise had been the district attorney for Mayes County for over two years. He had previously been an assistant prosecutor for David Vinzant, district attorney. One day Wise abruptly disappeared from work.[35] He left saying he was going to lunch and would be back later. He did not return but later sent in his resignation. Next thing you know he had filed for his boss's position. Adding injury to insult, he won the election.

Shortly before the election, Wise reported to the press that, while he was working for Vinzant from mid-1970 until February 1972, he was required to donate $50.00 a month toward Vinzant's re-election campaign.[36] Vinzant replied to Wise's criticism, saying it was politically motivated. "Sure he

Gloyd McCoy

gave, but it wasn't anything he didn't want to do," Vinzant said. "At the time he was happy to contribute to my re-election, but I guess he's changed his mind."

Wise had higher political ambitions than being district attorney. He had his eye set on the statewide office of attorney general. However, because of a future mishandling of a book contract, the public became outraged against Wise and he would finish last in the Democratic primary election.

The book deal which would ultimately lead to Wise excusing himself from the prosecution of the case was described in the *Washington Post*:

> It was also revealed that [Sid] Wise shared sensitive investigative reports with a former newspaper reporter with who he was going to write a book. The reporter, Ronald L. Grimsley, was hired on as an election campaign worker and eventually ran a newspaper classified ad seeking investors in the book venture. The telephone number listed in the ad was for a telephone at Wise's campaign headquarters.[37]

Wise would participate in the actual investigation of the murder at the crime scene. His participation in the actual investigation was an annoyance to the agents of the Oklahoma State Bureau of Investigation. Wise could be seen walking around Camp Scott wearing a derringer in his belt. He was described as a "pistol packing prosecutor."[38]

OSBI agents were trained in crime scene investigation. They were also territorial. They did not like interference from prosecutors who, in their minds, were just elected lawyers. An old adage is that every prosecutor is just one election away from being a defense lawyer.

The agents were also not impressed with the skills of Sheriff Weaver. Some of them had actually investigated Weaver when an ouster action had been instituted over his alleged public intoxication in Langley. OSBI agents believed the Mayes County officials were in their way and no help.

With regard to Wise, agents felt he was just a publicity-hunting politician. In the days following the murders, Wise would hold up to three press conferences a day at the main gate of Camp Scott. Wise, to the dismay of the OSBI agent in charge of the investigation, had given himself a title: Investigation Coordinator.

Crime scene tape went up around the Kiowa area of Camp Scott. Even bulldozers were brought to the area; although, they were never used. As night approached, spotlights were brought in so the investigators could continue working through the night.

The news three girl scouts had been killed was leaked to the press. News media flocked to the scene. The television stations broke into regular programs to make the announcement of the tragedy. Radio stations were making the announcement over and over. All Oklahoma media sources sent representatives scurrying to get there and get any information.

The state of Oklahoma was soon in an uproar. Shock! Dismay! Horror! There were many ways to describe the mutual anguish Oklahomans felt after they heard the heart-breaking news. The event would become one of those where you would always remember how and when you first heard the news.

Apparently, the news was leaked by an Oklahoma Highway Patrol official. Pam Henty, a member of the Oklahoma News Broadcasters Hall of Fame, was, at the time, working as a reporter at KTVY News, Channel Four, in Oklahoma City, Oklahoma. KTVY was the affiliate of the National Broadcasting Corporation (NBC). On that Monday, she had arrived at work and began calling some of her sources to see if there was any news.

Ms. Henry called the Oklahoma Highway Patrol Division Office that covered the northeast part of the state of Oklahoma. When told of the murders, she said, "I froze momentarily. In years of making such calls, I had never heard such a gruesome tale."[39]

Ms. Henry immediately went to Ernie Schultz, the station's information director. She said, "The shakiness in my voice conveyed the seriousness of the event."[40]

Chief photographer Darrel Barton heard Ms. Henry's announcement. He grabbed a map and quickly plotted the quickest way to get to Locust Grove. Within minutes, Barton and a reporter were on their way to Camp Scott. Shortly thereafter, Channel Four broke into the regularly scheduled programming and announced the bad news.

When parents, relatives, and friends of all the campers heard the awful news, they, of course, panicked. Some waited by the telephone hoping for good news. Many, after receiving little information about their child's safety, drove to Camp Scott to join a mile long line of cars full of concerned family members as well as the media.[41]

Parents parked their cars on the side of the narrow Cookie Trail. They ran to the front gate of the camp. They would not be told of their daughter's status.

The parents had to wait for hours under the blazing sun. The air was choked with the dust of the Cookie Trail. It was an unforgettable scene of hysteria.

Reporters were kept waiting at the camp's entry gate until the grounds were secured. Eventually, the reporters were taken on a tour of the area but were not permitted to view the crime scene. Later, authorities clamped tight security on the camp and reporters were denied access to the area.

Arrangements were made to return the other girls to the Tulsa headquarters. The other campers were not told of the deaths. They were taken to a creek that ran through the camp. Some of the girls were questioned by law enforcement before they left. Camp staff would be questioned over and over as law enforcement agents looked for any clue they could find.

Parents in Tulsa were called and told to await the buses at the main office of the Magic Empire Council. The name "Magic Empire" was now holding no believability. "Tragic Empire" now being a more suitable name.

Parents were not told whether their child was or was not one of the victims. Family members had many anxious moments until the buses arrived and their child bounded off the bus.

The returning scouts were surprised to find their parents upset. They had no idea the ordeal their parents and relatives had endured awaiting the bus.

Scout officials watched as parents were reunited with their children. Many parents grabbed their child and immediately left. Stacks of luggage were left behind. Parents and family members were concerned only with the important fact that their girl was alive. Most of the girls would never attend a camp again.

The families of the dead girls were notified. Richard Guse became outraged when he learned that, before he was notified of his child's death, Girl Scout officials called their lawyers and their insurance company. The families' disenchantment with the way they were treated would be a major factor in the decision to file a multi-million dollar lawsuit against the Magic Empire Council. Guse, however, one of the most offended, did not join in the civil suit.

Upon learning the victims' names, the press began harassing the families for comments. Richard Guse gave some of them photographs of his daughter in order to get them to leave. Guse would later report that, when scout officials came to notify him of his daughter's death, he was told there had been an "accident." He learned how his daughter died from television reports. It was the same way for the other parents. They were told of an "accident."

One news photographer, Michael Wheat of Pryor, had been allowed on the grounds of Camp Scott by Sid Wise. Wise asked him to take some photographs of the dead girls. Wheat was asked to take photographs of the dead girls despite the fact that the OSBI photographer had already taken the needed photographs.

Years later, Wheat was despondent about his taking of the photographs of the dead girls. "I still remember the faces of the three girls, Lori, Denise, and Michele. I took their pictures before the ambulance took them away."[42] The parents of the three girls would also remember their faces—before they were taken away.

an oklahoma
prairie fire

The murders of the three girls shocked and sickened the entire state of Oklahoma. The murders would become the preeminent news event in Oklahoma for several years. The fact the victims were so young and innocent was a primary factor for the interest given to the matter. However, another factor adding to the shock factor was, at the time, multiple murders were a rarity in Oklahoma.

Prior to the Girl Scout murders, the most infamous state multiple homicide occurred in northwest Oklahoma near Woodward. Four members of a rural family were murdered in their home.[43]

In September of 1974, Mervin Thrasher; his wife, Sandra; their children, Penelope (Penny), age five, and Robert, age eighteen months, were found shot to death in their farmhouse. The couple had been bound and gagged and killed execution-style. The children were killed while they slept in their beds.[44]

The bodies of the Thrasher family were discovered by Bob Patee; Patee was Mr. Thrasher's supervisor at his place of employment, Michigan-Wisconsin Pipeline Company.

Patee twice called Mr. Thrasher on the telephone to tell him he needed to show up for work. The first time was at 4:30 a.m. Thrasher came to work to help Patee repair an engine. He then went home.

Patee called again at 8:00 a.m. Thrasher said he could not come to work for a couple of hours. He never showed up. Patee did not think that was odd because it was Labor Day, and employees were not required to work.

The next morning, Thrasher did not show up for work. Patee tried to telephone him but got no answer. Patee decided to stop by the Thrasher home when he finished work.

Patee arrived at the house about 10:30 p.m. on September 3, 1974. The house was dark. With the aid of a flashlight, he began to look through the windows. He saw the body of Mrs. Thrasher lying on the floor.

Terrified by what he saw, Patee went and got the Woodward police. When investigators entered the house, they found both Mervin Thrasher, age twenty-eight, and his wife, Sandra, age twenty-seven, lying face down on the bedroom floor.

Mervin Thrasher's feet were tied together and his hands bound behind his back. He had been shot in the head three times.

Sandra Thrasher was tied in a similar fashion as her husband. However, her feet were also fastened and tied up to her hands. She had been shot in the head twice.

The two children were in bunk beds in another room: eighteen-month Robert in the bottom bunk, shot twice in the head. Five-year-old Penny was in the upper bunk. She was shot three times in the head.

Investigators had the opinion the baby, Robert, had been sitting up when he was killed due to the position they found him. The killer had looked the baby in the eye and shot him. Then he added one more shot for good measure.

The entire Woodward area became petrified with fear. Lights were kept on all night. Late night drivers toward the town of Woodward, who were unaware of what had occurred, were surprised to see the town so well lit.

Every time a dog would bark outside it seemed the local police and sheriff would receive a call. No one knew if the killer or killers were still in the area or if it could happen again. Doors that had usually been left unlocked were now checked and rechecked.

Citizens were worried their locks would not hold if their house were chosen next. Fear is always a terrible emotion, but it is especially so when it appears in a place that it does not usually frequent.

No murder weapon was found at the crime scene. However, it was ballistically determined all four Thrashers had been killed with a .22 rifle belonging to Mr. Thrasher. Shell casings were found in the bedroom. The casings matched shell casings found in the former Thrasher residence in Guymon, Oklahoma.

Bobby Wayne Collins, a nineteen-year-old service station attendant, was eventually convicted of the murders. One of the investigators was buying gas at the station where Collins worked. He noticed Collins's shoes had soles that matched the prints found outside the Thrasher house.[45]

Collins was questioned. Collins confessed to having once burglarized the house.[46] However, he claimed he was not in town at the time of the murders.

At trial, Collins took the stand in his defense. He said, six days before the murders, he had borrowed a car from his cousin and gone to Enid, Oklahoma, in an unsuccessful attempt to find a job. The cousin would not corroborate Collins's story.

Collins was convicted and sentenced to death. At the time, a sentence of death was mandatory in first-degree murder cases. Later, his death sentence was reduced to life imprisonment as a result of a 1972 United States Supreme Court decision, which, in effect, caused Oklahoma's death penalty statute to be unconstitutional.[47] Collins is still serving his sentence in the custody of the Oklahoma Department of Corrections.

Collins was represented by Stephen Jones, an Enid attorney. Jones would later represent the most infamous criminal defendant in Oklahoma history, Timothy McVeigh. McVeigh was the accused in the Oklahoma City Murrah Building bombing case.[48]

At the time Jones was representing Collins, he was a candidate for United States Congress. There was speculation among many that Jones lost the election due to his representation of Collins.

The rarity of multiple murders was soon a thing of the past in Oklahoma. In 1978, six employees of an Oklahoma City steakhouse were murdered in what was then the worst incident in Oklahoma City history.[49]

The murders of Lori, Denise, and Michele were a front page news item for days in the state's various newspapers.[50] The outrage against the killings was universal. The tragic news soon spread across America.[51] CBS news anchor Walter Cronkite mentioned the murders during his news broadcast.[52]

who did this?

The investigation began immediately. The woods surrounding the camp were vigorously searched for any clue. Fighting heat, snakes, ticks, and endless brambles of brush, the investigators scoured the area. Ticks were a major hazard in the search. One deputy was covered with 197 ticks after he finished his day of searching.[53]

The headline in the state's major newspaper said, "Officers Hunting 'Maniac' in Slaying of Three Girls."[54] The "maniac" term had been uttered by Mayes County Sheriff Pete Weaver, "We've got a maniac somewhere around. This is horrible. It's the work of a demented person."[55]

In July of 1977, the Associated Press Oklahoma news executives invited Dr. Robert Phillips, a clinical psychologist, to speak at their annual meeting. Dr. Phillips had been a psychologist for twenty-five years. He spoke on the profile of the killer.[56] He basically agreed the murders were the work of a "maniac." Twenty years later, an article about the murders described the perpetrator as a "monster."

Whoever committed the murders, according to Dr. Phillips, did so because he hated happiness, innocence, and decency. The best way to degrade those things was to violate the young girls. "Something happened during this man's life to make him feel inferior and built up a passionate hatred in him. He hates being alive, and in killing, he is taking revenge on a world he believes has mistreated him."

Phillips said the murderer probably did not plan on killing all three girls. He got caught up in the savage emotion, and the beast in him emerged. Phillips concluded by saying the man, who had no order in his life, tried to put things back in order by cleaning up the blood and putting two of the girls into the sleeping bags.

Although he did not tell immediately tell the press, Sheriff Weaver was already mulling the possibility he knew who had committed the crimes. That man was Gene Leroy Hart, a man who Weaver knew all too well.

For most of his life, Hart was not referred to by his full name, Gene Leroy Hart. His mother, family, and close friends called him "Sonny." The media began the practice of using his full name.

Hart did not fit the profile suggested by the psychologist. In fact, prison records showed that Hart was in no need for any type of psychiatric services and had been a well-adjusted inmate who got along with his fellow prisoners. However, sometimes law enforcement officials, especially in a high profile case, can attempt to pound the proverbial square peg into the round hole.

Hart was a convicted felon who had escaped from Weaver's jail. He had been on escape status for years. His mother lived two miles from Camp Scott. Weaver did not immediately bring his name up as a potential suspect.

At first, any potential lead was covered. OSBI director, Ted Lemke, said the state mental hospitals were contacted to see if anyone had been discharged to the area. Authorities also checked with the Oklahoma Department of Corrections and the State Pardon and Parole Board to see if any known child molesters had been released in the area.[57]

The first clue, one that was at first called "slim," was a flashlight found near the girls' bodies with tape on the batteries matching that used to gag the victims.[58] There would be a lot of discussion about the flashlight later at the trial of the accused. The lack of the accused's fingerprints on the flashlight would be one of the most discussed aspects of the criminal investigation.

The prosecutors would argue the flashlight was important because there was some tape on it that matched tape found in a cave two miles from camp that Gene Leroy Hart had supposedly used. The defense would stress the important point that the flashlight did not have Hart's fingerprints on it. At trial, the defense would have an argument against every piece of the prosecutor's evidence. The prosecutors had lots of evidence that Lori, Denise, and Michele were killed but no evidence as to who killed them.

A near-by landowner reported "a good deal of 'vehicular' traffic was heard on a remote road adjacent to the camp about 2:30 a.m."[59] At the time, this report caused people to believe several persons may have been involved since the report implied several vehicles had been in the area. After Hart was charged, the vehicular traffic aspect was never discussed in the media again.

The first person to be arrested as suspect in the crimes was a forty-four-year-old unemployed Locust Grove man named Floyd Smith.[60] Smith had been booked in adjoining Ottawa County. He was arrested by the Oklahoma Highway Patrol under "suspicious circumstances" at 1:45 a.m. He was arrested on State Highway Ten near Grove, Oklahoma.

Sheriff Pete Weaver said, "We are very interested in this man. We definitely want to talk to this person. We have reasons to believe that he could possibly throw some light onto the Girl Scout Camp slayings."[61]

Smith was not held long. The next day it was reported Smith had been eliminated as a suspect.[62] The so-called "suspicious circumstances," it was later learned, was that Smith had a Locust Grove address.

A few days later, Weaver reported another suspect. A forty-year-old mental patient with a history of psychiatric confinement was being sought for questioning. Weaver admitted, however, this individual, whose name was never reported, at that point "was not a serious suspect."[63]

Weaver also reported investigators had received numerous false confessions and crank calls. One telephone caller had been traced to Belleview, Washington.[64] Such calls and false confessions have always been a problem in highly publicized crimes.

"we have our man"

Although he had been at the camp from the start of the investigation, Mayes County Sheriff Pete Weaver did not immediately state to everyone who he thought was the probable perpetrator. He mentioned the name of Gene Hart to his deputies and to Sid Wise. Later, however, Weaver suggested to everyone Gene Leroy Hart could have committed the murders.[65] Law enforcement would also later try to connect Hart to a murder in Craig County. However, they found evidence that eliminated Hart as a suspect in that case.[66]

Hart, age thirty-four, was a convicted felon. He had escaped from Weaver's jail and had been on the loose for four years. Weaver had not been able to catch him. He had been teased by other law enforcement officials and citizens about not being able to catch Hart. Importantly, Weaver stressed Hart's mother lived within a mile of the camp.

The investigation suddenly centered on Hart. Charges were quickly filed on Hart accusing him of murdering Lori, Denise, and Michelle.[67] Although certain physical evidence at the scene of the murders might tend to show more than one offender, once the investigation shifted to Hart, there was no mention of any possible accomplice or any multi-perpetrator theory.

Gene Leroy Hart was born on November 27, 1943, at the Indian Hospital in Claremore, Oklahoma. Hart's father, Walter Hart, never came to see his son as a child. Hart was a full-blood Cherokee Indian.

On the day his trial started, Hart was described in a newspaper article as follows: "Hart, the one-time football hero from Locust Grove, Hart, the student with the high IQ, Hart, the convicted rapist, kidnapper and jail escapist. Hart, the soft-spoken, well-mannered prisoner who has read more than 100 books since his capture."

Hart's mother, Ella Mae Buckskin, was devoted to him. She was most supportive of her son, whom she called "Sonny." Just as years earlier she had faithfully attended his football and basketball games, she would later attend each and every court appearance. Ironically, she would miss the verdict announcement because she had left the courthouse while the jury deliberated. She did not think they would return so soon with a verdict. She arrived after the verdict was read.

Ella Mae Buckskin was the first person to have a television set in the town of Locust Grove. People would come from miles around to get their first look at television. Ella Mae was happy to let people watch it. At the time, she never envisioned television's eventual magnitude and that her son would one day be the state's television focus.

Ella Mae Buckskin was a kind-hearted woman. She regularly attended Pentecostal Holiness and Baptist churches in the area. She only had a ninth-grade education but was able to raise a large family by herself, and she was proud of the fact she had raised all her children without the help of a babysitter.[68]

Hart had three brothers and a foster brother, three sisters and a half-sister. He also had a son, Donald Eugene Hart.[69] Hart married young, divorced early, and his ex-wife made it difficult for him to see his son. At the time, Hart's son was fifteen. Hart had not seen his son in ten years. Hart's wife left him when he received his first felony conviction.

In 1960, Roger Morris moved from Fort Osage, Missouri, to coach football at Locust Grove. He was hired with the hope that he would make the Locust Grove Pirates into winners. Locust Grove had only had a football team for five years and had won a grand total of nine games in those five years. One of the first players to visit Morris was "the Cherokee Indian boy from across the street."[70]

Morris would describe Hart as "the best boy I ever coached." He described Hart as "college material." "It was a shame he never got an opportunity to prove it. He got married out of high school right away. I think things just went kind of downhill after that."[71]

Morris believed Hart could have obtained a scholarship to Northeastern Oklahoma A&M Junior College in Miami, Oklahoma. The junior college was a place where football players from small schools or with bad grades could go and possibly impress a four-year college into recruiting him. At the time of the murders, stories swept the state that greatly exaggerated Hart's abilities. There was a story, untrue, that he had been recruited to attend the University of Oklahoma by Bud Wilkinson. There was another story, also untrue, that he had rushed for two thousand yards in one season. Another story, the most probable one, was that Hart was scheduled for a tryout at the junior college and simply did not show up.

During Hart's junior year football season, the team won eight games and lost two, one of the losses was by forfeiture. That season, Hart played primarily as a lineman. Prior to the start of the season, Morris asked Hart to switch from running back to line. The coach told Hart there was a surplus of backs but few tough linemen. Hart agreed to the switch for the "good of the team."

The team lost a showdown of undefeated teams in game seven. Locust Grove played Coweta High School, and despite trailing only 6–0 at halftime, lost 34–0. That loss kept Locust Grove out of the state playoffs.

In Hart's senior year, 1962, the team won seven games and lost three. Hart played fullback in the team's split T offense. He was also a team captain. Dewey Talley, an assistant coach, who would later become a guidance counselor at Pryor, said he recalled a game where Hart literally knocked another team's best running back out with a tackle.[72]

W. H. Sanford, an offensive tackle and defensive end on the 1961 team said Hart "was kind of shy." He also said, "He was a good athlete. He was kinda high-tempered. But we all were then. I knew he wouldn't back down from anything. He just acted like all the rest of us."

The local's fondness of Hart came from the fact he had been a part of the first successful teams from Locust Grove. Oklahoma small towns historically worship their local football stars. Hart was named the school's top athlete his senior year. He also played basketball.

Many of the newspaper stories about Hart referred to him as a "football hero." However, the articles did not give any details. At the time of Hart's football days, the town of

Locust Grove did not have a local newspaper. Thus, there were no game-by-game reports for review.

The Oklahoman, in Oklahoma's centennial year, named the best football player for each town in Oklahoma during the previous 100 years. Hart was not named the best player in Locust Grove history. The player named the best was Jeremy Hooker who played for the Pirates in the early 1990s. Hooker was a standout linebacker and running back.[73]

Hart being Indian was significant. During the early '70s, there were important cases involving American Indians. There was the standoff at Wounded Knee, and there was the trial and conviction of Leonard Peltier, a case that is still controversial today.[74] Hart's case, at the time, fit into the niche of controversial cases involving American Indians.

Rennard Strickland, an Indian historian, lawyer, and at the time, dean of the University of Oregon College of Law, wrote the following:

> I have been perplexed by a strange duality in American Indian law and policy. Over the years I have explored America's schizophrenic attitude toward native people. Non-Indian citizens, see Indians alternatively, and often simultaneously as "Savage Sinners" and "Redskinned Redeemers." The Indian is visualized as the devil incarnate and a savage model for selection. Historically for policy makers, there are two Indians—one good and one bad.[75]

To those who knew Gene Leroy Hart, he was a "good" Indian. In the hundreds of articles about the case, except for law enforcement officials, prosecutors or members of the victims' families, not one negative statement was ever recorded. No one who had known Hart would go on the record and speak ill of him. The family of the victims were never overly critical of Hart.

Hart was almost a saint, at least as far as his contemporaries were concerned. They knew of his past criminal record, but they still were convinced that he was a good guy and could not and did not commit the murders. He was undoubtedly the most popular criminal defendant in Oklahoma history.

Hart attended the Locust Grove public schools for his entire school career. Hart was a member of the senior class of 1963.[76] There were fifty-four members of his senior class. The graduation speaker for the commencement ceremony was Charles Angle, dean of students at Oklahoma A&M College of Miami, Oklahoma. One wonders what the graduating senior Gene Hart thought about his future as the commencement speaker talked of life's future possibilities.

After graduation from high school, Hart held several jobs, including working for the Grand River Dam Authority. Hart also would become a convicted burglar and rapist.

Hart pled guilty to having bound and raped two pregnant women and the burglary charges. Yet his criminal record did not diminish the respect he had from the Locust Grove locals.

Family members said he pled guilty to his first convictions of burglary because he had been told he would receive a suspended sentence. Instead he was sentenced to imprisonment. He later was paroled on those charges. There were legal attempts to vacate the prior convictions, but these efforts were futile.[77]

Friends of Hart would even defend him against the previous rape convictions. A reporter wrote: "Hart supporters, who are convinced he was being framed, aren't bothered by his plea of guilty ten years ago to raping and kidnapping two young Tulsa women and locking them in the trunk of his car." His friends, according to the reporter, say the two women went with him willingly from a Tulsa tavern and got in the trunk to hide from their husbands, and that he entered the guilty plea only because he was afraid of being convicted by a jury and given a harsher sentence.[78]

Jimmie Don Bunch was in the Tulsa County Jail awaiting to be transferred to prison for a burglary conviction while Hart was incarcerated on the rape charges. Bunch, in an affidavit issued in 2007, said Hart denied the rape charges. Bunch, under oath, swore, "Gene Hart assured me that the Tulsa authorities were framing him for the rape he was charged with because he was an Indian and ex-felon."[79]

During his trial, Hart was allowed to hold a press conference in the law library of the courthouse. The press conference was well choreographed by his lawyers. Bob Martindale of the *Tulsa World* wrote, "Gene Leroy Hart, breaking his public silence for the first time, described himself as a religious family man who can sympathize with the parents of the Girl Scouts."[80]

The press conference lasted thirty minutes. Hart refused to discuss his ex-wife. He denied that he was having a "personal relationship" with a nurse from Corpus Christi, Texas, who had supposedly moved to Pryor. He said, at one point, "I am not a hero."

Hart had been on the lam from the law for some time. Supposedly he had been hiding out in the hills near Camp Scott prior to the murders. Although the search covered a wide area of forest and there were statements Hart knew how to live off the land, no evidence was ever shown that he actually lived outside for any significant period of time.

While law enforcement and others were scrounging the hills of Mayes County looking for him, Hart was staying in the houses of others.

John Zelbst, a law student from Lawton, Oklahoma, who helped the defense lawyers, got to know Hart well. He said it was obvious Hart knew a lot about hunting and fishing as it was a favorite topic of his. However, Hart admitted to Zelbst he could not "live off the land" as his ancestors could do. Hart escaped from the Mayes County Jail in Pryor, Oklahoma, on May 20, 1973.[81]

Hart was being held in Mayes County awaiting a hearing on an application for post-conviction relief on one of his convictions. Hart was twenty-nine at the time of his escape. Another prisoner, Larry Dry, age twenty-three, from Salina, Oklahoma, also escaped.

Hart had actually escaped twice from the Mays County Jail. The first time he escaped, Sheriff Pete Weaver theorized Hart and Dry cut through reinforcing rods that made up the bars across the cell doors sometime during the night. A main door leading out of the cellblock was locked. The two men apparently hid in a utility closet until a guard unlocked the door sometime around 7:00 a.m. on a Sunday morning. When the door was unlocked, the two men apparently fled out the back door. It was thought an accomplice was waiting nearby to hustle the two men away from the jail. Hart was captured eleven days after his escape. A former Pryor service station operator, Tom Jones, was given credit for his capture.

Hart and Dry had holed up in a vacant house in the country near Strang, Oklahoma. Jones and his family, who had agreed to rent the house, came to the location one evening. Jones's kids found Dry hiding in the attic. Dry convinced Jones he was using the place as a refuge. Jones even agreed to take Dry to the home of an acquaintance of his, Bonnie Martinez. When Jones returned, his kids had discovered Hart hiding in the attic. Hart had threatened the family with a sawed-off shotgun. Jones recognized Hart from a prior conversation. Jones convinced Hart to give him the shotgun. Law enforcement was contacted, and Hart was returned to jail. Subsequently the next day, Dry, in the company of his parents, gave up and came back to jail.[82]

On September 16, 1973, Hart again broke out of jail.[83] Sheriff Weaver speculated Hart was able to escape with the aid of friends who slipped him a hacksaw, which had enabled him to saw his way to freedom.[84] During the escape, Hart was said to have crossed the roof of the courthouse and dropped to the ground before disappearing. Hart's escape was a major source of embarrassment for Weaver. After his escape, Hart had been seen numerous times in the Locust Grove area and even in Tulsa. Many people thought he just went about his business with no concern that he would be captured. Lots of people saw Hart. Yet Weaver had been unable to apprehend him. In a later civil case, Weaver would testify that he, prior to the murders, had begun to intensify his search for Hart.

Two months before the murders at Camp Scott, a Mayes County deputy almost captured Hart. The deputy came upon Hart as he was walking down a road leading to Locust Grove. Hart noticed the deputy driving toward him and fled into the woods.[85]

From the start, there were those who had the opinion Hart was nothing more than a scapegoat. One reporter said:

> Sheriff Pete Weaver never convinced me he had the right guy. He said all the right stuff, but it had the smell of 'rounding up the usual suspects.' More

than one member of the Oklahoma City and Tulsa broadcast media mentioned in our discussions that Gene Leroy Hart was a little too handy to blame this on.[86]

Supporters of Hart, then and now, believe law enforcement had tunnel vision with regard to Hart.[87] Angie Jake, editor of the *Tulsa Indian News*, said, "[Hart] pulled the wool over their [law enforcement officer's] eyes for so long and he frustrated them. So, when he popped up, they blamed it on him."[88] *The Washington Post* printed comments concerning similar viewpoint the wrong man had been charged:

> There are people in these wooded Ozark foothills of Eastern Oklahoma, it seems who, don't feel the law got the right man. That opinion is rooted in personalities and local politics, in perceived prejudice against Indians as well as the evidence itself. The result is an uneasy feeling that the real killer is still loose.[89]

The Washington Post also discussed the lack of Hart fingerprints at the crime scene:

> In the course of the investigation, authorities announced that an excellent set of fingerprints were found on one girl. It did not match Gene Hart's, and later the officials would say the only print really recovered was that of a policeman who had touched a photographic plate used in the fingerprinting process.[90]

When Hart's name was first mentioned as a potential suspect, some law enforcement officials, including Sid Wise, were skeptical. Wise said the crimes did not "fit" Hart.

However, Larry Dry, Hart's previous escape partner was interviewed. Dry described Hart as a sexual pervert who liked young girls. It was Dry's damaging comments that convinced the doubters that Hart was their man.

Dry described Hart as a "sexual deviate" who could not live without sex. Once, according to Dry, Hart wanted to rape two young girls who were swimming. Dry said he had to threaten Hart with a shotgun to stop him.[91]

Dry's credibility was suspect. He was looking to get out of prison early. The State did not call Larry Dry to testify. The decision to not call him was supposedly made during a meeting with defense counsel during a break in the trial. At the start of trial, defense counsel had filed a motion to exclude Dry's testimony. It was denied. Yet later the prosecutors agreed not to put on the evidence regarding Hart's supposed sexual characteristics. Dry was released early from prison because of his cooperation in the Hart investigation. However, he was in and out of prisons over the next decade. He was last released from prison in 1996.

The filing of charges against Hart was also spurred by the discovery of some wedding photographs in a cave near Camp Scott. Some squirrel hunters discovered the photographs in the cave. It was subsequently discovered that Hart had been a photographic assistant at the Granite, Oklahoma, prison and had assisted in the development of the photographs. On the wall of another nearby cave, a message was scratched into the stone: "The killer was here." Defense lawyers for Hart would later argue that the photographs had been planted in what became known as the cellar/cave by Sheriff Weaver or someone acting on his behalf.

the manhunt

The search for Gene Leroy Hart was intense.[92] Over 400 law enforcement agents would eventually be part of the search.[93] At one time, the Federal Bureau of Investigation had forty agents assigned to the case. It would take ten months of searching to capture Hart. Lieutenant Don Mentzer of the Oklahoma Highway Patrol was the main leader of the manhunt, although there were others standing by waiting to take credit.

The Washington Post reported: "Some 400 people would come to look for Hart. Some were drunk, and others arrested for marijuana. A group of Vietnam veterans from Tulsa, calling themselves 'the Spooks' claimed they would find Hart in eight hours. They were given a chance but they failed."[94]

The Tulsa World, Tulsa's daily morning newspaper, published an appeal to Hart to turn himself in to the authorities. The newspaper never heard from Hart. The article stated:

> *The Tulsa World* has been told that you fear for your safety if you should surrender to law enforcement officers. If this is so, we would offer you help in seeing that you are able to give yourself up without harm. We also have the assurance of Governor David Boren that he will use the power of his office to help assure your safety."

The search for Hart continued to be reported daily in the press.[95] The manhunt was the key item of interest in Oklahoma.[96] Special tracking dogs from Pennsylvania were brought to the crime scene.[97] The dogs tracked a scent from the murder site, but their tracking ended at a pond. The pond was dragged in hopes of discovering a possible weapon. No such weapon was found.

Criticism of the investigation started early. A Tulsa dog handler criticized the investigation, saying the Pennsylvania dogs were brought into the area too late to do any good. During the search, one of the dogs was killed when run over by a motorist. Another dog died later of heat prostration.[98] There was talk that the dogs had died because an Indian medicine man had put a curse on them. These same dogs had been used in the hunt for Marcia Trimble, previously mentioned. The dogs were no help in that case either.

Sheriff Pete Weaver had an explanation for why the dogs had lost the scent. According to Weaver, the fleeing suspect "must have jumped from tree to tree like a coon."

On June 24, 1977, hundreds of law enforcement agents and volunteer citizens band radio operators stationed themselves around a four-mile area. SWAT team officers swept the area, but no one was found.

Outside of the area, an Indian hitchhiker was arrested but soon released. The anxiety of this hitchhiker must have been great. Imagine walking down a road, thumbing for a ride, and then be arrested as a suspect in a triple homicide.

On June 25, 1977, a helicopter with special heat-sensing devices capable of registering the presence of human bodies was flown over the search area. Nothing was discovered. On June 27, the helicopter was again flown over the area. Again, nothing was found. With the nature of the crimes he allegedly committed and the fact he could not be captured, Hart was becoming, to some, the ultimate "bogeyman."[99]After five days, the intense search of the woods and hills near Locust Grove ended. A highway patrol spokesman said the search for Hart was stopped "primarily because there hasn't been any information that we knew what specific geographical area he was in."[100]

At one point in the search, there was a report that warning shots were fired at someone. After that a ban was instituted on searchers regarding the carrying of weapons.[101] As the sixth-month anniversary of the hunt neared, law enforcement officials continued to report they would eventually catch Hart. While being interviewed by reporters, Sheriff Weaver stood gazing up at the dark hills in northeastern Oklahoma; he grimly observed, "Some folks disagree, but I say he's still in there somewhere. We'll get him. No man can hide forever."[102] FBI agents continued to come and go into the rugged Mayes County hill country. Three agents of the Oklahoma State Bureau of Investigation had been assigned to the area almost around the clock.

Sheriff Weaver advised reporters he had turned his regular duties over to his under-sheriff so that he could devote full time to the investigation.[103] Weaver and Sid Wise believed Hart was "constantly shifting from house to house in the hills south of Locust Grove holing up with relatives and friends."[104]

Weaver would often offer to take reporters on hikes into Camp Scott and give them a tour of the places searched by law enforcement. The reporters would later return to the sheriff's office loaded with ticks. Weaver would then laugh at them with his deputies after they left.

Ella Mae Buckskin, Hart's mother, was continually harassed by law enforcement officials. She claimed her son had not been in Mayes County for years. "They've gone over my house with a fine-tooth comb, and they've harassed me. But he's not around here. I don't think he is even in Oklahoma."[105]

Weaver denied that Ms. Buckskin was being harassed. He volunteered to take a polygraph if Ms. Buckskin would take one. The American Indian Movement officials threatened to stage a protest if Ms. Buckskin and other Hart family members were not left alone. There was a report that FBI agents pulled their guns on Buckskin's eight-year-old nephew.[106]

Once Ms. Buckskin was confronted by agents at a grocery store after she had bought some chewing tobacco. They approached her and asked her who she was buying it for. The agents thought she might be buying it for her son. She paid for the tobacco and went outside. She then opened up the tobacco bag and put some in her month. She then spat some of the tobacco at the agent's feet.

One official, who requested he not be identified, said, "He [Hart] [is] probably sitting on a curb in Albuquerque, New Mexico, while we're out hunting here."[107] Weaver vowed he would catch Hart. "I vow we'll get him," he said. "It may be the next five minutes—maybe the next five years."[108] Ironically, when Hart was captured, Weaver was not part of the group that apprehended him.

During the time Hart was on the run, reports began to surface he was tiring of the running and hiding. Hart, however, had supposedly expressed fears of "having the hell shot out of him, if he surrenders."

"we got him"

Hart was captured on April 6, 1978, at 4:15 p.m. at a three-room cabin in Cookson Hills, south of Tahlequah, Oklahoma. The cabin was owned by a local Indian man, Sam Pigeon. Pigeon was later charged with the crime of harboring a fugitive. William Smith, another Cherokee Indian, was also charged.[109] Their charges were eventually dropped after Hart's acquittal and death.

Professor Rennard Strickland, in a speech published in 1998, recounted the incident of Hart's capture. He wrote that the OSBI had forced the wife of a Cherokee leader to reveal where Hart was hiding:

> Most Cherokees did not believe Hart was guilty. The ancient Cherokees had a traditional system of justice that allowed the religious leaders to use "a sacred city of refuge" where he might grant sanctuary. The leader of the Keetowahs extended this protection of religious sanctuary to Gene Leroy Hart and hid him in the Cherokee Hills. After about two years, the Oklahoma State Bureau of Investigation essentially kidnapped the wife of Keetowah Cherokee Chief who had granted Hart sanctuary. The investigator threatened to arrest her and suggested they would also imprison her seven children

if she did not reveal where Hart was hidden. She told them where Hart was, and he [William Lee Smith] was subsequently arrested.[110]

Pigeon's cabin was located fifty miles from Camp Scott. Hart had stayed at the cabin for approximately eight months. Pigeon called Hart "Drum."[111]

OSBI agent Harvey Pratt described the cabin as a "tar-papered shack." The cabin only had three rooms. The OSBI agents would search the cabin and report that no incriminating evidence was found. Later, a search warrant was obtained for a second search of the shack. The second time around the OSBI said they found some items, a corncob pipe, glasses, and some newspaper clippings of photos of some cheerleaders, which linked Hart to Camp Scott.

Defense counsel for Hart would later say the items were planted the second time around, and if the items were in the building, they would have been found the first time. Defense lawyers would make the sloppy investigation a key part of Hart's defense.

Hart had walked out of the cabin and noticed the presence of law enforcement. Hart ran back into the cabin and tried to escape out the back door. The cabin had been surrounded. Hart was captured without incident.

The capture of Hart was described by OSBI agent Harvey Pratt:

> We had the place surrounded. I came in from the back, and as we approached, I saw him open the back door. He stuck his head out, saw us, shut the door and went back inside. By then, we had agents enter from the front who took him down. They cuffed him and carried him out around the side of the house.[112]

Gloyd McCoy

When captured, Hart was dressed in a striped tank top shirt with cutoff shorts and high-topped tennis shoes. He had gained thirty to forty pounds since last seen. Hart was also wearing a pair of women's glasses, the type that were horned-rimmed that tapered to a sharp point. The type of glasses he was wearing are often referred to as "cat glasses."

As Hart was being taken to a transport vehicle, it was reported he called an agent a profane name and said, "You or the OSBI will never pin those murders on me." This statement was the only statement ever made by Hart to the OSBI or law enforcement that related to the murders. The statement was in no way inculpatory.

Before the OSBI took Hart from the site of his capture, the agents took turns posing with Hart for photographs. Each one wanted a lasting memory of their trophy catch. Some of the agents still have the photograph with them and Hart proudly framed and in a place of prominence.

The hunt for Gene Leroy Hart was over. The search had taken ten months. Over 10,000 man-hours were reportedly expended. No details were given as to how the figure of 10,000 hours was determined. One must ponder if time spent wondering where Hart was located was included in the huge total. Estimates were that two million dollars were expended by the State of Oklahoma in capturing Hart.

After his capture, Hart was taken to the OSBI office in Tahlequah. He was then transported to the Oklahoma State Penitentiary in McAlester, Oklahoma. He was transported in a three-car convoy. Hart sat in the middle of the backseat of an unmarked car flanked by two officers. That car was preceded by an OSBI vehicle. A highway patrol cruiser was in the rear of the convoy flashing its red light.

Upon arrival at the prison, the convoy was halted at the front gate. The guard took down the names of the passengers. The convoy was allowed to enter.

Inside the prison compound, the news media and photographers were waiting. Hart was taken out of the vehicle in full view of the spectators. He appeared oblivious to the flashes from the cameras. Hart made no statements as he walked into the prison. Hart's legs were shackled. His arms were gripped tight by two law enforcement agents. Upon his entry inside the facility, there was silence. The silence was broken. Security Chief, Melvin E. "Bud" Tyler noticed the cut-off shorts Hart was wearing. He, trying to be humorous, asked, "You been jogging?" Hart made his only comment of the evening, "No, I haven't."[113] Hart was every criminal defense lawyer's ideal client. He knew when to keep his mouth shut.

Hart's arrival at the prison in front of dozens of reporters is reminiscent of the famous scene witnessed by millions of Americans when Timothy McVeigh was walked out of the Noble County Courthouse in Perry, Oklahoma, after being arrested for bombing the Murrah Building in Oklahoma City. Another such comparable scene was when Lee Harvey Oswald was being transported from one jail to another in full view of the media. He was shot and died.

Indian leaders were outraged by the scene of Hart being led into the prison while shackled. Millie Glago, of the American Indian Center in Oklahoma City, said the media was "playing up the case." She also accused the media of presuming Hart was guilty. She said, "The overall impression of the Indian Community is the State of Oklahoma already has convicted Hart."[114]

Sam Pigeon, the man who harbored Hart, was a sixty-year-old Cherokee Indian. He worked in a nursery in Tahlequah taking care of trees. He preferred to speak the Cherokee language rather than English. He told reporters he let Hart stay in his crude three-room cabin because "he didn't do it."

Pigeon was aware Hart was a suspect in the Girl Scout murders. When asked why he had not reported Hart was staying with him, Pigeon again said, "'Cause he didn't do it." Hart had stayed with Pigeon for almost eight months.

Hart and Pigeon did not speak much to each other. Hart understood the Cherokee language but did not speak it. According to Pigeon, when the two did talk, it was about hunting and fishing.

Hart spent much of his time reading magazines and newspapers. He would also lift weights during the day.

Pigeon would leave for work every day at 6:30 a.m. and return at 6:30 p.m., and Hart "would still be there." Hart was a good housekeeper, according to Pigeon.

On June 10, 1978, criticism was levied toward Oklahoma's governor, David Boren, and his attempt to aid the discovery of Hart. The criticism was levied by Hart's sisters. The newspapers were more than glad to publish the criticism, as any item involving the case was eagerly awaited by the populace.

Hart's sisters, Nancy Baker and Millie Littledove, were critical of Boren supposedly promising parole to a convicted car thief and escape artist in exchange for helping locate Hart during the manhunt. The sisters accused Boren of joining the prosecutors in an attempt to "railroad" their brother.[115] The term *railroad* would be mentioned in the closing argument on Hart's behalf at his trial.

The convict Larry Dry had been signed out of the Oklahoma State Reformatory in Granite located in western Oklahoma on March 28, 1978. Hart was captured on April 6, 1978. Dry was recommended for parole by the Oklahoma Pardon and Parole Board on April 26. Boren approved the parole on May 18, 1978.

Dry said, "I knew just about where Hart was and then they got the rest of the information from another person." An aide for the governor confirmed Boren granted Dry a leave from prison but denied he had promised Dry a pardon for his cooperation. Boren's position apparently was it was mere coincidence Dry got parole after he cooperated.

Sheriff Weaver was relieved Hart had been captured, "This is a big load off my shoulders. We were lucky to get him when we did. The foliage is coming out, and if it had gotten any heavier, he probably would have taken off back to the hills, and we would have been still searching." Weaver said, when Hart returned to the Mayes County jail, special precautions would be taken to avoid him escaping for a third time.

"He's a good runner," Weaver said. "But this time he will have no visitors, and we are keeping a special guard on top of his cell every minute of the day and night."

On April 26, 1978, it was reported an informant had been paid $5,000 for information regard Hart's whereabouts. The information had supposedly led to the capture of Hart. Ironically, Professor Rennard Strickland, as earlier mentioned, said the OSBI learned of Hart's location by coercion of David Smith's wife. Strickland had been hired by Smith to write a history of the concept of sanctuary in the Cherokee religion in case he had to go to court.

Sheriff Weaver said the informant was paid soon after Hart's arrest. He would not tell the identity of the informant. The money had been paid to the person through an intermediary.

"There were a number of people active, giving information. I don't know who got the reward, and if I did, I wouldn't be at liberty to say,"[116] Weaver said.

"It could have been one of Hart's family, it could have been a friend, but I'd never tell—we already have enough homicides being investigated here,"[117] Weaver said, obviously implying Hart or Hart supporters would have the informant killed if his or her identity were made known. Three thousand of the $5,000 total came from donations collected by residents of Leesburg, Florida, who, according to Weaver, had "put on some kind of campaign"[118] when they heard about the Girl Scout murders. The rest of money came from assorted, private contributions.

One newspaper article stated that a cousin of Hart, Jon Clayton Potts, age twenty-three, of Locust Grove, Oklahoma, had given "valuable information" implicating Hart in the sex-slaying of three Girl Scouts."[119]

Doris Milner's grandfather said he was relieved that Hart had been captured. Walter Milner, however, expressed doubt on the guilt of Hart. He said, "I am not convinced that he [Hart] is the one who committed the crime, but believe me, it's a real relief knowing that at least they have something now."[120]

going to court

The homicides had occurred at Camp Scott, near Locust Grove in Mayes County. The county seat of Mayes County was Pryor, Oklahoma. Legal proceedings in *State of Oklahoma v. Gene Leroy Hart* would be held in the courthouse in Pryor.

Hart's first court appearance was set for Tuesday, April 6, 1978. The initial appearance was moved to 3:00 p.m. from its original time of 1:30 p.m. The delay was "[d]ue to a conflict in the use of Governor Boren's private aircraft which was to be used to transport Hart to Pryor."[121] Hart was being transported from the Oklahoma State Prison in McAlester to Pryor for his first court appearance.

An estimated three hundred people congregated on the courthouse lawn to await Hart's arrival. There was a sign erected on the lawn. It said, "Help Justice, Gene Leroy Hart and family." Upon his arrival, Hart was escorted into the courthouse by an entourage of uniformed highway patrol troopers. He was shackled.

There was no demonstration from the crowd as Hart was marched toward the courthouse. Just as Hart entered the building, a woman in the crowd yelled, "He didn't do it!" Several other women were crying.

Hart made a passing glance toward the spectators and then turned his eyes to the courthouse door. He was taken up three flights of stairs to the assigned courtroom. The courtroom was filled with people awaiting the proceedings. Throughout the first proceeding and all future proceedings, the courtroom would be filled with spectators.

The initial appearance or, as often referred to, the arraignment, is the proceeding where the defendant is brought before the court, the charges explained to him, bail set, and other issues addressed. Hart appeared at the proceeding without counsel.

District Attorney Sid Wise read the first Information against Hart. The Information is a document setting forth the charges against an individual. In Oklahoma, an Information is filed upon the authority of the district attorney. An Information is not required to be submitted to a grand jury for approval.

This Information charged Hart with the murder of Denise Miller. After the reading of the lengthy document, Hart told the judge he would waive the reading of the two remaining charges. The judge refused this request. The remaining two charges were read in full to Hart. Hart pled not guilty to the charges.[122] Bail was denied. The three charges were consolidated for the purposes of the preliminary hearing.

The next day's issue of the *Daily Times*, Pryor's daily newspaper, ran a front page editorial. The editorial stressed Hart was innocent until proven guilty.[123] This editorial is probably the only time in Oklahoma history that a newspaper spoke out asking that someone charged with murder be afforded their constitutional rights.

Following the initial appearance, Sheriff Weaver met with the media. When asked if Hart had made any statements, Weaver told the reporters that Hart had not yet been interrogated.[124] He would never be questioned by any law enforcement official. Apparently, Hart was well aware that he had the right to remain silent.

Weaver then began to pontificate. Weaver expressed concern about Hart's prosecution, saying that sometimes cases are brought against a defendant "on fact" but defended sometimes successfully merely "on theory." According to Weaver this "legal fiction" style of argument has its roots at common law. "I hope I don't see it happen in this case," Weaver said.[125]

the right to counsel

There was much interest as to what lawyer would represent Hart. Hart received numerous letters from prominent lawyers and not so prominent lawyers volunteering to provide him legal representation.

Eventual Hart's attorney, Garvin Isaacs, has said Hart could have had any lawyer he wanted. F. Lee Bailey, who had gained fame representing "the Boston Strangler" and Sam Shepard, sent a letter. Later in his career, Bailey would represent Patty Hearst and O. J. Simpson. He would not, however, represent Gene Leroy Hart. Neither would Melvin Belli, a prominent civil litigator from San Francisco, who specialized in high-stakes personal injury cases and would from time-to-time take a high profile criminal case in order to enhance his reputation. His most notable criminal defendant client had been Jack Ruby, the Dallas bar owner who had killed presidential assassin Lee Harvey Oswald on national television.

At the time of the Hart case, there was no state public defender system. Unless an accused had funds to hire an attorney, the local lawyers would be appointed to criminal cases on a rotating basis. The pay for such legal work was abysmal. Many judges and Oklahoma legislators believed that the lawyers should do court-appointed work as a charity on behalf of the court. The system had many flaws. There were many complex criminal cases that ended up having a defendant represented by the local bank's lawyer or a lawyer who had just graduated from law school and had little experience in murder cases.[126]

D. C. Thomas, a noted criminal defense lawyer who would play a small role in Hart's case, once stated: "If you asked me what the second worst thing that could happen to you, I'd say be charged with a felony and be rich. If you asked me the worst thing that could happen, I'd say be charged with a felony and be poor."[127]

Oklahoma now has a statewide public defender system. Today, if Gene Leroy Hart were charged with a capital murder, he would immediately have two lawyers assigned to represent him as well as an investigator. Any needed experts would also be provided at no charge.

During Hart's trial, his defense lawyer asked the trial judge to reimburse the defense for $8,850 for expenses such as psychologists, chemists, photographs, and fees for a jury consultant. The judge denied the request saying the court fund was almost broke. "So is the defense fund," counsel said.[128]

Unless Hart and his family wanted to rely on the Mayes County court to appoint him an attorney, they would have to find and hire their own lawyer or lawyers. His family set out to find someone. There was a top criminal defense lawyer in Pryor at the time. His name was Tony Jack Lyons. Lyons was a former air force colonel. He had tried and won over fifty murder cases.[129] His trademark was a bright red blazer. However, Lyons had had previous dealings with the Hart family, and they with him. Both wanted nothing to do with the other. Sid Wise always said Tony Jack Lyons was the best defense lawyer he ever faced.

Initially, Hart was going to be represented by Larry Oliver. Oliver, a full-blooded Cherokee, ran a law office in Tulsa, Oklahoma. He was hired by Hart's mother. Oliver subsequently filed a request to withdraw from the case when he learned that other lawyers were going to replace him.

Oliver was quoted in 1998 saying some harsh things about his former client, Hart. He said, "There was apparently a dark side to him."

Oliver claimed to have spent many hours with Hart before he withdrew as his attorney. "I'm not sure you'd trust him with your granddaughter. I read him, and I can tell you my reading was not favorable to him. I thought there was a strong possibility he could have done it. There was a bad side to him."[130]

Oliver made reference to Hart having a drinking problem. He said, "He didn't drink any more than I did. But I wasn't affected by it as much as he was." Oliver refused to elaborate.[131] He did, however, state that Hart had a "karma, charisma."

Following Oliver's withdrawal, the court appointed Larry Poplin, a Pryor lawyer, to represent Hart for a brief period until new counsel had officially entered an appearance. Oliver tried to make it appear he withdrew because he thought Hart was guilty. Years later he would make derogatory comments about Hart. The statements made years later were certainly unethical as they violated the concept of loyalty to a client.

Eventually three lawyers entered an appearance to represent Hart as a team: Robert L. "Duke" Wheeler, Garvin Isaacs, and Gary Pitchlynn. That team did not last long as

Wheeler withdrew after a dispute with his co-counsel prior to the start of the preliminary hearing. Apparently, Wheeler wanted to actively question witnesses despite the fact he had not done much work in the preparation. There were also reports of disputes over money or the lack thereof.[132] Isaacs and Pitchlynn would stay on the case.

Jimmie Don Bunch, who would later embarrass Garvin Isaacs during his testimony at Hart's preliminary hearing, in an affidavit took credit for Hart hiring Isaacs to be his lawyer.

According to Bunch, when Hart was apprehended by authorities he was brought to the prison at McAlester, Oklahoma, and placed in a cell next to Bunch on Death Row Unit. Bunch said,

> At the time I was personal friends with an attorney named Garvin Isaacs out of Oklahoma City and Norman, Oklahoma. I really liked and trusted Garvin Isaacs, and I advised Hart to employ Mr. Isaacs as his attorney to defend him in the murders of the three girlscouts [sic].[133]

Garvin Isaacs has never told fully how he became Hart's lawyer. Bunch's statement about being Isaac's friend must be evaluated by Bunch's later actions in the case that will be fully discussed.

Garvin Isaacs was thirty-three years old at the time of this case.[134] He had Indian heritage in his family background.[135] Isaacs would work on the Hart defense for 359 straight days, most of it non-stop.

Garvin Isaacs grew up in Apache, Oklahoma. His father, Garvin A. Isaacs, was superintendent of schools. His mother was a home economics teacher. Garvin was a high school basketball standout. He was an all-state basketball alternate.[136] He scored thirty-one points in a game against Cement High School in the state playoffs.[137]

Isaacs was active in the 4-H Club in high school. He won a statewide speaking contest and the right to participate in a national contest in Columbus, Ohio, in 1962.[138] Isaacs would mention 4-H in his closing argument in the Hart case.

Garvin Isaacs attended Texas Christian University on a basketball scholarship. In fact, he played on a historic team. He played on the first integrated basketball team in the history of the Southwest Conference.[139] Isaacs and the player who integrated the team got into a fight during an unofficial practice. The fight was not race based. Later the two became lifelong friends.

Isaacs had graduated from the Oklahoma City University School of Law. He had worked as both a public defender and prosecutor in Oklahoma County. He spoke with a tone that was unique. His voice was a combination of a southern accent, Texas drawl and an Oklahoma accent. It was hard to describe, but people loved the way he talked. He talked loud and fast. He was as tough as a boot. He was looking for a case to let the State of Oklahoma know that he was *the* criminal defense lawyer to hire. His enthusiasm was the main reason Hart agreed to let Isaacs represent him. He had never been defense counsel in a murder case.

Pitchlynn, a native of Wewoka, Oklahoma, was a graduate of the University of Oklahoma with a degree in journalism. At the time he began work on the Hart case, he had only recently graduated from the Oklahoma City University Law School. Pitchlynn would gain a lot of respect for his role in the Hart case. He would later describe his experience as a "great adventure."

Pitchlynn was an American Indian. He, like Hart, was a high school football player. He played quarterback for the Wewoka Tigers.

Hart, in an interview after his trial, only days before he died, told of his first meeting with his lawyers: "The very first day I met Garvin Isaacs, Gary Pitchlynn, and Duke Wheeler, I said, 'There is no way they [the prosecution] can get a conviction.' And we maintained that from the start to the finish. It went according to our plan."[140] Duke Wheeler was a lawyer who worked with Isaacs. He did not last long as a co-counsel. He and Isaacs had a dispute over money and strategy. Wheeler and Isaacs would part company.

After Isaacs and Pitchlynn were chosen to represent Hart, a flap developed about an attempt to persuade Hart to change lawyers. Two men, Bud Welch of Pryor and Quinton Smith of Tahlequah, were allowed to visit Hart at the Oklahoma State Prison. Warden Hess had permitted the visit by the two men citing a "special emergency visit" provision. Hess had received a telephone call from powerful Oklahoma State Senator Gene Stipe of McAlester, Oklahoma. Stipe was a longtime state senator. He was also a leading Oklahoma trial lawyer.[141] Stipe told Hess the two men were coordinators of an Oklahoma defense fund. Hess later learned they were not involved with any organized fund drive. Hess would not have allowed the men to visit Hart if he had known the true facts.

Hart's sister, Nancy Baker, complained the two men were part of a plot to obtain a phony confession from her brother. Welch, a bail bondsman, denied the allegation and said the visit was "to help the boy…and see if he was satisfied with his representation." Welch wanted to tell Hart that Stipe, "the greatest lawyer in the whole country," was willing to take his case.

Isaacs and Pitchlynn, in interviews years later, told how their lives had been threatened during their representation of Hart. According to the two lawyers, the threats were not so much from enemies of Hart, although there were such threats, but from the "criminal element of Mayes County" who feared detection of the killer because of the lawyers' attempt to establish an alibi for Hart. Threats became so frequent that Isaacs began to carry a gun. At one point, Isaacs asked for protection from the highway patrol but his request was denied.[142]

Early in the case, Isaacs called his longtime friend and fellow lawyer Barry Cousins of Lawton, Oklahoma. Isaacs told Cousin to "get as many guns as you can find and head to Pryor." Cousins did so. Cousins also brought along a law student John Zelbst.

The defense team rented office space in a two-story building in Pryor. The building was owned by a retired dentist. The lawyers would have the entire second floor. Not only would the lawyers and any helpers that came along work there, they would live there. The rent was $200 per month. Mattresses brought in by the Hart family and supporters were laid across the open room. Sleeping bags were laid on top of the mattresses. There was access to the roof. Sometimes Garvin Isaacs would go on the roof and talk to reporters from above. The place became known as "the Hart Hotel." The building was across the street from the courthouse. For months there was constant activity in "the Hart Hotel."

Hart's lawyers made their first appearance at a motion hearing held on April 18, 1978. The prosecutors wanted to obtain saliva, blood samples, and hair samples from Hart. At the hearing, Garvin Isaacs was asked if the defense had any objection. Isaacs answered, "We'll give you all the spit you want from Gene Leroy Hart and all the blood if you don't take more than a pint." The defense was granted access to copies of written statements connected with the murder investigation, all technical reports, photographs, and copies of chemical, medical, and toxicology findings. Throughout the process, defense counsel was constantly having to go to court to get access to the State's evidence.

there's a new prosecutor in town

District Attorney Sidney Wise was discovered to have entered into an agreement to write a book about the upcoming trial. This news caused a public outcry. Folks did not appreciate Wise trying to make money off the tragedy. The outcry would be a factor in Wise being replaced in the case by S. M. Fallis, Jr., district attorney of Tulsa County. His full name was Sevier Moreland Fallis, but everybody called him "Buddy." Reportedly, there was a behind-the-scene attempt to get Fallis on the case. The victim's parents believed that Wise could not handle a case of this magnitude. Originally, Fallis and Wise were supposed to be co-counsel. Eventually, however, Wise completely withdrew from the case. The outcry over an advertisement seeking "investors" for Wise's book project and the fact the family of the girls were concerned about his ability to prosecute such a significant case began an effort to have Fallis appointed as a special prosecutor.

Fallis, at the time, was forty-five years of age and considered a top prosecutor. He was five-foot-six and had a dynamic personality. He was once described as "a diminutive, cigar-chomping prosecutor."[143] When he went to court, he won. He had a conviction rate of well over 90 percent.

He was known as a "gang-buster." Fallis's toughness would often lead to personal grief. His home was once robbed and left in shambles by vandals. Once a shotgun blast ripped the rear of his parked car. An anonymous caller said the next shot would be between his eyes. Once an escapee from jail told a reporter he and an accomplice had once wanted to gun down Fallis in his front yard. He was reported as saying, "We came this close to killing Buddy Fallis. The only reason we didn't gun him down was because someone told us he had round-the-clock protection, and we decided not to risk it."[144]

Fallis liked to say that all his legal life he had been prosecuting the "scum who prey on innocent people." Fallis was tough, conservative, and sometimes controversial. He once considered filing "blasphemy charges against a movie theater."[145] The last blasphemy charge in Oklahoma had been filed in 1941. Fallis was criticized in 1980 for filing criminal charges in victimless crimes. Shirley Barry of the ACLU said, "A prosecutor like Buddy Fallis, who seems to be looking for victimless crimes to prosecute, is really making our whole criminal justice system unworkable."[146]

According to some, Fallis would use intimidation to strike fear if a witness did not go his way. Dr. Tom Kuker, a chiropractor, charged with possession of narcotics, said Fallis wanted him to testify against his brother. According to Kuker, Fallis said, "if he did not cooperate, he [Fallis] would ruin the Kukers through the news media."[147]

One of Fallis's greatest victories occurred in 1980. He prosecuted a defendant for assaulting and raping a Catholic nun. The jury recommended a sentence of 1,700 years. That sentence was an Oklahoma record. Fallis, during an emotional closing argument, pleaded with the jury to not turn this "monster" loose on society.

After the jury returned the verdict, Judge Jay Dalton told the jury: "I feel this is a very good example of why the Supreme Court was wrong in their ruling as far as death sentences in rape cases are concerned."[148] Ironically, Fallis had asked the jury to "only" impose a 350-year sentence.

Fallis had been the district attorney since he was thirty-one years of age. He had previously been the chief prosecutor for Tulsa County, which basically meant he was second-in-command. He would eventually hold the district attorney position, always running unopposed, until 1981 when he resigned.[149] Opponents of Fallis had little luck in persuading anyone to run against him.[150]

Fallis believed in strict enforcement of the law. He would not hesitate to protest the early release of anyone he convicted.[151] Fallis was not shy about letting folks know his opinion on matters. Despite the loss in this case, Fallis remained quite popular. Despite some criticism from the defense bar and appellate courts for certain trial tactics, Fallis was admired by his colleagues in the legal profession both in his criminal and civil careers.

A joint announcement was made by Fallis and Wise. Wise told the press, "I felt that there was definite need to assure that someone remained familiar with the State's case in the event the court proceedings go beyond my term." He also said, "While I question whether these delays [requested by defense counsel] will be granted by the court, I did feel that the continuity of the case be preserved in order to assure the State of effective and equitable representation."

Wise would not blame himself for the fact Fallis had to be put on the case. He chose to blame what he considered to be dilatory tactics of defense counsel. He said his term was likely to expire before the trial started and someone would need to be ready.

At the press conference, Fallis was asked why he had become involved in the case when it was outside his district. Fallis noted the three victims were from his district, two from Tulsa and one from Broken Arrow, Oklahoma. He was entering the case to "serve the ends of justice."

Sheriff Pete Weaver expressed elation at the announcement. Weaver said, "A case of this magnitude deserves the best and in Sid Wise and Buddy Fallis, I think we have the very best."[152]

No matter what anyone thought about Buddy Fallis personally, his reputation was that he was a tough man to beat. Although Weaver had described Fallis and Wise as being a team, Wise was not on the team. He would have little to do with the case except make occasional comments to the press. Whether he knew it or not, Wise was going to be phased out.

Although Wise announced he would still participate in the preliminary hearing and trial, he eventually withdrew completely from the case in November of 1978. His involvement in the book scheme and other accusations against him was causing public skepticism to grow against the prosecution. In order to avoid the appearance of impropriety and, undoubtedly, pressure from state and local officials, Sid Wise completely removed himself from the State's team. Wise had to admit the complaints against him were "clouding the issues."[153]

Wise had lost support from the public. Hart supporters, in order to mock Wise, printed up some T-shirts that said, "Gene Hart for Attorney General." A common joke/statement was that if Hart was actually on the ballot for attorney general he would get more votes than Wise. Another bumper sticker that was often seen during this time read, "Pryor, the Hart of Gene Country."

Fallis needed a co-counsel. He called upon Ronald Shaffer, his top assistant in the Tulsa District Attorney's office. Shaffer was a most competent prosecutor. He had started his career in the Tulsa County Courthouse as a clerk. He eventually worked his way up to prosecutor and then to district judge. He started his legal career in 1957 as a clerk and retired in 2006 as a judge at age seventy. The only business address he ever had was the Tulsa County Courthouse. Shaffer was a quieter version of Fallis. Once during a closing argument in a murder case, he argued a mock question to the defendant, "How many rights did you advise [the victim of] before you pulled the trigger?"[154]

raising money

Neither Gene Hart nor his family were wealthy. Funds would have to be raised to fund his defense. Hart's sisters wrote letters to numerous publications asking them to print their solicitations to "all Indian people and the general public for funds to defend Gene Leroy Hart."[155]

Local fund raising events were held.[156] Over four hundred people showed up for one event—a gospel singing and chicken dinner.[157] One Hart supporter was surprised at the number of attendees. "I didn't think this many people would show," said Nancy Baker.[158] One Locust Grove resident, who asked not to be identified, said 85 percent of the community believed Hart was innocent. He also said the citizens of Locust Grove doubted he could receive a fair trial.

At one point during the evening, one of the musicians, Bill Grass of Locust Grove, stopped the music to remind everyone why they were there. He said, "Gene Leroy Hart's needin' some help. Your contributions will help him fund his dream to be free of this."[159] The event raised $1,160.00. Another fundraiser raised $1,400.[160]

Twelve hundred people turned out for a "hog fry" dinner to raise funds for Hart's defense. The event was held at the Cherokee Heights Community Center in Locust Grove.

The menu was hog fries and chicken and dumplings. The cost of the meal was $2.00 a plate. Nine-year-old Tobias Smoke commented, "I even chipped in an extra quarter because I wanna help him. I don't think he done it."[161]

The Cherokee Nation would provide the major portion of the money raised for Hart's defense. The Cherokee Nation Tribal Council would vote to donate $12,500 to the attorneys defending Hart. The October 14, 1978, minutes of the Cherokee Council meeting shows the following:

> It was pointed out that Mr. Hart has been dubbed by the news media as a full-blooded Cherokee Indian. Gary Chapman made a motion that [the] Council approve the appropriation of $12,500 for the attorneys of Gene Leroy Hart, to be used for defraying the cost of expert witnesses and trial transcripts in order that the allegations presented a trial can be determined to be true with the greatest degree of certainty as possible. In doing so, the Tribal Council takes no position on the guilt or innocence of Gene Leroy Hart, but asserts its desire that a fair trial be afforded. Second by Houston Johnson.[162]

"The decision was not easy," said Cherokee Chief Ross Swimmer. Swimmer said the funds would come from tribal revenues unrelated to state or federal funds.

Eventually, over $20,000 was raised for the defense. In the defense of Timothy McVeigh for his role in the Murrah Building bombing, the United States paid $10 million for legal expenses.[163] Garvin Isaacs gave the following quote in 1997 regarding the fees paid for McVeigh's defense:

> This is the most outrageous, most public murder case in history and the money spent to defend Tim

McVeigh means no one can say he was discriminated against. It's up to the jury to decide the case, not us. And whatever they decide, I'm satisfied that Tim McVeigh got a fair trial.[164]

During the fundraising time, it was reported some of the proceeds were stolen. A gallon jar with a homemade sign saying, "Help Justice, Leroy Hart, and Family" was sitting on the counter of the Cookson Hills Bar owned by Mary Jo and Clarence Potts. After the bar was closed one night, someone broke into the bar and took the jar, which contained at least $50.00.[165] Mr. Potts was against the fundraiser. He called his wife's fundraising scheme "just plain stupid."[166] Mr. Potts thought Hart was guilty. He may have been the only Locust Grove resident to be quoted with that opinion.

Locust Grove citizens did more than just donate money to the cause. They provided undiminished support. Some townsfolk even opened their homes so Hart's relatives would have a place to stay during the court proceedings.[167] Near the end of the trial, the defense team had virtually no money. There was not even enough money to buy food. Reporters learned that if they needed an interview, they needed only to invite the defense team member to dinner. Barry Cousins had read about a wealthy family in New York who had provided funds to an American Indian on trial in California. He sent newspaper clippings and a request for help. One day, out of the blue, a member of the family showed up in person with groceries and a large check. The defense team was elated.

the preliminary hearing

At a preliminary hearing, a prosecutor is required to prove two things: (1) that a crime has been committed, and (2) there is probable cause that the charged defendant committed the crime. In Oklahoma, a preliminary hearing is presided over by a special district judge, a magistrate appointed by the elected district judges. A special district judge will handle certain matters such as misdemeanor cases, arraignments, small claims actions, and other assigned maters. In the Hart case, the assigned judge was Special District Judge Jess B. Clanton.

A preliminary can often be a perfunctory proceeding. Since "probable cause" is all that is required, it is not difficult in your run-of-the-mill case for the prosecutor to get the judge to find enough evidence to meet that standard. If the probable cause standard is met, the defendant is then "bound over" for trial, meaning he will have to go to trial. The preliminary hearing in this case was anything but perfunctory.[168] From the defense side, it was obvious that Garvin Isaac's mission was to establish himself as the "big dog." He was going to try to score as many points as he could with the media and learn as much as he could about the prosecution's case as he could.

In a rare move for a preliminary hearing, the defense was going to put on evidence. The defense was going to give an advance viewing of their defense that someone else committed the crime.[169].

A benefit of the preliminary hearing is the defendant has an opportunity to hear evidence of the State and cross-examine these witnesses. At the time of Hart's case, the preliminary hearing was one of the few ways that defense counsel could learn about the State's case. Years later, certain discovery rules were imposed in Oklahoma, which required disclosure by the prosecutor of certain reports and evidence.

Defense lawyers were able to have the preliminary hearing continued the first time it was scheduled.[170] The lawyers were not so lucky the second time they tried to get a continuance. Judge Clanton denied their request.[171]

The preliminary hearing would start, and the evidence against Hart would be made public. At the start of the preliminary hearing, tensions in Pryor were high. Those in charge of security were taking no chances of anything happening to disrupt the proceedings. Sheriff Weaver announced both uniformed and plainclothes guards, "all well armed," would be in the small courtroom where the hearing was to take place. "We're not disclosing the number we will have on duty," Weaver said, "but we've got our guard up and security will be adequate throughout the courthouse."

Judge Clanton ruled seating would be on a first come, first serve basis. The seating capacity of the courtroom was under 100. All spectators would be subject to a search before entering the courtroom.

Lori Farmer's mother told the press, "I'm going to be here every day" to learn as much as she could about the death of her daughter. She acknowledged that many Locust Grove and Mayes County residents were convinced that Hart was innocent. She said, "People who don't know more about it than we do shouldn't say they don't believe he did it."[172] A courtroom spectator, Locust Grove resident Norman Fleming, was quoted as saying, "I'm here because I want to be one hundred percent sure they've got the right man—not ninety-eight percent sure or ninety-nine percent sure."[173]

The preliminary hearing in *State of Oklahoma v. Gene Leroy Hart* made Oklahoma legal history. The hearing would be the first court proceeding to be televised on closed-circuit television at another location.

The courtroom at the courthouse held only ninety-six people. Two hundred more could view the proceedings on three-color monitors set up in the Pryor Municipal Auditorium. The closed-circuit viewing received favorable reviews. Ian Fleming, news director of channel six in Tulsa, commented, "This is fantastic—it's worked out better than we expected it would."[174]

The proceedings in the actual courtroom remained traditional. The proceedings at the auditorium were more casual. Spectators would talk amongst themselves. Some would offer running commentary. When the judge entered the courtroom, someone in the auditorium said, "Here come the judge." The televising of the preliminary via closed circuit was such a success that there was talk the entire trial might be televised. Defense counsel nixed that idea. The Oklahoma Supreme Court in guidelines established for televising court proceedings had said that both sides had to agree. Garvin Isaacs formally objected to televising the trial saying it would turn the proceedings into "theater" and the participants into "actors." It is unfortunate that the trial was not video recorded. Such a taping could have been a historical prize of Oklahoma's most controversial trial.

Records in the Mayes County Court Clerk's office showed that 176 witnesses had been subpoenaed to testify. Fifty-six of the witnesses were subpoenaed by the State.

Throughout the proceedings, Gene Leroy Hart would be monitored by the spectators and the press. His every move would be watched by someone. Throughout the preliminary hearing and later throughout his trial, Hart would be on his best behavior. One reporter described Hart's demeanor as follows: "Throughout the first three days of the preliminary, the dark-haired Hart, sat between the defense lawyers writing notes and seldom raising his eyes to watch witnesses."[175]

The State of Oklahoma's first witnesses were camp officials.[176]

Carla Wilhite, during cross-examination by Garvin Isaacs, confirmed another unusual incident occurred three or four days before the slayings. Wilhite was at the camp's staff house. She heard a strange noise at a door. The watchdog began barking. Wilhite investigated but found nothing.[177] Wilhite confirmed to Isaacs during questioning that a rain-soaked towel that belonged to one of the counselors was taken as evidence from their tent. The towel was confiscated because it had blood on it, which she could not explain.[178] There was much speculation a note would be admitted into evidence during the preliminary hearing, which would show a death threat had been made. However, it was never introduced.

Reporter Robert B. Allen of the *Daily Oklahoman* reported, "[B]oth the prosecution and defense indicated they had no such note to present as evidence, and there were indications it no longer existed."[179] The article disclosed that the note had been found and given to the camp director who thought it was a joke and threw it away. Ben Woodward, camp ranger, testified, "two tents had been found mysteriously slashed shortly before the Girl Scouts arrived on June 12 [1977] for a week's encampment."[180]

A "camp ranger" was at the camp. One would suppose that one of his duties would be to patrol the camp at night. However, he must have been asleep if he was present the night the girls were murdered. If he was at the camp, one must wonder why his assistance was not sought by Carla Wilhite when she heard the sounds in the night.

Barbara Day, Camp Scott director, testified for the State at the preliminary hearing. On cross-examination by defense attorney Garvin Isaacs, she told of seeing a mystery car outside the camp gate after all 137 girl scouts had arrived. She said the vehicle was "not American made," and there were four individuals inside the car.[181]

During the preliminary hearing, Larry Mullins, a crime scene technician for the OSBI, testified. His testimony would later be stressed during the trial by defense counsel. Mullins testified regarding fingerprints that were found on a flashlight found near where the three girls slept. None of the fingerprints found could be matched to Hart.[182]

After three days of the preliminary hearing, the prosecutors had failed to link Hart to the killings.

The Daily Oklahoman reported, "Still after three days of testimony by twelve witnesses in a preliminary hearing, there had been no evidence to link Gene Leroy Hart with the savage slayings, which shocked both the state and the nation."[183] The article stressed, "[o]nly six times has the name of Hart come up in the crowded third floor Pryor courtroom."

At one point during the preliminary hearing, defense counsel alluded to the possibility that a homosexual counselor could have slain the Girl Scouts.[184] At one point, Garvin Isaacs asked a counselor if she had any homosexual tendencies. The counselor, Carla Wilhite, snapped back, "No." She told Isaacs she did not know of any gay persons in the Scout organization, and then added when asked if she was homosexual, "Well, I am not one."[185]

The prosecutors attempted to link Hart to the crime scene by telling the judge about certain items found in a cave.[186] The prosecutors presented evidence that photographs found there belonged to Hart, These items might have persuaded the judge, but they would not later persuade the jury,

The prosecutors presented evidence regarding hair found at the crime scene. An OSBI chemist had microscopically compared hair found at the scene to hair samples retrieved from Hart's head, per a court order. The chemist, Ann Reed, said they were similar. Garvin Isaac's cross-examination of the chemist on her "hair" testimony was long and intense. He was able to get the witness to admit she could not say Hart was actually the Camp Scott killer. She said, "I cannot identify a person by hair comparison." She did say, "However, those hairs came from Mr. Hart or from somebody with the same microscopic characteristics."[187]

At one point, apparently upset by Isaacs's weakening his witness's testimony, Fallis leaped to his feet to object. He complained about Isaacs's repeated questions regarding whether hair of the counselors at the camp had been compared with the hairs found at the crime scene. Isaacs took offense at the objection. Soon he and Fallis were engaged in a heated exchange. "You may run the courts in Tulsa, but you don't run them in Mayes County," Isaacs snarled at Fallis.

Judge Clanton grabbed his gavel and began hammering. The pounding echoed throughout the courtroom. "I hope this is the last time I have to do this," Judge Clanton said to both lawyers.[188] Defense counsel were taking the offensive. Getting Fallis riled up was part of the defense strategy.

On June 14, 1978, an interesting story developed about an individual with supposed knowledge about who committed the murders. *The Daily Times* reported, "A man [Tex Baker, age fifty-one], who allegedly hitchhiked from Texas to Pryor to present evidence that camp counselors, not Gene Leroy Hart, were responsible for the murders of three Girl Scouts, was arrested for child molestation."[189] As he was being taken to jail, Baker was heard to say, "This is that Pryor County justice."

At the conclusion of the prosecutor's case, Garvin Isaacs demurred to the evidence and asked for a dismissal. A demurrer basically argues that the prosecution has not met its burden of proof. The request was denied. The preliminary hearing would continue. It would now be the defense's turn.[190]

Usually at a preliminary hearing the defense does not present any evidence. However, the defense does have a right to put on evidence. In this case, it would be seen that it was a good thing that the defense did put on evidence. One of the strategies of defense counsel was to give the prosecutors an idea of what they faced. The defense lawyers were not trying to win the case at the preliminary hearing. They wanted to show the prosecutors that they were going to defend Hart to the ultimate.

A teenage Locust Grove man who once may have given Gene Leroy Hart a ride testified. He testified he was threatened with felony charges unless he helped the prosecutors put Hart at the scene of the murders.[191]

Jack Lay, an agent for the OSBI, testified a twenty-year-old New Mexico prison escapee, Rikki Green, had confessed to the murders of the girls in 1977. The OSBI had discounted the confession. Lay said Green was not considered a viable suspect because he was "hazy" when questioned about details of the murders. "I asked him how he committed the crimes, and he couldn't remember," Lay told Isaacs during questioning

Green told Lay he had entered the camp with two other persons, one of them described as a part-Indian male from Tulsa. Green said he was "high on drugs" and had murdered the three girls. Green had been fingerprinted but no blood or hair samples were taken.

Green had been given five polygraph examinations and, according to Lay, had "flunked" them all. Lay said, "We were pretty sure he was lying from the start to keep from going back to New Mexico."

The judge began to get upset with the length of the proceedings. He said, in order to expedite the proceedings, he was considering the possibility of night proceedings. He never did resort to night court.

Fallis began to complain to the judge, saying the defense lawyers were on a "fishing expedition" and they "[were] imposing on the court's time." Fallis complained the "attitude" of the defense counsel was "let me run out and find another witness." Fallis told Judge Clanton he planned on filing a motion to prevent a "seemingly never-ending procession of witnesses." Judge Clanton told Isaacs to move his case along.[192]

Fallis never filed any motion to hurry the defense. He preferred to just complain. After the day's proceedings, Isaacs met with reporters and responded to Fallis's gripes. He said, using a baseball analogy, that the prosecution has had its time "at bat and now it's ours. We've got a lot more to offer."

The defense called Danny Creekmore to testify at the preliminary hearing. Sheriff Weaver had testified previously about information Creekmore had given him. The information was Creekmore had met Hart in a cave shortly after the murders. Creekmore was a sixteen-year-old runaway being held in juvenile detention in Tulsa. Creekmore said he "made up" the story because "he thought a reward would be paid."[193]

Travis Coverdale, who lived in a rural area near Locust Grove, said a "stranger was jumped" on property near his sister's land four days after the triple slayings. He later saw two men walking down a road. Sheriff Weaver's office was notified. "Both of the men—they were white—were taken into the sheriff's car, but that's the last I have heard of them," Coverdale testified.[194]

"the defense calls jimmie don bunch"

The defense called a prison inmate named Jimmie Don Bunch. Garvin Isaacs had interviewed Bunch, an OSP inmate in his cell on June 5, 1978. Isaacs called him to testify, thinking he would stand by a tape-recorded interview and sworn statement. Isaacs believed Bunch would testify state agents had asked him to lie against Hart.

Bunch, in an affidavit sworn in 2007, stated Buddy Fallis and Ron Shaffer had him brought to their office in Tulsa. According to Bunch, Fallis showed him photographs of the dead girl scouts and asked him if he could, in good conscience, lie for the man who had "mutilated" three "little girl scouts." When Bunch took the stand, his testimony was a jolt to defense counsel.[195] He changed his story.

Rather than testify he had been asked to lie against Hart, Bunch began telling a story that his statements to Isaacs were lies and that Isaacs knew they were lies. On the taped interview with Isaacs, Bunch reported a prison guard named Pulschney had promised him a "one-way ticket home." Bunch could be heard on the tape telling what he had said in response to the guard's offer: "And I said, you mean you are trying to say that if I get up on the stand and say that Gene Leroy Hart admitted the murder that you will guarantee my parole? He said I am saying that the OSBI will get you out of there on parole."

According to Bunch, Garvin Isaacs had promised him a parole if he would testify as a witness in favor of Hart. He and Isaacs had supposedly negotiated before the tape recorder was turned on. The major weakness in Bunch's testimony is apparent. How could Garvin Isaacs promise parole to anyone? He had no authority. At the time he was an unknown defense attorney. He had no such stroke.

Bunch was a seasoned convict. He should have known that Isaacs's lack of authority to come through on such a promise was readily apparent. The tape recording contradicted Bunch's version of the events. During the playing of the tape, one could hear Garvin Isaacs ask, "Have I promised you anything for saying this?"

"No, sir," replied Bunch. He then told Isaacs, "Garvin, there is nothing you could promise me. I don't think you could get me out of here. I am doing this because I feel they are bum rapping the man. When I am saying bum rapping, I believe they are trying to frame him."

Bunch could also be heard on the tapes saying,

> I want to go home as bad as anybody, but I have got to live with myself, and if it means getting up there and lying on Gene Leroy Hart for something that the man didn't do I would serve every day on death row, and I am sure that I will receive some kind of retaliation from this, for coming up here and telling the truth.

At the preliminary hearing, Bunch said he was incarcerated near Hart. He and Hart had discussed the case several times. Bunch asked Hart if he was guilty. "I don't know," said Hart.

Hart allegedly told Bunch he had been smoking "reefer and drinking wine for several days." According to Bunch, Hart said he had woke up in a cave with blood all over him. "That's when I really knew he had committed the murders," Bunch said.

An outraged Isaacs accused Bunch of lying and repeatedly asked Bunch why he had signed a transcript of a recorded statement in which he had claimed that he had been pressured to testify against Hart. Bunch, who was serving a twelve-year sentence for kidnapping and escape, admitted he signed the statement to help Hart but insisted the statements he had made were not true.

On cross-examination by Buddy Fallis, Bunch said the only threats he had received were from Isaacs. According to Bunch, Isaacs had told him that, if he did not testify as Isaacs wished, "Tulsa law enforcement officers will put a bullet between your eyes."

This statement by Bunch is not credible. Why would Tulsa law enforcement help Hart's lawyers?

In a 2007 affidavit, Bunch said Hart, after he returned to prison, came to him and told him that "he wasn't angry at me" and that he really "regretted" what happened to the three girls. Isaacs was naturally upset about Bunch's testimony. He said, "I've had it done to me before, but never like this.[196] Hart, who was usually described as calm and displaying no emotion, was said to be "really depressed and mad."[197]

After the defense rested, Judge Clanton bound Hart over for trial.[198] The judge said he "[found] a crime of murder in the first degree ha[d] been committed and that there was probable cause to believe that the defendant, Gene Leroy Hart, committed the crime." The judge made the same ruling in all three cases.

Hart displayed no emotion as the decision was aired. The ruling came on the fourteenth day of the preliminary hearing. The ruling to send Hart to trial may not have been the most exciting event of the day. For excitement nothing much can exceed a bomb threat. An anonymous caller called the court clerk's office and told Deputy Clerk Vicki Deffenbaugh, "There's a bomb set to go off in the courthouse at 10:30."

Ms. Deffenbaugh notified Eloise Gist, the court clerk, who advised Judge Clanton. At 9:31 a.m., a recess was called. At 10:34 a.m., Judge Clanton was notified no bomb had been found. Twelve minutes later, the preliminary hearing restarted.[199]

On July 1, 1978, previous to the bomb threat, it was reported security of Hart was "increased." "Friday's session was marked by security measures that seemed to catch spectators by surprise. Hart was taken from the Mayes County Jail across the street from the courthouse on a run and went through a different door than he usually did." Sheriff Weaver reported "certain activities" in the community had prompted new security measures. [200]

Subsequent to the preliminary hearing, the *Daily Oklahoman* published an editorial critical of the preliminary hearing.[201] The editorial complained that "[j]ustice stumbled and stalled but finally made it to the finish line just ahead of extreme boredom and public impatience." The editorial was critical of the defense lawyers, saying they had turned the proceedings into nothing more than a "fishing expedition." This editorial was a far cry from the sentiment expressed in the Pryor newspaper that Hart was "presumed innocent." The editorial went on to say "[t]hey were not the first defense lawyers to employ the device." The editorial was critical of Judge Clanton. The editorial pondered why the judge did not cut off questioning at an earlier point in the proceedings. The editorial was also critical of the Hart supporters: "It's a pity that our society is yet so unsophisticated that the cry of 'persecution' must be anticipated anytime a minority-race member is brought to trial." The last paragraph of the editorial called for a change of venue. [202]

The editorial challenged defense counsel statements that the trial could not take place until the following year: "[T]he trial should not be put off until next year, as defense lawyers are suggesting might be necessary." The editorial acknowledged Hart deserved a fair trial, but that there was also a need for a "prompt disposition" of the case.

Following the preliminary hearing, it was reported a man had signed a local motel register with the name "Gene Leroy Hart." Sheriff Weaver was told by an unidentified informant the man planned to cause "trouble." The informant had been evasive and could not say what the man planned to do. Weaver told reporters the threats were "nothing out of the ordinary in a case of this magnitude which received this much publicity." Whether the information was reliable or not, the man, the so-called "Gene Leroy Hart," did not cause a disturbance.[203]

getting ready for trial

The Hart defense team may not have had much money, but they did have a lot of paper. The lawyers representing Hart were not shy about filing motions in support of their client.[204]

Most of the defense motions were written by Barry Cousins, a lawyer who played an active part in defending Hart but stayed behind the scenes. Cousins' role was to file every imaginable motion he could think would apply to the case. By the end of trial, over sixty written motions were filed by defense counsel. Defense counsel, in the motions, attacked the failure of the State to disclose evidence the defense lawyers were entitled to review. The defense filed motions to suppress evidence, motion to prevent evidence of other crimes committed by Hart to be introduce, motions to prevent imposition of the death penalty.

Isaacs had convinced the judge that the prosecutors should file written responses to all defense pre-trial motions. The purpose, Isaacs said was to insure a proper appellate record was available. A strategic reason for filing the motions was to keep the prosecutors busy. To this day, prosecutors in Oklahoma hate to respond in writing to defense motions. If you can keep a prosecutor in the law library or at his/her desk writing and researching, there is less time to work on the presentation of evidence.

On April 23, 1978, a motion was filed saying Hart could not get a fair trial because the prosecutors and law enforcement officials were leaking information that Hart was an escape risk.[205] The defense team complained about a lot of things.

The *Daily Times* published a story in which Garvin Isaacs complained because a Cherokee County assistant district attorney had chosen not to release a composite drawing of a suspect in a violent rape. The story said Isaacs was "angered."[206] Isaacs was upset because he wanted to make the argument that this individual might have killed the Girl Scouts. Until the day of trial, defense counsel was continually asking for more time. The judge, however, held the reins tight. All continuance requests were denied including one right before trial.[207]

the judge

In every criminal trial, a key player is the judge. The judge in *State of Oklahoma v. Gene Leroy Hart* would be the Honorable William Whistler. Judge Whistler served as a judge in Craig, Rogers, and Mayes County.

Prior to a trial, the lawyers always want to know what makes the judge tick or what are his/her viewpoints. Whistler was well respected. He had actually been a practicing lawyer. Today, district judges in Oklahoma are usually former prosecutors. Candidates for district judge run advertisements saying they are endorsed by law enforcement.

Whistler was forty-five-years old when he ran for associate district judge. He had been practicing law out of a Vinita office for twenty-two years. He would win the election and become a judge.

Whistler was a graduate of the University of Oklahoma College of Law. He was a former president of the Craig County Bar Association. He was a member of the American Legion.

A case in which Judge Whistler stirred up public criticism from some was *State of Oklahoma v. Zoella Mae Dorland.*[208] That case had been tried a few years before Lori, Denise, and Michele were murdered. Zoella May Dorland

and her husband, Clarence, lived in a trailer park in Catoosa, Oklahoma. The couple had three small children. Patti Adamson lived next door.

On February 4, 1975, Clarence was shot and killed while he was in the doorway of Adamson's trailer. Zoella was charged with murder. Claremore lawyer Jack Gordon, Jr. was appointed to represent Zoella. There was not much of a defense available. "She shot him through the heart with a .44 magnum in his girlfriend's trailer, right next to hers."

The case would be prosecuted by Sid Wise, district attorney, and Bill Higgins, assistant district attorney. It would be Jack Gordon, Jr.'s first murder trial. The jury deliberated six hours before finding Zoella guilty. However, she was not found guilty of murder. The jury found she was guilty of a lesser degree of homicide, first-degree manslaughter. The jury recommended she spend four and one-half years in prison.

The controversy in the Dorland case arose at the formal sentencing. Judge Whistler, obviously believing Zoella should not go to prison, imposed a suspended sentence. The next day's headline: "Killer Goes Free." Judge Whistler showed by his decision he would not always follow the prosecutor's recommendation.

In the Hart case, Judge Whistler allowed individualized *voir dire* of potential jurors, lengthy questioning of jurors, and excluded some of the State's evidence. Judge Whistler had a tough job to do in the Hart case. No comments have ever been printed in which Judge Whistler was criticized for any of his rulings. No media has put the blame of the State's loss in the case upon Judge Whistler.

After the trial, Judge Whistler called members of the victim's families into his chambers. He told them, "Sometimes for our system to work, the guilty have to go free." Whistler would come close to granting a mistrial due to comments made by Fallis in closing arguments. He believed Fallis had perilously come close to commenting on Hart not taking the stand during the trial. The issue would have been a centerpiece of an appeal if Hart had been convicted.[209]

the oklahoma trial of the century begins

The trial of Gene Leroy Hart remains the most controversial trial in Oklahoma history. Some might argue that the trials of Timothy McVeigh and Terry Nichols were the trials of the century. There is no doubt that they participated in the crime of the century. Hart's trial was an event of real controversy. The case was like a sporting event in which the outcome was not predestined.

During a press conference held during the trial, Hart expressed his attitude about being the center of attention in this event. "I have no desire to be here," he said. "Maybe I represent the fears and doubts that many people have about a case like this in the system that we have."[210]

The case would be one of the first death penalty cases in Oklahoma since Oklahoma had reinstated the death sentence. The United States Supreme Court in 1972 declared current state death penalty statutes unconstitutional. Fallis was outraged by the decision. States, including Oklahoma, revised their statutes in order to pass constitutional muster. At the time of Hart's trial, Oklahoma had not executed anyone since 1966.

There was an article that reported the trial would bring a million dollars of economic impact into Pryor.[211] The article said Gene Leroy Hart was one of Pryor's "biggest industries."

A local beautician was quoted as saying, "We've got a bonanza in our lap. I think my business will jump a lot, especially with all the women coming to town."

Tom Hoxie, executive director of the Pryor Area Chamber of Commerce, in the same article, said, "It is not all that good that it takes a trial to spark the economy, but these are the facts with what we must live with during this time. I hate to use the old bromide 'it's an ill wind that blows somebody good,' but so be it."[212] Richard Guse, Michele's father, was asked if he was offended by the story about the economic impact of the trial concerning his daughter's death. He answered no.[213]

Guse took the opportunity to praise the town of Pryor. "You have so many good things going for you," Guse said of Pryor. "I just want to let the people of Pryor know that this is a real nice community, and I would hope the people would not chose sides and become divided on this." He also said, "I don't have any right to condemn anyone. I don't believe the people of Pryor would like anything better than to turn back the clock of time."[214]

Unfortunately for the town of Pryor, the economic boom never materialized. Although there was some increase in business during the preliminary hearing, the trial did little economically to the town coffers.[215] The motels did a brisk business. One motel owner said his motel was hosting reporters from the *New York Times*, a Fort Smith, Arkansas, newspaper, and Oklahoma City and Tulsa papers. Other places hosted reporters from Dallas and Chicago, affiliates

Gloyd McCoy

of the National Broadcasting Company and the American Broadcasting Company and representatives from radio, television, and newspapers from across Oklahoma.[216]

The eyes of the entire state of Oklahoma would be on the Pryor courthouse. The trial would be the feature of every Oklahoma newspaper and television news report until it concluded, and even afterward.[217]

Prior to the start of trial, the Oklahoma Court of Criminal Appeals, entered a ruling regarding Hart's access to certain material. The court ruled unanimously Hart's lawyers should be given any evidence the State had, which might tend to clear him. The State had argued and won at the trial court level that any such evidence was work product and should not be given to Hart. The Court of Criminal Appeals ruled former prosecutor, Sidney Wise, had forfeited the State's right to keep its work product private when he gave investigative reports to a former newspaperman, Ross Grimsley, who had contracted with Wise to write a book about the slayings.[218]

Defense counsel had also asked the Oklahoma Court of Criminal Appeals to disqualify the prosecutors on the case based on the alleged impropriety of Wise. At the time, there was no better prosecutor than Fallis. The defense was hoping to get him booted out and get a lawyer not as skilled. Unanimously, the court denied the request. Fallis and Shaffer would try the case as planned.[219]

Defense counsel had, prior to the start of trial, vigorously pressed for postponement based on their lack of access to the State's evidence. The lawyers, after exhausting state avenues, even took the unusual step of trying to convince the area federal court to stop the trial. This attempt failed. The Honorable Dale Cook denied the request saying, "It is well settled that a federal court should not enjoin a state prosecution or any state judicial proceeding except for the most exigent circumstances."[220]

"I'm just glad very glad the time is approaching that we will finally go to trial. It's been nearly two years since the tragedy of Camp Scott and I think the public has a right to see this thing through to its conclusion," Sheriff Weaver told the press.[221] Weaver also pointed out a bit or irony. The day the trial would start was the sixty-seventh anniversary of the founding of the Girl Scouts of America in 1912.

When Hart arrived in court on the first day of trial, he did not look like a man who had spent months in jail. In fact, he was quite dapper. Except for the circumstances, especially the guards, he could have easily passed for an attorney. His new clothes had been brought to him by his family. He was wearing new glasses, and his hair had been neatly trimmed. He appeared calm as he watched the proceedings begin.

Bettye Milner, the mother of Denise, was in the court-room almost every day of the trial. She commented on Hart's dress and demeanor. She said the jurors "weren't able to see past Hart's slick courtroom image. When Hart walked into the trial, you saw a well-dressed intelligent Indian man with a briefcase. You didn't see the Hart he was. We expect some-one to look like a murderer, and it doesn't always work."[222]

The courtroom was filled with spectators. Family members of Lori, Denise, and Michele, members of the media, and interested citizens filled every seat in the courtroom. There had certainly never been a case with this much noto-riety in Pryor or for that matter Oklahoma. There was a lot on the line. Not only was Hart's life at stake, but there were careers on the line and reputations.

The lawyers on both sides were striving to achieve the status of hero. Of course, they would never have said so. However, generically speaking, prosecutors and defense lawyers, even those who appear mild mannered, have tremendous egos and ambition. Such lawyers think they can do anything. The case would certainly alter all the participants' lives, even the non-lawyers.

As the trial began, no one was certain of its outcome and what effect it would have on the futures of those involved. Both sides were confident of victory. It would be a legal battle of the ages. Neither side feared the other.

The *Tulsa World* predicted the intensity displayed during previous court hearings by the lawyers would continue. "Bitter clashes between Isaacs and prosecutor S. M. Fallis—who strongly dislike each other but stop short of publicly saying so—are expected to continue during the trial."[223]

One story, regarding Isaacs and Fallis, which received no mention in the newspapers at the time, was the way the taller Isaacs would try to intimidate Fallis and make him mad. When the lawyers would approach the bench to make an argument, Isaacs would often nudge Fallis with his elbow or step on his foot intentionally. Fallis never complained but would often stand back from the bench. The judge would often call him forward so he could be heard. At one point in the trial, Fallis objected when Isaacs stood between him and the judge.[224]

Fallis was not used to such tactics. With less-talented defense lawyers, he could be intimidating and somewhat of a bully. Top quality lawyers were treated in a more gentlemanly manner and most of them thought he was a "great guy." None had tried Isaacs's tactic of using prosecutorial tactics on Fallis. The plot, well conceived, was to get Fallis mad and get him to forget the case. Make it personal. Get the jury to like the defense better than the prosecutor. If the jury did not like Isaacs's manner of attacking Fallis, they would have the kindly, quiet, and well-prepared rookie lawyer, Gary Pitchlynn.

Lawyers and persons who watched the performance of Pitchlynn were quite impressed, and to this day, he receives rave reviews from those who were there. At the time, Pitchlynn had a full beard. It made him look professorial.

Isaacs, despite being over thirty, still had somewhat of a baby face. The lawyers' personalities were different, but together they made a good team. Insiders say they never heard them argue amongst themselves to any great extent.

Pitchlynn did not seek the spotlight. He was glad that Isaacs like to mingle with the press. He had plenty to do.

On the day the trial started, the *Tulsa World* reported: "A source who has privileged information of the triple murder investigation says that the prosecution's case is 'strong.' But the source maintained that it is not 'invulnerable.'"[225] The trial would start twenty-one months and five days after the deaths of the three young girls.

Judge Whistler estimated it would take two weeks to try the case.[226] It would take a month. It would take ten days to pick a jury.

the decision will
be in your hands

In America, a defendant in a criminal case has a right to have his fate decided by a jury of his peers. The right to a jury trial is available for minor crimes all the way up the crime chart to first-degree murder. In the Hart case, three times the usual number of names of potential jurors were drawn in anticipation of the trial. Twelve people from the list would be chosen. Not only would the defendant's guilt or innocence be determined, his life would be at stake.

During jury selection in Oklahoma, the trial judge begins by asking questions of the jury usually involving identification and the potential juror's background. Under Oklahoma law, after the judge completes his preliminary questions, both the prosecutor and defense counsel get a chance to question jurors. Other states and the federal system only allow the judge to question prospective jurors; although, both sides are allowed to submit relevant questions for the judge's consideration.

The jury selection procedure is especially important in highly publicized cases. It is important to ensure jurors were not tainted by what they had heard from television news reports or read in the newspapers.

Jury selection is one of the most important parts of a trial for both the prosecution and the defense. Both sides want jurors that they feel will be amenable to their side of the story. In other words, they want to stack the deck in their favor.

Potential jurors can be excused for "cause." A prosecutor or defense attorney can ask that a potential juror be excused from jury service if there is some reason why that juror could not be fair. For example, if a prospective juror had already formed an opinion of the case, it could be presumed the juror could not be fair.

In cases involving the death penalty as a sentencing alternative, a prospective juror can be excused for cause if he/she cannot consider the death penalty as a possible punishment. Alternatively, a defense lawyer would ask to excuse a potential juror for cause if the person would automatically impose the death penalty and not consider life imprisonment.

The lawyers are also allowed to use peremptory challenges. Generally speaking, a lawyer can use a peremptory challenge to excuse a potential juror for any reason. Each side is given a certain number of peremptory challenges. Once there are twelve jurors and there is no basis to excuse any for cause and each side has exhausted its peremptory challenges, the jury has been established.

Jury selection is both an art and a science. Much has been written by legal commentators on the proper way to pick a jury. Every lawyer has a theory. The United States Court of Appeals for the Fifth Circuit once said of jury selection, "The selection of a jury is a call upon experience and intuition. The trial lawyer must draw upon his insights and emphatic abilities. Written records give us only shadows for measuring the quality of such efforts."[227]

Gloyd McCoy

Some lawyers use jury consultants to help pick juries. The defense was assisted in their efforts to pick a jury by Cathy Bennett, a psychologist from Santa Barbara, California. Bennett was allowed to sit at counsel table and assist the defense lawyers in screening and evaluating the potential jurors. Bennett said, "I only accept cases I believe in."[228] She said, "We're looking for jurors who are independent minded, will give the guy a fair shake and will listen to the evidence and will not give over to peer pressure."

Bennett had received notoriety in the Indian community by assisting in the cases that evolved after the Wounded Knee situation in South Dakota. She had a bachelor of arts degree from the University of Florida. She had a master's degree in humanistic psychology. Bennett's primary advice to the lawyers was simple: ask the potential jurors open-ended question. The answers to open-ended questions will reveal a persons thoughts, and that will be far more revealing than yes or no answers. She would lecture on this method her entire lifetime.

When Bennett was quoted in the paper after the first day of trial, Judge Whistler told Bennett and Isaacs, "I am going to admonish you and Miss Bennett not to comment on the case. If she does not care to abide by that, she'll become a spectator at that point."

Buddy Fallis had complained of Bennett talking to the press. Ironically, after Bennett had been admonished by the judge, Fallis talked to the press and said the "State did not think it was necessary that those called for jury duty be psychoanalyzed."

Fallis had never participated in a case in which defense counsel had so diligently went through the process of selecting jurors. Fallis would have been satisfied to take the first twelve people put in the jury box. That is unless they were American Indian, lived in Locust Grove, and didn't believe in the death penalty.

The defense needed its jurors "psychoanalyzed." Bennett may well have been the most important non-lawyer on Hart's team. No witness testimony was as helpful to Hart as her advice. She helped pick the jurors who would believe in Hart's defense and not convict him merely because he had been charged.

Both sides talked to the press. Many of their quotes were broadcasted or printed. The statements by the lawyers helped increase the notoriety of the case. At the time, it was rare for a judge to impose a gag order prohibiting lawyers from commenting to the press. Today, one of the first orders signed by a trial judge in a highly publicized case is to impose an order prohibiting commentary by the lawyers to the press.

The jury selection procedure in this case had been modified. Judge Whistler had agreed to allow individualized jury selection. Rather than question the jurors as a group, the court would allow separate interviews of each potential jurors. In a case involving publicity and high emotions, one does not want to have a juror's answer to a question taint the other jurors.

Judge Whistler began jury selection with what he referred to as his "patriotic speech." "If war is too important to leave to generals," the judge told the prospective jurors, "justice is too important to leave to the lawyers."

During his questioning, Judge Whistler repeatedly asked the jurors if the fact Hart was an Indian would influence their decision. He also questioned the venire about their attitude on the death penalty and whether or not they had already formed an opinion of the case. A main emphasis of Judge Whistler's questioning was the potential juror's willingness to follow the law.

After Judge Whistler finished his questions, the prosecutors were allowed to question the prospective jurors. Following their questions, defense counsel had their turn. It was estimated that defense counsel spent four times longer asking questions than did the prosecution

Judge Whistler indicated early he would not be moved by jurors who claimed a hardship. When defense counsel Isaacs asked a juror be excused because of an illness in her family, the judge said, "The trial is going to be a hardship for everyone. If I use that as grounds, Mr. Isaacs I wouldn't have a jury."[229]

During jury selection, the defense was far more active. One exasperated potential juror, after lengthy questioning from Garvin Isaacs, told the defense lawyer his grueling questioning was "making me feel guilty."[230] In addition to the tedious and often prying questions by Isaacs, the defense team had a dozen law students led by John Zelbst canvassing the county checking out jurors.

The law student's questioning of the townspeople about the potential jurors angered many of the people they approached. "I don't appreciate some of the things they were asking," one woman said. "They were pushy, and I won't let them come in here again."[231]

The second day of jury selection saw a heated argument. Isaacs, during questioning of a potential juror, suddenly turned toward Ron Shaffer and accused him of "tampering" with the juror. Isaacs' charge was Shaffer was trying to tip an answer to a potential juror by body language or gestures. "If you've got something to say," Isaacs snapped, "would you come up and state it?"

Shaffer responded by asking the judge to have Isaacs direct his questions to the prospective juror. Isaacs then directly accused him of trying to communicate with the juror.

Judge Whistler called the lawyers to the bench. He did not want the prospective jurors to hear him. "There's only one God in heaven and only one judge in this court, and I'm it," he snarled at Isaacs. He then asked Isaacs if he was "prepared to conduct yourself properly in this courtroom?" Isaacs responded, "Yes, sir—I'm just trying to represent my client as competently as I can."

Later during questioning, another flare-up occurred. Fallis objected when Isaacs asked a potential juror if she believed a prosecutor could be unethical. "The defense seems unable to abide by the rules," Fallis said.

During the jury selection, several Indians were excused by peremptory challenges used by the prosecution. Normally, peremptory challenges can be used to exclude a prospective juror for any reason at the discretion of the party. Normally, a lawyer is not required to give a reason why the person was excluded from service. Isaacs objected to the prosecutor's use of peremptory challenges. He argued the State was trying to systematically exclude Indians from jury service. The objection was overruled. That ruling was correct under the then state of the law. However, based on a United States Supreme Court case, that is not the law today. A prosecutor cannot use peremptory challenges based solely on race. The prosecutor would be required to give a non-racial legitimate reason for excluding the person.[232]

Judge Whistler was part Indian. Isaacs argued, at one point, the judge was "bending over backward" to show that he was not prejudiced in favor of Indians. Isaacs also complained the judge was showing prejudice to Hart by the "tone of his voice and attitude."

Judge Whistler emphatically denied the accusations.

Monday, March 12, 1979, was described as "the most frustrating day since the jury selection began a week ago."[233] Twenty-four potential jurors were paraded in and out of the courtroom. There were seven hours of questioning.

At the end of the day, only one potential juror, a young hospitality hostess at a resort who was also a high school drop out, made it through the process without being excused. At one point, Judge Whistler summoned the lawyers to the bench to discuss ways to make the proceedings go faster. At another point in the proceedings, the judge ordered the prospective jurors who were being kept in an adjoining courtroom to be moved to another location. The judge was fearful the prospective jurors could hear the questioning and formulate answers designed to get themselves excused from jury service.

Sixteen prospective jurors were excused because they had already formed an opinion about the case. Other potential jurors were removed for varied reasons, from opposition to the death penalty to being close friends of the Hart family or close friends of witnesses who were expected to testify. One man was excused because he was a relative of Hart. A Pryor saleswoman was dismissed because she felt "animosity" toward a law enforcement officer who was expected to be called as a witness.

Although she had previously been admonished not to talk to the press, jury consultant Cathy Bennett was quoted in the next day's *Daily Oklahoman* as saying she had "never seen anything like it" in the seventy-five trials she had been involved.

One question Garvin Isaacs would ask the potential jurors was, "What is your favorite television show?" Fallis, in an attempt he said to "speed things up," began asking the question. When Fallis mentioned he was trying to "speed things up," Isaacs jumped from his chair objecting, "Judge, I object to him continually saying something about saving time." The objection was overruled.[234]

The jury selection process drove Fallis crazy. He especially got cantankerous when Isaacs spent sixty-eight minutes questioning one prospective juror. At one point, Fallis asked a potential juror, "If I stood here for an hour, would that make you any more of a qualified juror?"[235]

Isaacs later objected to a statement by Fallis that "too often the victims are ignored." That objection too was overruled.[236] Although the jury selection process was proving to be tedious, members of the community still continued to attend the proceedings. "It fascinates me," said Gerald Manley of Pryor. Manley, age forty, had sat through all of the jury proceedings, as well as all the motion hearings and all but one day of the lengthy preliminary hearing.

Manley had to attend a funeral on the one day he missed. Manley lived only five blocks from the courthouse. He would awaken at 5:30 a.m. and begin standing in line in the dark for one of the coveted courtroom seats. "It's better than TV," he said. Manley had "been there since the beginning and would be there until the end."

Priscilla Dougherty and Doreen Colvin drove twenty miles each day from Locust Grove to attend the proceedings. "We just want so bad to find out who killed the girls," said Dougherty. She added, "We don't think this boy Hart had anything to do with it," Colvin said. "The only thing we wanted from the first for Hart is a fair trial." Colvin had many questions about the case. She hoped that, by attending the court proceedings, her questions would be answered.

Jack Headrick, who lived between Pryor and Locust Grove, had also been a regular attendee of the proceedings. He arose every morning so he could complete his work at his job in time to attend the afternoon trial sessions. He usually arrived at the courthouse at 2:00 p.m. and would stay until the close of court business. Headrick said, "Sometimes we stand in line two or three hours to get into the damn thing." Headrick, at the time, had a seven-year-old daughter who was a member of Camp Fire Girls. "She's going back to camp this summer, not here, but somewhere," he said. "As a parent I have to know. I want to see the evidence for myself." He also said, "I'm here to see he [Hart] gets a fair shake because he's guilty, we're talking about taking a man's life. And if he's innocent, then that means there's someone still out there lurking about."

On the last day of jury selection, Garvin Isaacs attempted to have Sheriff Weaver and Undersheriff Al Boyer removed from their seats directly across from the prospective jurors. Hart thought the two men were spying on the potential jurors and also on defense counsel. He wanted the men "removed from the courtroom or have them moved to another area."

Judge Whistler denied the request. Isaacs quipped, "I see the hypnotic eye coming my way on occasion." Laughter rippled through the courtroom. Even Judge Whistler broke into a wide smile. Isaacs was referring to the fact Weaver had recently completed a special course in hypnosis. At the time, many law enforcement agencies were using hypnosis as a way to supposedly refresh the memories of witnesses. The argument against the procedure was that it was unduly suggestive.

Years after the Hart trial, the Oklahoma Court of Criminal Appeals issued an opinion which would not allow a witness who had been hypnotized to testify. A murder conviction from Cleveland County, Norman, Oklahoma, was reversed because of the possible suggestive implications placed on a witness's mind. The case was never retried. Today, hypnotically enhanced testimony is generally unacceptable.

Judge Whistler continually commented he had never sat in on such a slow-moving jury selection. When the process ended, he said, "We can finally see the light at the end of the tunnel."[237] As the jury selection was coming to an end, each side began exercising its peremptory challenges.

Defense counsel used their final peremptory challenge to excuse a Pryor postal worker.[238] After ten days and the questioning of 113 people, six men and six women were seated as jurors.

The jury included three housewives, a basketball coach, a utility foreman, an industrial plant manager, an inventory clerk, a supermarket checker, an airline employee, a pipefitter, an apprentice electrician, and a former den mother for a Cub Scout group who worked at an antique shop. Six of the jurors were from Pryor, five from Adair, and one from Spavinaw. No Locust Grove native made it to the jury.

The jurors ranged in age from thirty to fifty-nine. "I think we've got a good jury. The system works," Judge Whistler stated.

Garvin Isaacs told reporters, "We are happy with the jurors. Hart is happy with them. We feel comfortable."[239]

The prosecutors did not express publicly whether or not they were "happy" with the panel of jurors.

During the ten days of jury selection, thirty-nine potential jurors were excused by the judge for cause after they said they had already formed an opinion about guilt or innocence. Fourteen other potential jurors were excused for cause because of their views about the death penalty. Seven of the fourteen said they could never vote for the death penalty in any case. Seven said they favored the death penalty as the sole punishment for a murder conviction regardless of the circumstances.

Judge Whistler requested the news media not print the names of the jurors.[240] The judge wanted to "lessen the chance pressure would be applied to them or their families." Ironically, after the verdict was announced, the *Tulsa World* published the names of the actual jurors. [241]

The jury was sequestered. They were housed at a local motel.[242] The jury spent their evenings at the Holiday Hotel. They were allowed to visit their families for fifteen minutes per day. An OSBI agent was there to monitor their conversations to ensure that there was no discussion of the trial.

the case starts

At the beginning of the actual case, defense counsel made some arguments to the judge. Defense counsel advised the judge they were prepared to stipulate with the prosecution where the bodies were located and each specific cause of death. Isaacs argued the prosecutors were offering certain photographs not for any proof of a relevant issue but to arouse the passions not only of the jury but the community.

Isaacs was making a good point. The prosecutors were running the risk of an appellate reversal due to the fact the cause of death was not an issue. The issue was not how the girls were killed or if their deaths were homicides. The issue was *who* killed Lori, Denise, and Michelle. The offer to stipulate on evidence is a technique often attempted by defense counsel in a criminal case to keep certain evidence from the juror's view. It rarely works. In order to have a stipulation, both sides must agree. Fallis, upon hearing the offer to stipulate, stated the prosecutors "were not prepared for a stipulation at this time."[243]

There was no way the prosecutors were going to give up the opportunity to present testimony and photographs detailing the horrific deaths of the three young girls.

A final motion in limine was also argued by defense counsel. Defense counsel sought to prevent the State from calling Larry Dry, the prisoner who had escaped with Hart from the Mayes County Jail, to testify to Hart's alleged conversations on sexual matters. The motion was denied.[244] The State, however, never presented the evidence.

The jury was instructed as to the law governing a trial. The jurors could not discuss the case among themselves until all the evidence had been presented, the arguments of counsel complete, and the applicable law charged. The jury would be allowed to read newspapers, but only after reports of the trial were cut out by court personnel.

Defense counsel moved the court to allow Gene Leroy Hart to give his own opening statement. Judge Whistler overruled the defense motion on the grounds that he could possibly make a legal error while delivering his statement.[245] Defense counsel was trying to pull a fast one. Under no circumstances did the defense want to put Hart on the stand. No matter how much they prepared Hart, the risk of putting him on the stand against an experienced prosecutor like Fallis was too great a risk. If Hart would have been allowed to present a canned opening statement claiming his innocence, the jury would have basically heard his version of the events. He would not have to face cross-examination. Neither would he be required to be placed under oath.

If Hart had been convicted, the judge's ruling refusing his request to give his own opening statement might have been an issue for appeal. However, although a defendant has an absolute right to represent himself, courts have usually held a defendant does not have the right to from time to time make an appearance as his own lawyer. Defendants have to make a choice, a lawyer or themselves. Hart

Gloyd McCoy

would have been foolish to make the choice for complete self-representation.

The idea that Hart should be allowed to give an opening statement in which he could, in effect, give a statement of the facts without the fear of cross-examination had some basis in Oklahoma history. In the Thresher case mentioned earlier, Stephen Jones put his client on the stand right before he was to give a closing argument. Collins made a statement to the jury before Jones gave his closing argument. The reason this was allowed was because the prosecutors made no objection.

Opening statement is the part of the trial in which the parties tell the jury what to expect. Each side gets to tell the jury the story of the case. One of the usual themes in a defense opening statement is that the jury should keep an open mind until all the evidence is presented.[246]

Buddy Fallis gave the opening statement for the State of Oklahoma.

As required by Oklahoma law, Fallis read to the jury the three murder charges against Hart. He then briefly told the jury the events that had taken place on or about the time of the murders and what type of testimony they could expect to hear. He finished his opening by telling the jury the State would prove beyond "any" reasonable doubt that "Gene Hart did in fact commit the crimes."[247]

Garvin Isaacs gave the opening statement for Hart. The jury was told to pay particular attention to the time and date of certain testimony. More specifically he asked them to pay close attention to testimony concerning photographs found in a cave near the camp. The photographs had supposedly been developed by Hart when he worked as a photography assistant while incarcerated at the Oklahoma State Reformitory in Granite, Oklahoma.[248]

"Keep your eyes on the pictures" Isaacs cautioned. "Watch those pictures. They are going to tell you a lot. They are going to tell you that Mr. Hart is an innocent man." Hart's defense to the photographs was they had been planted by Sheriff Weaver. Hart would argue the photographs had been confiscated when he was originally booked into the county jail prior to his escape. The photographs were then put in a cave to incriminate Hart.

Prior to trial, the *Washington Post* had reported on the alleged planting of the photographs:

> Sheriff Weaver declined to discuss whether the pho-
> tographs were among Hart's possession when he
> transferred him for a hearing from state prison in
> 1973. But it has been learned Hart says the photos
> were left behind in his wallet when he escaped out
> of Weaver's jail on September 16, 1973.[249]

Isaacs also told the jury that members of Hart's family were going to "put their freedom on the line to testify for the accused." Eventually, his mother would be the only family member to testify. She would testify that Hart was elsewhere at the time of the murders.

Isaacs concluded his remarks by saying the following in dramatic fashion: "I have come here to tell you what Mr. Hart would have said, if the court would have allowed him to talk." Surprisingly, the judge did not take offense to Isaacs's criticism of his prior ruling not allowing Hart to give his own opening statement.

No objection was made to the last statement. The prosecutors should have objected. Isaacs was implying Mr. Hart

142   *Gloyd McCoy*

was being denied a right, which he wasn't. Although Buddy Fallis objected to a lot of defense counsel's arguments or actions, he failed to object at certain key times.

One of the things a lawyer must do in his opening statement is show some enthusiasm for his cause. In the trial of Timothy McVeigh, for example, defense counsel Stephen Jones told the jury: "I have waited two years for this moment."[250]

At no point in the *State if Oklahoma v. Gene Leroy Hart* either side show a lack of enthusiasm.

The State's first group of witness included the three Kiowa Unit counselors, the director of Camp Scott, the director's husband, and the camp ranger. These witnesses testified to the events leading up to and including the discovery of the three dead girls.

Later, during the trial, the prosecutors called various law enforcement officials to testify. Reporter then and now lawyer Richard Rouse of Oklahoma City related this story about certain testimony:

> Several of the trial observers mentioned to me that during the trial, one of the deputies was testifying about searching a cave that had been occupied by someone. There was a pile of human feces that they dug through in a search for evidence. When asked what was used to dig through the piece of shit, he announced he had used a (Re)Elect Pete Weaver for Sheriff poster. [That remark] brought a huge gaffaw from everyone in the courtroom.[251]

Prosecutor Ron Shaffer called state of Oklahoma Assistant Medical Examiner Dr. Neill Hoffman. Dr. Hoffman had conducted the autopsies of the three girls. When Dr. Hoffman was called to testify, Garvin Isaacs stood up. He asked the judge to advise the families of the victims that the "gruesome" autopsy photographs were being admitted into evidence despite numerous objections. Judge Whistler denied the request. Again, Isaacs offered to stipulate to the cause of death. Again, the prosecutors refused the offer.[252]

Dr. Hoffman's testimony was upsetting. His descriptions were vivid. Naturally, a vivid description of an autopsy by nature is upsetting. He described how he first saw the girls. The first girl he saw was Denise Milner. She was laying on her back on top of her sleeping bag. "She was nude from the waist down and had some black shiny tape on her night shirt. Her hands were also bound by the same tape, and I had noticed three large areas of injury about the head."[253]

Dr. Hoffman also said Milner had absorbed laceration and tears to the vagina. He surmised that the tears and laceration were "probably" caused by a blunt object, most likely a male sex organ. On cross-examination, Dr. Hoffman admitted he did not in fact know that a male sex organ had caused the injuries. Dr. Hoffman concluded his testimony with statements regarding the autopsies of the other girls.

Following the testimony of Dr. Hoffman, the prosecutors called Oklahoma Highway Patrol Troopers Charles Newton and Leon Rice. The troopers testified regarding two crumpled photographs that had been found in a cellar-cave area near Hart's boyhood home. The cave was three miles from the murder scene. Three days after the murders, two squirrel hunters had came upon a cave and discovered the photographs. The photographs were of a wedding and were supposedly the property of Hart.[254]

The State next called Anne Reed, a crime scene investigator with the OSBI. She was to testify about "hair" evidence. Today, such evidence would be subject to much more scrutiny than it was at the time. "Courts are now confronting challenges to testimony [and evidence] whose admissibility has long been settled."[255]

The State's case depended on the "hair" evidence. At the time, the evidence was admissible. Currently, such evidence is deemed unreliable by the courts. Hair matching evidence is without standards for identification. Such evidence is scientifically unreliable and, thus, inadmissible. The state of the art of hair analysis has not reached the level of certainty to permit expert testimony that a defendant's hair is microscopically consistent with hair samples found at the crime scene. Observers believed Hart's case had been damaged by the "hair" testimony.[256] However, the jury was obviously impressed with Garvin Isaac's cross-examination of the witness.

The State's witness, Janice Davis, is now deceased. She committed suicide. Years after the Hart case, Ms. Davis's forensic testimony came under a great deal of controversy. In fact, there was a great deal of concern as to the reliability of forensic analysis in Oklahoma after 2000.[257]

There is always tremendous pressure on law enforcement to solve high profile crimes and harshly punishing the perpetrator. This factor often leads to the presentation of dubious evidence such as Janice Davis's "hair" evidence and the "sperm" evidence about to be discussed.

The prosecutors called Dr. John McLeod to testify. Dr. McLeod's testimony was a comparison of some "deformed" sperm taken from Hart's underwear and compared to semen taken from the crime scene. This testimony was presented, despite early reports in the investigation that no semen was found at the crime scene.[258]

The complaints of defense counsel about McLeod's testimony obviously were persuasive. Jurors, at the time, due to the lack of scientific foundation and other factors, especially when such evidence as here, was presented in a "statistical matter" could become confused or be persuaded to discount such testimony. [259]

One newspaper reported that expert witnesses from the State discussed the hair and sperm samples but "[t]he experts admitted such tests could not positively identify the source of the hair and sperm."[260]

During the State's case-in-chief, the jurors were taken to Camp Scott so they could see where the events occurred. Interestingly, the judge, the prosecutors, and defense counsel did not go with the jurors.

The jurors were taken to the site by deputies who had been instructed to not talk to the jurors. The jurors were instructed not to talk to each other or the deputies.[261] In writing of the jurors' visit to Camp Scott, a reporter wrote, "The question of how one person could kill and rape three girls without being heard has not been answered in the trial."[262] The jurors by viewing the scene may have determined that it would have been impossible for one person to have committed the crimes.

the hart defense

After the prosecution rested its case, the defense lawyers seriously considered not putting on any evidence. The defense is not required to take the stand and testify and is not required to put on any evidence. Garvin Isaacs said, "I began calling some witnesses because I think the jury expected us to present some evidence. Right now they may be hung up, but I didn't think they'd bring back a conviction."[263]

Ella Maye Buckskin was the first witness for the defense. She appeared represented by a lawyer. The reason she appeared with a lawyer was to reinforce the opening statement comment that Hart family members would testify but would risk charges being filed on them. Ms. Buckskin testified her son had been at her home on June 3, 1977. Also present at her home was her brother, Groundhog Sulletemke, who was deceased at the time of the trial. Ms. Buckskin said the two men stayed only a short time and then left to go to Tulsa. The point being Hart was in Tulsa and could not have killed the Girl Scouts.

The State attempted to admit statements from investigators who said Sulletemke made statements to them that did not corroborate Ms. Buckskin's testimony. Judge Whistler denied the attempt to introduce the statements.

The basis for the ruling was that Sulletemke was deceased and could not be cross-examined by defense counsel about his remarks. To admit the evidence would have been building reversible error into the record.

Hart returned to his mother's house three or four days after the murders of the three girls. Ms. Buckskin told him of "visitors" to the house, meaning law enforcement was looking for him. Hart went back to Tulsa, according to Buckskin.[264]

The defense called Sam Pigeon to testify for Hart.[265]

Pigeon was the Indian medicine man whom Hart had stayed with up until the time of his capture. Pigeon did not testify directly. He used the services of an interpreter who spoke the native Cherokee language.

Pigeon was called to rebut evidence presented by the prosecutors. These witnesses testified that a corncob pipe and blue hand mirror that was allegedly stolen from Camp Scott had been found in Pigeon's cabin after Hart's capture.

Pigeon testified, through his interpreter, that he had not seen the items in his cabin at any time. The defense's other argument regarding the pipe and the mirror was that they were planted like the photographs in the cave. The first time the three-room cabin was searched, the items were not found. On a subsequent search, they were found. Defense counsel vehemently argued the OSBI agents had planted the items the second time they searched.

The defense also put on evidence that another person had committed the crimes. Joyce Paine and her son, Larry Short, testified Bill Stevens, who at the time of Hart's trial was serving time in a Kansas prison,[266] came to their home near Okmulgee, Oklahoma, on the morning the scouts were discovered. Both said Stevens, age twenty-three, had

Gloyd McCoy

scratches on his neck and arms and red stains on his boots. Mrs. Paine claimed the flashlight recovered at the camp death scene was the same one she had loaned Stevens about a month before the slayings.[267]

A waitress from Choteau, Oklahoma, testified that a photograph of Stevens resembled a man who came into the café where she worked on the morning the bodies of Lori, Denise, and Michele were discovered at Camp Scott. Choteau was only twelve miles from Camp Scott. Denise Boyd, the waitress, said of the photograph, "It looks too much like him." She told how the man had taken his shirt off and kept looking at his hands. Boyd had contacted defense counsel after she had seen a photograph of Stevens on the news.[268]

Following the Hart trial, Mrs. Paine and her son were charged with perjury because of their testimony. A mistrial was declared when the jury deadlocked at seven to five for conviction. During that trial, the State of Oklahoma called Stevens to testify. The State did not call him during the Hart trial. Stevens testified he was working in Seminole, Oklahoma, on the day of the slaying. The two individuals were never retried.[269]

The State missed an opportunity. The defense was claiming someone else did the crime. What better way to rebut this testimony than to have the person actually testify? The *Washington Post* reported Stevens had been eliminated as a suspect: "Stevens, who is serving prison time in Kansas for conviction of rape and kidnapping, was eliminated as a suspect by prosecutors who said the hair and sperm found on the bodies of the victims were not his."[270]

This was one of the most important prosecutions in Oklahoma history. Yet the prosecutors did not call as a witness the person the defense was saying did the crime. The failure to call Stevens might have had some strategic rationale. However, any strategy excuse is weakened by the fact the State went to all the trouble to extradite Stevens to testify in the perjury trial. His testimony was needed at the Hart trial. This failure was a missed opportunity for the State.

The defense called Tom Kite to testify. Kite, now a lawyer in Oklahoma City, was one of the Vietnam veterans who participated in the manhunt for Hart. Kite testified about remarks made by Sheriff Weaver about Hart.

Weaver told Kite falsehoods in order to get him to think of Hart as dangerous. Weaver had supposedly told his deputies that, if they brought Hart in alive, they would lose their job. Weaver also told Kite that Hart's fingerprints were found at the crime scene, which was false. He also had told Kite that Hart was armed and dangerous. Weaver's trial testimony was that he could not remember making such statements. [271]

Weaver told Kite that Hart was making a circular route through the area and that he was on a pattern to return to Camp Scott. Weaver had no basis for such a statement. He told Kite that his group should hide and wait for Hart to return. Apparently, Weaver was trying to teach a lesson to Kite who had made statements to the press that former soldiers could find Hart if given the chance.

Weaver's attempt to teach Kite a lesson backfired. His treatment of Kite made him look like a liar and showed the pettiness of his character.

The defense called experts to rebut the hair and sperm analysis presented by the State. The *Washington Post* summarized the defense testimony: "The prosecution built its case on the point that hair and sperm found on the victim's bodies was probably Hart's. But experts said no possible comparison is possible in such situations."[272]

John T. Wilson, chief chemist of the Independence, Missouri Regional Crime Laboratory, said he had studied the reports of the State's witnesses. He said the test conducted by Dr. McLeod showed the presence of sperm but "beyond that I couldn't place any importance on it." Wilson, who was being paid $250 for appearing as an expert witness, agreed with the findings of the State's witness that hair found on the body of one of the girls had the same microscopic characteristics as Hart. However, he said it was impossible to identify a person by hair alone.[273]

Herbert Maxey, a former employee of the Oklahoma Health Department, testified for Hart. He said that he agreed that hair and sperm, even though characteristically similar, were not enough to accurately identify an individual. Maxey said more accurate hair testing could have been done. He said more accurate testing would have been possible with the use of a neutron activation oven. According to Maxey, such equipment costs about $400,000 and is used primarily by the FBI.

Maxey, a private consultant, said hair may look similar and give a race clue, but "[t]hat is as far as it goes." He said testing is not adequate if all that is used is a microscope.

On cross-examination by Mr. Fallis, Maxey held firm, stating again, "You can't identify anybody by sperm or even by hair." Maxey said he was not familiar with Dr. McLeod's work. However, he said his analysis using statistical methods "really doesn't tell us anything."

In 2009, Mary Long, a former OSBI chemist who now works for the Oklahoma Indigent Defense System, commented on the OSBI's forensic analysis capabilities at the time of the Hart trial:

> The laboratory capabilities at the time were not too great. Identification of blood, seminal fluid and sperm and other fluids, ABO typing on blood products, secretor testimony for ABO group substances in water based bodily fluids; nothing that even comes close to individualization with biological stuff.[274]

A young Girl Scout, Kim Lewis, was called as a witness. The young girl entered the courtroom with her mother. The scout testified that on the night of the murders she and a counselor and other girls came upon a man in the dark with a flashlight. The girl testified that the man was white and over six feet tall.

Gary Pitchlynn was the defense lawyer asking the girl questions. Dramatically, he asked Hart to stand. Pitchlynn asked the girl if Hart looked like the man she saw on that dark night. She responded, "He doesn't look very much like the man I saw."

Pitchlynn the handed the girl a photograph of Bill Stevens. He asked the girl if the man in the photograph looked like the man she saw. She said, "Yes." At that point, despite rebuttal testimony that other girls did not see Stevens, reasonable doubt may have been established.

the last witness

The defense's case-in-chief ended with the testimony of Allen Little. The next day's *Daily Oklahoman* had a lead article headlined "Hart Defense Rests With Dramatic Volley."

> The former jailer's testimony was among the most damaging leveled against the prosecution's case by defense lawyer Garvin Isaacs, who is attempting to convince the jury Weaver nursed a bitter grudge against Hart because of his escapes, and that it may have prompted Mayes County lawmen to "plant" evidence.

Little testified for thirty-five minutes. Afterward, he told reporters he was "shaking in his clothes."

Following his testimony, Little had asked Judge Whistler for police protection and a law enforcement escort from the courthouse. Judge Whistler denied the request. He told Little, "Get Mr. Isaacs to escort you."

Little, when he worked as a jailer, had seen the photographs taken by Hart in Weaver's office. He remembered the fact because he also remembered there was a car part there as well.

Following Little's testimony, the defense rested.

Gene Leroy Hart did not testify. The jury would later be instructed they could not use that fact that he had not testified against him as evidence of guilt.

The decision of whether or not a defendant should take the stand is a tough call in any case. O. J. Simpson did not testify in his murder trial.[275] The decision of whether or not to testify is one of the few decisions in a trial in which a defendant can overrule his lawyer. If the defense lawyer does not want his client to testify, the client can tell the court that he wants to testify anyway.

The only other decision that an accused can overrule his lawyer is the decision as to what plea to enter. If a defendant wishes to plead guilty, he cannot be stopped from doing so even if the defense lawyer believes that he could defeat the prosecution's case.

Prior to the start of the trial, the *Tulsa World* had predicted Hart would not take the stand:

> Hart probably won't take the stand, ostensibly because he doesn't want to implicate the people who helped harbor him for five years. But more realistically would be his fear of facing prosecution questions about his past convictions and the nature of his crimes.

In cases in which a defendant has prior convictions, the dilemma is that a defendant may need to testify, but his testimony can be impeached with his prior convictions.

The ultimate result in the trial shows Hart not taking the stand was the proper decision. When something works, it was effective representation. When it does not work, it can often be a claim for ineffective assistance of counsel on appeal and in collateral action.

After the defense rested its case-in-chief, the prosecutors called thirteen rebuttal witnesses. The defense then called five additional witnesses to rebut the prosecutors' rebuttal witnesses. At the end of the trial, seventy-six witnesses had testified.

On March 28, 1979, Judge Whistler adjourned the trial. The next day he would read the jury their instructions. Following the instructions, closing arguments would begin. Although he could have, Judge Whistler would not place any limitations on the time to be used in closing argument.

closing argument
of the state

By law, the prosecutor makes the first closing argument and then, because the prosecution has the burden of proof, is allowed a second or rebuttal closing argument. Unlike an opening statement, the lawyers are allowed to comment on the evidence and make points to the jury. Generally, lawyers are given wide latitude in making their argument. However, historically lawyers, especially prosecutors, have been known to push the envelope.

During the closing argument, all the lawyers were emotional. As legendary Texas plaintiff lawyer Joe Jamail has said, "If you are not emotionally involved, your client is not getting your best effort."[276]

Ron Shaffer made the first closing argument for the state of Oklahoma: "Ladies and gentlemen, I want to tell you that we appreciate your patience with us. I know you all are tired. I am too. We're all tired. But don't let fatigue interfere with what must be done under the evidence in this case."

Traditionally in closing argument the lawyers thank the jurors for their service. This is usually done in the opening moments. The practice not only reminds the jurors of the importance of their job but allows the lawyer to get used to speaking in an oratorical fashion after extended periods of only asking questions.

Shaffer began apologetically. He implied to the jurors that there might have been reason for the jurors to be impatient with the prosecutors. He got away with a legal conclusion or personal opinion that Hart committed the crimes. Defense counsel could have objected. He goes on to say, "We had three little girls in that Girl Scout camp brutally murdered, sodomized, and raped by Gene Leroy Hart. Gene Leroy Hart is the man that is here today. The little girls are why we are here today."

Shaffer began a theme that is echoed throughout the argument of the prosecutors that the "girls" are the "reason" the case is taking place. The prosecutors stressed the tragedy of the event.

He continues,

> Given a chance, if I may, I wanted to go over some of the items that we found there that this man left behind and are the things that came in the way of evidence from the bodies of those three little girls.
>
> We have the death scene at Camp Scott, and what do we find? We find two little girls zipped up in the sleeping bags, one of them tied up with her little hands behind her legs where he had raped and sodomized her. We had another little girl who was laying there dead, zipped up in a sleeping bag, little Lori Farmer. She had been raped. And if you recall Dr. Hoffman's testimony, that even occurred after the little girl was dead. And then we have little Doris Denise Milner, even though she can't be here today,[277] she left you all some evidence, some evidence pointing toward Gene Leroy Hart.

The prosecutor here made good use of the horrific crime scene. In most murder trials, prosecutors use the fact that the victim is not there. This argument was objectionable as being an attempt to elicit sympathy for the victims. Defense lawyers are not required to object to every argument that may technically improper. Shaffer said there is "evidence pointing to Hart." He did not enumerate what evidence he is talking about but digresses to talk about Hart being an Indian.

> Gene Leroy Hart, the man that says, "I am a Cherokee," and he puts a man like Sam Pigeon on that witness stand for you that says he's a religious man and his main part of his religion, if you recall his testimony, said that he helped anybody that came to his door. He used that old man just like he used those little girls at Camp Scott on June thirteenth, not because he's an Indian, because he knows that that is the kind of religion that man had. I'm proud of the little bit of Cherokee that I've got running through my veins. He uses his, and that is what is not right insofar as he's saying and getting what he got from Sam Pigeon.

Shaffer digressed to discuss "Indian" matters. He claimed Hart "used" Sam Pigeon. The evidence was that Sam Pigeon knew what he was doing and had volunteered to help Hart. Defense counsel could have objected to the remark that Hart had used Pigeon like he had used "those little girls." However, defense counsel probably knew the statement made no sense. The fact that Shaffer had Indian heritage is not relevant to anything.

Now let's look at the evidence a little bit. We had forty-eight witnesses, I think, on behalf of the State. We've got 125 exhibits that you all will have the opportunity to look at.[278] Now what do they show? That's the whole important thing about this trial. And if I can, let me go over it a little bit. If I misstate any of it, forget it; throw it out the window. Do the same thing for the other lawyers in this case.

Prosecutors like to tell the jury how much evidence has been presented by them. This is a sly way of arguing quantity alone can overcome reasonable doubt. The number of exhibits and witnesses called was a good point. A bad point was telling the jury to disregard anything he misstates. As an advocate, a lawyer should believe he never makes a misstatement.

Out at Camp Scott we have the little Milner girl. She is bound with her hands behind her back. They have a cord wrapped around and tied behind her back. And that there was some black duct tape wrapped around and tied to her little hands. And that there was some black duct tape additionally wrapped around her little hands as they were tied behind her. There are her little pajamas with black tape again, black duct tape, draped around her little shoulders, holding her arms down. That tape came from the roll that was laying there next to the tree where the bodies of the little girls were. And if you recall the officer's testimony, her hands were tied first because of the way the tape was matched up to the roll, because in between the tape on her little wrists was the tape on the—on the top of her, across the back of that little girl's hand was hair from Gene Leroy Hart. And what did we find on the tape on

Gloyd McCoy

the top of that little girl's pajamas? Hair from Gene Leroy Hart.[279]

A person can not be identified by his hair. Hair isn't like a fingerprint. He goes on to say, "And what did we find from the inside of those little girls' bodies, in different cavities, was the sperm of Gene Leroy Hart."[280]

Tests that would say conclusively that the sperm was that of Hart were not available at the time. The remark should have been countered with an objection.

After seeing, here's the flashlight. That flashlight was laying there when Gene Leroy Hart left the scene in a hurry, probably when the alarm went off. The flashlight is interesting because we know that flashlight is connected with the cellar/cave area. Because what do we know? We know the killer was at the cellar/cave area before and after the crime. Because we know at the cellar/cave there is a roll of masking tape left there. And we know that that masking tape matches the tape that was around the flashlight. It was prepared beforehand. Premeditation. Just like the gag around the little Milner girl's neck. A rag, like a towel or a piece of washcloth rolled up with a piece of trotline cord through it, with loops on both ends, and then sewn up with needle and thread. Premeditation, that's what it's called.

And the plastic around the flashlight to keep it from being shown or to keep anybody from seeing the light so he could get around in the woods like Larry Dry said they also did when they was walking across the fields and hiding from the law. Remember all of those things. We also know that Gene Leroy Hart was back at the cave/cellar after the crime occurred. And how do we know that? Because Susan Embrey, the little girl's counselor, had her glasses stolen, and they were recovered at the cellar/cave area. So we know he was there before and after.

Mr. Shaffer should have reminded the jury at this point that when Hart as captured he was wearing women's glasses. Such a statement would have bolstered his argument that women's glasses at the cellar/cave could be linked to Hart.

And there's another piece of evidence found at that cave, grimy as it might be. A piece of newspaper just happened to be from the April 17, 1977, *Tulsa World*. The paper matched and was from the exact same paper found in the flashlight from the April 17, 1977, *Tulsa World*.

After we get to the cellar/cave area, you say how in the world is that going to connect Gene Leroy Hart with the killing of these little girls? Well, he, by his own attorney's stipulation, was raised in that area at that particular location because that was his, as they said, boyhood home. Larry Dry tells you how they hid out there at the cave/cellar area. And we also have a little item called a photograph of two girls. Now that might be as insignificant as heck except when you look at the other things connecting Gene Leroy Hart with those particular photographs. The photographs were developed by him. You heard Mr. Lindville's testimony didn't you? Developing the photographs after Mr. Lindville had taken them—the photographs as the way of the girls who were happened to be visitors of. So we know he had access to those pictures to begin with.

There is another thing about those photographs, and if you recall one of the testimony [sic] yesterday or the day before, I lose track of the days, Art

Lindville, if I recall correctly the right officer had received a picture from Mrs. Buckskin, Gene Leroy Hart's mother. Look at that photograph. Compare that photograph of Gene Leroy Hart's ex-wife to the photographs found there at the cave/cellar area. There is a very, very strong resemblance between the two women. Look at those photographs. Examine them. Compare the photographs with the ones found in the cave/cellar area.

Counsel says that was all planted by Pete. Shame on you, Pete! If you haven't got any more sense than to put something so insignificant as pictures. If you're going to plant something, then he has no business in being a police officer and a law enforcement officer. My God, if you are going to plant something. He's got enough sense to go out there and plant prints—fingerprints, they're a lot better. Give him a little bit of credit. If Pete knew who they were why in the name of God did they have to publish those in the newspapers and on TV to even find out who those women were? It doesn't make any sense, unless you want to buy their smokescreen, and that's all any of it is.

The last paragraph was the prosecutor's attempt to dispel the defense argument that Sheriff Weaver planted the evidence. No mention was made of the defense's last witness who saw the photographs in Pete Weaver's desk long before the murders. The prosecutor also did not refer the jury to Weaver's own testimony that he did not plant the evidence.

The evidence is un-contradicted that Gene Leroy Hart did this. There has been no witness say Gene Leroy Hart didn't do it. That was all smokescreen, every bit of it.[281] Remember, when people put their hand on that Bible and they raise their right hand, that doesn't mean they're always telling the truth on that witness stand. That's what you folks have got to determine in this case. Who are you going to believe in that regard concerning the smokescreen? It's an old lawyer's trick. You think that a lawyer would trick you? How many times did you hear that in *voir dire*? Do you think a lawyer would put up a smokescreen for a defendant?

The use of the term "smokescreen" was improper. Also, the remarks about "uncontradicted" evidence is a back-door way of commenting on Hart's failure to take the stand. As such, the remark is improper. No objection was made by defense counsel.

Common sense. The judge tells you in that last part of your instructions that one of the things you should not leave out here in the courtroom when you go back in there to deliberate is your good, old, homegrown, common sense. Take it with you. Look at the case. Look at the evidence, and use your common sense in balancing it out and see who are you going to believe in putting all of this evidence together.

There's another little thing that is called evidence, and it's a little mirror and a little corncob pipe. Those little old items don't mean a whole heck of a lot to anybody I don't suppose, except they just happen to be found down there in that house of Mr. Sam Pigeon where Gene Leroy Hart had his things. And the smokescreen comes on again. These are planted too. Again, isn't that kind of dumb if you're going to plant something like these two items. Mr. Chrisco dow[n] there stuffing it in Sam Pigeon's bedroom where Gene Leroy Hart was staying. If

Gloyd McCoy

you are going to stuff something in there you're going to plant something, why do you spend a month and a half or two months calling all of those little Girl Scouts to find out who it even belonged to? Why wouldn't you take something out of the Kiowa Camp instead of the Choctaw Camp where Karen Mitchell was staying? Give them a little bit of credit; don't buy that smokescreen stuff. Gene Leroy Hart had these items, this little mirror and this little pipe in his possession that were taken that very night from the locker of Karen Mitchell in the Choctaw Camp. That again connects Gene Hart to the crime scene because of the place where he was arrested is the place these items were recovered.

Then we come back to the testimony of Dr. McLeod and the testimony of Ann Reed concerning the hair. Ann tells you that the hair—and how many were there? Not just one hair. She found hair in the wrist bindings and that tape of the little Doris Denise Milner. There were hairs of Gene Leroy Hart on the tape on the top of her pajamas. Isn't it strange that for three different areas that hair is found that belongs to this man. Isn't it strange that there are six or nine, depends on how any you want to call the ones in the bindings, there are either six or nine hairs that match in every microscopic characteristic that that little girl used in making her determination on the hairs. Even his own witness agrees with Ann Reed on the hair exemplar.

And there's a couple of other things about that testimony that we might not have overlooked that he put on the witness stand. And that's the little Brooks girl and Mrs. Buckskin. Do you remember what Mrs. Buckskin said about the fact that he had on—Gene Leroy Hart had on boots, suede, or high top shoes I believe she described them, that were suede when he came back home in three days after the crime occurred, which was the same day that Willie Thompson and Mr. Colvin found the cave/cellar area and when they felt that somebody was watching them. Do you remember that testimony?

And remember also the little Brooks girl who told you that she saw some boots that night by the latrine, flashing the light, and described those and identified those in the photograph. The very same ones he had on when he was arrested. The very same boots. One other thing and I'm—but it's kind of interesting to me, the fact of other items taken from the house of Sam Pigeon. What kind of man would cut out pictures of little cheerleaders in all of those poses and keep those stuffed in a sack with his dirty clothes?

A man who roams the woods. A man who knows all of these areas. Gene Leroy Hart. Don't let your common sense stay in the courtroom, take it with you when you go back into that jury deliberation room.

One other thing about the plan, if you're going to plant something at the cave, Pete really had to be stupid. He not only had to plant some photographs, he had to run up there with that roll of masking tape and chunk it down on the ground by the cellar, and he'd have to use that some kind of newspaper, run up there and chunk it down on the ground around the cellar, and you had to take those glasses that were found to be Susan Emery's that were broken and in the case, and you had to run up there and throw them down on the ground. He would have been a pretty busy guy. Except for Willis Thompson, who didn't have anything to do with law enforcement, he was out there hunting squirrels. And he and his buddy came upon the site and identify the items that they saw laying out there in the weeds.

This is a crime by a man roaming those woods, roaming the Girl Scout camp, Gene Leroy Hart. The evidence points toward Gene Leroy Hart, and it satisfies everybody that Gene Leroy Hart is what happened to those little girls.

The evidence "satisfies everybody." Who is everybody? Mr. Shaffer did not tell the jury who is "everybody." If "everybody" is law enforcement, the remark is objectionable. The only "everybody" who must be satisfied is the jury.

Don't let those little girls be put out of your mind anything that's happened in this case. [sic] The evidence for Gene Leroy Hart is evident.

You've all been seeing in the last three weeks, and I guess we're going into our fourth now and are almost through with it, the judge is here to protect this man and make sure that the evidence is put on correctly. He has his defense lawyers to aid in that regard. He has twelve people sitting on the jury to determine his fate.

That Bible that you all saw everybody put their hand on and take an oath to our God to tell the truth, there's a part that you ought to remember. There's a verse called Mark and its in chapter nine, verse forty-two, and it talks about little children. And it says: "Whoever shall harm these little ones, it is better that a millstone be hung around his neck and he be thrown to the depths of the sea."[282]

The ending statement was dramatic. It was also egregiously improper. Courts are universal in ruling that such argument is highly prejudicial. In a close case, appellate courts do not hesitate to grant new trials on such arguments. One can only speculate why an experienced prosecutor would make such a known improper argument that could cause a conviction to be reversed. Defense counsel should have objected to this quotation of scripture.

closing argument
of the defense

Following Mr. Shaffer's closing argument, it was the defense lawyer's turn.[283] Both defense lawyers made arguments to the jury. Splitting an argument between two defense lawyers is not an unusual practice. Mr. Pitchlynn gave the first part of the argument for Mr. Hart.

Mr. Pitchlynn used a soft-spoken voice in giving his portion of closing argument. This approach was in sharp contrast to the loud voices of both prosecutors and his own colleague, Mr. Isaacs.[284] Pitchlynn stayed up all night before the day of his closing argument. He practiced his closing over and over.

> Ladies and gentlemen of the jury, I hope you are afraid of it. I hope you will abide by it. It's a very serious consequence, and I want you to understand that responsibility. Old lawyers have a saying, it goes kind of like this: When facts support you, argue the facts. When the law supports you, you argue the law. But when neither the facts nor the law support your position, then you scream and holler, and you pound on the table[,] and you roll in the floor, and

you do whatever you have to do to get the attention of the jury.

Now my associate, Mr. Isaacs, is a little loud, but he was born that way. You probably know people like him.

But when Mr. Fallis gets up here and starts to screaming and hollering in your faces, crying for blood and vengeance[,] and starts pounding on the table and rolling in the floor to get your attention, then you're going to know what he knows that neither the facts nor the law supports anything other than the innocence of Gene Hart.[285]

Mr. Pitchlynn's introduction was outstanding. The argument set a theme for the jury to consider—that the prosecutors had to be dynamic in order to cover their lack of incriminating evidence. Strangely, the prosecutors did not object. The lack of objection allowed the jury to believe that the "old lawyer saying" was true. Also, Mr. Pitchlynn did well in making light of Mr. Isaac's loudness. He was able to portray Mr. Isaac's as loud while portraying Mr. Fallis as deceitful.

What have we been doing here for the past four weeks here? We didn't come into the courthouse to mourn those little girls. We're sad about those little girls. And we owe those girls and their families mourn [sic][;] this is public mourning. We owe those families, and we owe those children the duty to find the truth. Today that's what we're here for. We didn't come here for vengeance or an excuse. That's what we're here for, is to find the truth.

Mr. Shaffer's theme was the case was about the girls. Mr. Pitchlynn counters by telling the jurors what the case is really about. However, a defense lawyer takes a risk by saying a criminal trial is about truth. A criminal trial is about "beyond a reasonable doubt."

> And what is the truth? The truth is that these families have lost three precious little girls. They were brutally murdered at Camp Scott. The truth is also that this man was charged immediately after that and before the evidence was, was ever, ever gathered and ever studied. The truth is that these men and Sheriff Weaver and the OSBI directed [an] investigation that was never designed to find the truth, but was designed for one purpose, that purpose being to convict this man. One purpose.

> We asked you a number of times to take your positions in this jury box and have an open mind [i]to listen to the testimony from this stand, all of the testimony, before you arrived at any conclusions or any opinions as to the innocence or guilt, to get to the truth and the facts.

> I hope that each and every one of you, all twelve of you, can look this man in the eye right now and being honest to him and say ["]I've done that,["] because if you have, if you truly have, then you are not going to [find him guilty]. I mock most of it. You're not going to be persuaded by loud oratory. You are not going to be persuaded by how they use language, descriptions of what happened at Camp Scott, as they've played a stage professional on your emotions.

> We're all human. We're all angry about what happened out there. But what we're here for is not to be

angry but to find the truth. I hope that's what you all try to do.[286]

We talked about hunches, speculations, and we've attempted to try and bring you the facts, because that's not their job. Their job is to convict him. Our job is to come in and show you the facts. That's what we've tried to do.

You've heard the testimony from this stand about being by the flashlight. We know whose flashlight that was. They knew whose flashlight that was. Who told you? Where did that testimony come from? We brought you the facts. And it's your job to take those facts and put them in order and find him innocent.

Mr. Shaffer noticed his fingerprints. I'd also point out the footprints. What happened to the footprints? There were footprints in the blood in the floor of that tent. Those two footprints [would lead] to the murderer. We don't know [whose footprints those were.] I hope they don't know.

They ought to [be able] to identify them. You asked them what happened to the fingerprints? We know there were fingerprints on the lens of that flashlight, but we know it wasn't Gene Hart's. They even told us it wasn't Gene Hart's. Whose was it? We don't know that either.

Mr. Pitchlynn was now talking about a new theme. The so-called "Some Other Dude Did It" defense. Mr. Pitchlynn did not need to prove who the "other dude" was. He only had to present "reasonable doubt" that it was not Hart but someone else. The weak point in the State of Oklahoma's case was the lack of Hart fingerprints at the scene. Defense counsel hit that issue hard.

We know whose flashlight it was and where it came from. We have an idea of how it got there. Still seen—it was seen in that tent a week or two weeks after the murder of those little girls. And you saw the little girl take the stand, cry, and look you all in the eye and say "I'm sorry, but I had to come up here."

Try as they might the prosecutors know the best memory of all of us [was] a small child, that a small child saw out there that night, she didn't see it. And she took that picture out of the group of seven or eight pictures without any hesitation, without any problem. She showed that picture as the face of the man she saw that night. There was no question in her mind. And she took the stand and she looked at all of you scared and she told you what she saw. She told you that she picked that picture out. And we showed you. Whose picture was it? The picture of the same man at the scene that Monday morning in the Midway Café, Chouteau.

The young girl's testimony that she saw Bill Stevens at the camp is highlighted here. The prosecutors never adequately explained what was wrong with her testimony.

Nervous, upset, restless, worried. The same man that went to that tent on Sunday night after his automobile broke down on Highway Thirty-Three, crept through that camp and went into that tent and murdered and assaulted those three little girls. The same man that today is in a penitentiary in Kansas for conviction on the same type of crime.

Mr. Fallis objected to the argument at that point. "[I]f it please the court, I am going to object...that is not a correct statement of fact not in evidence in this case." The objection was sustained.

> You know that it wasn't Gene Hart that was in the tent. You know that it wasn't Gene Hart that was seen on the creek. You don't know who it was. But we know that it wasn't Gene Hart.[287]

> Ladies and gentlemen, you are participating in the finest system of justice that has ever been conceived by man. Our system has a dual purpose. We have tried to point that out throughout this process. The purpose is first of all to protect the innocent. Secondly, to punish the guilty. Don't forget that. Don't forget that. There are two purposes in the process.

> The jury acts upon this system like brakes on a train.[288] If this system gets off track, then it's your duty and your responsibility to stop that system, allow it to back up and get on the right track and proceed. That's where we're at. It is time for the jury to put on the brakes. Our system is off the track. It is very much off. And now the bend is the conductor. He has failed to fix it. These people are the engineers, the firemen. That gentleman over there, Mr. Pete Weaver, Sheriff of Mayes County, he's the switchman[,] and he's the one that put his train on the wrong track from the start. You, the jury, can put on the brakes. This train is fueled by a lot of money from the coffers of the State of Oklahoma. The train is fueled by a lot of riffraff freight men and desires for personal gain. You carry a precious cargo. That cargo is a thing called justice. And in this case it is justice for a man by the name of Hart.

Mr. Pitchlynn began a new theme: Hart was railroaded.

In June of 1977 the previous district attorney in this district, Sid Wise, filed charges against Gene Hart in June. As I said, before the evidence had ever been gathered and the evidence studied[,] those charges were filed.

In October of the same year[,] this man, Sid Wise, contracted to write a book about this case. And somewhere through all of that time[,] he also found time to finish dead last in his race for attorney general of the State of Oklahoma. Okay, that deal left to all prosecutors to file cases with one hand and file profits with the other. So even though Mr. Wise is gone, the Mayes County railroad continued to run on. And like the old political rally train[,] every politician that could find room climbed on board. While Sid Wise hit the campaign trail, the governor of our state emptied the jail of outlaws who would swear to find Gene Hart.

The prosecutors let Pitchlynn get away with a lot. His criticism of Wise was not relevant and there should have been an objection.

Ladies and gentlemen, I am frightened by where we have come in this area to get to where we go right now. I am frightened because a system with the power and the money, a system with a motive, a good motive, to find truth, has been swayed to convict this man for the sake of authority. My only hope and your only hope and the hope of those people out there and the hope of Gene Hart is that this jury will act as a brake[,] and when you look at the evidence, when you weigh the evidence, you are going to understand something went wrong way back there.

The evidence is before you. You are twelve of this community, community full of people that I've gained a lot of respect for because of their convictions[;] they want to know the truth. They care for Gene Hart. Look at the evidence, and when you do[,] you will know Gene Hart didn't kill those little girls. We have done our best to show you that he didn't.

Time and money, it all ran out. We can't go any further. When you leave this room to deliberate[,] you are on your own. Thank you.

Garvin Isaacs gave the second part of the closing argument for Mr. Hart.

May it please the court and ladies and gentlemen of the jury. An old courthouse [was dedicated] and a stonemason put up a sign[,] and the sign says: "In this hall of justice [the] crown never loses, [the] crown never wins," and that's the true theory of our system of justice.

Mr. Isaacs was correct. In America, the prosecutor's job is not to convict but to see that justice is done. Such was announced by the United States Supreme Court in *Berger v. United States,* 295 U.S. 78 (1935).

We went through a lengthy *voir dire* process, it took eleven days, and went through a hundred and thirty some odd persons to get you twelve seated. We picked you because we felt like you were the fairest of people, and people who we would want to sit in judgment of us if we were on trial.

These remarks were designed to make the jury feel special—
that they were specially chosen because it was known they
could be fair.

> When the awesome power of the State of Oklahoma
> marched with all its forces pertaining to one man,
> the scales were unbalanced, they are not equal. The
> State's got a lot of money, got a lot of people work-
> ing for them. But our system of justice is set up in
> a way every citizen accused has some things going
> for him. Every man is entitled to the presumption
> of innocence.[289] Thank God for that. This man is
> entitled to this if he is accused and tried and pros-
> ecuted for any crime, the burden of proof of every
> element of the crime.

Although every defendant is presumed innocent, many
believe that it is difficult to apply the presumption when the
crime involves children.

> Probably the biggest thing in an accused's favor is
> this fact that he has the promises of twelve good
> people to apply the law to the facts and make deter-
> mination. I want to talk to you about things in this
> case this morning, things that trouble me. I may get
> emotional, I did a little bit ago when Mr. Pigeon
> was talking, but will you forgive me if I do[?]

> You went out to Camp Scout[,] and you saw this
> tent number eight, the tent where the little girls
> were[;] you saw holes sawed in the floor there.
> We've got a picture here of blood on—on some of
> the boards in that floor, and look at that picture,
> there's footprints there. You heard testimony about
> the footprints. Right here is a shoe that belongs to
> Gene Leroy Hart. There's no blood on his shoes.
> What did you—what's the type of material they're

made out of? That stuff would have soaked up blood like a sponge. And none of it is there. Took the shoes apart looking for blood and looking for hair. No blood or hair on any of these items.

There is blood on somebody because somebody was in that tent. The Brooks girl told you that she saw a man wearing shoes similar to those. She saw him there in the Quapaw unit, the next one over from the Kiowa Camp. She told you the fellow was wearing Khakis. Where is he?

I don't know where he is, but I can get two bloodhounds and A. T. Maxey[,] and some of the newspaper people said I look like a farmer watching his prize bulls perform when Mr. Maxey testified.

Well, I'll tell you what, you give me two bloodhounds and A. T. Maxey and a couple of technical evidence people like John Wilson and by golly we'll produce the man that was in the area of Camp Scott, seen by Clayton Potts[,] and you heard Clayton Potts tell you that Gene Hart is not the man.

Eyewitness identification throws all of this crap right out of the window. You heard the little girl tell you she'd seen a stranger there. We don't know if two of them were there. We don't know if one of them did it. We don't know if one of them held the light for the other. Gene Hart's fingerprint is not on this flashlight.

They go—they go on about this pair of gloves and about Gene being a fingerprint man at the Granite Reformatory. Do you see any blood on those gloves? Are you—I'm not going to sit there and let them tell me that he was wearing these gloves and that Gene L. Hart had these gloves on and Gene L. Hart went into the Girl Scout tent and murdered three little girls with no blood on the gloves. Now that's a bunch of baloney; you know it, and I know it.

Let's talk about the statement. That will tell you more about this case than anything I can think of. In 1973 Gene broke out of jail over here in Mayes County. You heard Mr. Al Little tell you about Gene was seen back there in the cell walking around trying to divert attention from the guys sawing the bars.

Well, after this case is over with we've got ten more to go and two of them are escapes from the Mayes County Jail and two of them are what's commonly known as malicious injury to public property. If you break out of jail[,] they don't get you for simply escape, they get you one to ten for sawing bars.

Mr. Isaacs tells the jury that Hart faces future charges for escape. The prosecutors did not protest.

You heard Al Little tell you that in 1973 he and this fellow John Ross looked in Pete's desk and that those pictures were in Pete's desk. Had more calls from more crackpots and more cranks since I've got involved in this case that I can believe. You wouldn't believe it. People call, I know who killed the three Girl Scouts. People—people tell you they know this and know that. I'm clairvoyant; I can see the past and tell you who it is. Look on page of your notebook, and I'll tell you the answer to those three questions. Well the three questions on page nine just happened to be what is your favorite television show, what's your favorite book, and which institution do you consider most important, the family and stuff like that. We've weeded them out.

We've talked to hundreds and hundred of people. To be sure, to be convinced that Al Little saw those pictures in that desk drawer we said[,] "well what else was in there?" And Al Little told us about seeing that picture in there with a carburetor that had been salted or sugar had been put in it, and also the picture of what he called a signal thirty. And he drew those pictures.

Now you heard Mr. Ross get on the witness stand and testify that he was friends with the sheriff. You heard Mr. Ross testify that he visited in the sheriff's home and the sheriff visited in his. I won't say no more about that.

Gene Leroy Hart was at his mother's house on May twenty-eighth of 1977. Jimmy Beck was there. Jimmy Beck saw him. Norman Carey was there. Jimmy Beck said he wasn't wearing these glasses. Now if I saw a guy walking down the street wearing those glasses, I would certainly remember him.

You know you look kind of strange when you have a pair of glasses like these. I wonder when you have a pair of glasses like these. I wonder what changed Mr. Beck's mind? Well, I have an idea that there that there was some money paid to Mr. Beck, just like the money that Norman Carey told you they paid him for telling them he saw Gene down there at Ella Mae's house.

Did you see Mr. Beck's jaw start to twitching when I asked him who he went to lunch with and what they talked about? He said they didn't talk about the case. This case has been on my mind day and night, twenty-four hours a day, talking about it so much my wife says[,] ["]you're going crazy, you're losing your mind.["] Mr. Beck is going to be a witness[,] and he's with the OSBI agents at lunch[;] you know what they're going to be talking about.

Gene's mother told you Gene was there on the twenty-eighth and told you he left on the—on the fourth day of June, on or about the third, with Groundhog Sandusky [sic] and went to Tulsa. She said he was wearing thongs. Groundhog's dead, and I can't bring him here to tell you, you know, [who] else had been to his house and who stayed with him. But you can see those OSBI reports[,] and you can see Groundhog's name in there a couple of times. The law won't permit it, under the circumstances, to call somebody to testify about what Groundhog told them. When you're a fugitive[,] it's awfully difficult to have friends, other than your family.

Mr. Isaacs brought a new reason to find reasonable doubt. He referred to the evidence that Hart was somewhere else at the time of the crime.

On June twelfth Clayton Potts told you about seeing the guy at a stream down there by Camp Scott, south of Camp Scott. He told you it wasn't Gene. Richard Day tells you about seeing a guy with a bottle of water. Remember me asking how tall the boy was and he said he was about my size. The Stevens were out there. They say they know who the fellow was. I don't know if they do or not. You know the Stevens were in the area. Richard Barber talked about a car up there at the gate of Camp Scott on the twelfth at about seven o'clock in the evening. Who in the heck was in that car? Nobody knows.

The little girls were murdered the night of the twelfth or the morning of the thirteenth. The next morning Floyd Cunningham is out there and he hears that man right over there talking to that man right back there about Gene Leroy Hart's mother. On the fourteenth the doctors, Dr. Hoffman, looked at those slides. No, wait a minute, I may be wrong. That may have been the thirteenth. No, on the thirteenth or the fourteenth he looked at the slides and didn't see any spermatozoa. And on the sixteenth these pictures Mr. Al Little saw in Pete Weaver's desk were found down n the cave/cellar area. I submit to you that the last place that a fugitive would go, a person who had murdered three little girls, is to his boyhood home within a softball throw of his aunt's house.

And on the sixteenth, the same day the pictures were found, you heard Mrs. Buckskin tell you that Gene came back home and Groundhog was with him. That the FBI had been there. Why was the FBI there? The man right over there knows because he sent them there. The—knowing that you're going to be accused of being in the area[,] you have got to remove yourself from the area. That's what Mr. Hart did. With three hundred and five years hanging over his head[,] it's a pretty good idea to move on.

Mr. Isaacs mentioned that Hart has three hundred and five years of prison time to do. Mr. Fallis would later complain that this comment caused the jury to acquit Hart. Fallis said, "Finding someone guilty of a crime is a difficult task and knowing he would still be behind bars might have made the decision earlier."[290] If the statement was so improper, one wonders why an experienced prosecutor like Mr. Fallis did not object.

Gloyd McCoy

On June the nineteenth[,] we've got the footlocker coming to the Locust Grove police department. We don't know who brought it there. We don't know who touched it. It wasn't accompanied—and those contents weren't inventoried. We know that the footlocker was in the Locust Grove police department for a period of approximately two weeks to a month and during that time there were law officers in the Locust Grove police department who had access to this. We don't know if that locker was locked or unlocked until Gary Campbell picked the [locker] in June or July—July the sixth, I believe he said, he finally checked the locker[,] but he doesn't remember what was in it.

We know that A.D. David was in the Locust Grove police department. We know there was other law enforcement officers in the Locust Grove department, and you heard A. D. David crawfish on me when I asked him had he ever been to Sam Pigeon's house. Do you remember him looking at the ceiling? And do you remember Mr. Chimyl saying that A. D. Told him that he knew how far it was from his house to Sam Pigeon's house and how are you going to know that unless you've been in your vehicle and gone down there.

Sometime after July the sixth[,] Tom Kite and spooks, the Green Beret, going to find the man in the woods. They come up here[,] and Sheriff Weaver tells Kite that Gene Hart's fingerprints are all over the house that had the tape in it. Well, we know there aren't any of Gene Hart's fingerprints on that house, anywhere in the house or about the house. And if those fingerprints had been there, we'd have heard about it. Don't know whose else's—uh—who else's fingerprints were in there.

Isaacs here mentioned Tom Kite's testimony that Weaver had lied to him. That testimony showed Weaver was a dishonest person and the jury could have inferred from that that Weaver was the type of person who could plant evidence.

> Sometime in August Karen gets the trunk back. Can't get the same open. She don't know whether Shammill used a paperclip on it to lock or was it something else he had done. August the sixth of [']77[,] you heard Sam Pigeon tell you about Gene coming to his house. January the twenty-fifth, 1978, OSBI expert, I think you'll have an opportunity to look at it, you might read all of it. They knew approximately where Gene Leroy Hart was on January 26, 1978. Knew he had been to William Lee Smith's house on January the twenty-sixth. They knew he had been at a stop dance, which is a religious ceremony for that particular religion that Mr. Hart and Sam does.

> And on April 6, 1978, they go to Sam Pigeon's house and capture Gene and search the house. And these trained law enforcement officers, the technical agents there, and they tell us that they didn't see this corncob pipe in that house.

The prosecutors never offer a meaningful explanation as to why these items were not found during the first search. The house was small and was not cluttered.

> They also tell us that they didn't take any of Gene's underwear out of Mr. Pigeon's house. They didn't pick up any of his clothes that was there. Mr. Bowles tells us that they paid an $8,000 reward on or about April the sixth. April the fourteenth Joyce Payne writes the sheriff. She gets no relief. She calls

the sheriff after April the fourteenth. He doesn't return her call.

April the nineteenth we got some exemplars. We gave the State of Oklahoma samples of Gene's hair, his saliva[,] and his blood. If you'll recall[,] those tests [show] that his hair was inconsistent with the microscopic material characteristics on the bodies of the three victims. They would have had to let him go.

May second, [we] filed a motion for all the inventoried lists of Gene Leroy Hart's property. You heard the sheriff testify about that yesterday. Mr. David wouldn't produce any lists. June the second we got an inventory list. I don't know what it's worth. You saw the way the sheriff keeps records. [One] piece of pink paper in here someplace, which is part of the business records of the Mayes County Sheriff's Office. I want to point something out to you in this property list. See right there where it says "miscellaneous" and its got "belt, nail clippers, ..."

Somebody was going to write something else in that blank, or they wouldn't have put a comma after the nail clippers.

By golly you don't come to the Mayes County Jail or any other jail in Oklahoma on a post conviction relief application, which is like a habeas corpus application, you're challenging something about a former conviction. It's constitutional. You don't come to one of those places without having all of your documents with you in an envelope. This thing doesn't say anything about the habeas corpus papers, where they were or what was being done.

If we'd had that envelope, or knew where the envelope was when Gene Leroy Hart broke out of the Mayes County Jail, we'd know how those pictures got into Sheriff Weaver's desk. Joyce Payne is still trying. She called a fellow by the name of Black in Oklahoma City to tell him about the flashlight and this guy's feet.

June the sixth, 1978, preliminary hearing. You heard Croslin Smith get on there and tell you during the middle of June Mr. Pitchlynn and I went down to Sam Pigeon's house, was down one night, and you heard him tell you that mirror and that pipe were not in that house, and they weren't. You know why we went down there.

You heard Richard Hogan tell you that he was in Sam Pigeon's after Gene was arrested and that since that time he's been in the house on numerous occasions, he hadn't seen this mirror lying on top of a refrigerator, hadn't seen this corncob pipe anywhere in that house. July the sixth of '78, preliminary hearing ended. A. D. Tells Campbell that he knows how many miles it is to Pigeon's house.

July the twelfth, OSBI goes back to Pigeon's. Goes back to Pigeon's house. Pigeon is not there. He's out in the field there at the nursery working. And he comes out with these items. And these pictures of the cheerleaders. And I thought there was going to be something, you know, something like out of the Playboy Magazine. I was kind of surprised when we got the pictures of a bunch of cheerleaders in here and it looks like a lingerie ad or something like that.

Joyce Payne is still trying to get in touch with somebody. Finally gets in touch with us in October. The sperm goes to New York. Okay, the sperm's in Tahlequah, to Oklahoma City, to Dallas, back to Oklahoma City and in October they decide they'd better take them to New York. Gotta have the 800-year-old man look at them.

November the seventh, no, wait a minute, October the fifth, it comes back to Oklahoma. November the seventh, sperm goes back to New York. December the twelfth, interview with Mr. Peters, Joyce Payne's common law husband who is in the penitentiary with Mr. Stevens. Who conducted that interview? The guy's right here[;] Mr. Thurman was sent up there to talk to him. January the sixth, talked to Old Peters again. February the twentieth stated on the report they get around to talking to Joyce Payne. We get the report the day before yesterday.

When I was in the 4-H Club[,] they told us that we'd ought to have a title for our time copy. If I was going to put a title on this one, I would entitle it "How to Convict an Innocent Man.["] I want to talk to you about that. We don't have the footprints off of the floor. There's no blood on Gene's shoes.

We've got Arthur Lindville, OSBI, trained technical investigator, who comes into the tent. He processes this tent. There's a bloody towel in this that's been used to wipe up blood. Doesn't even bother to process the dog gone thing.

Look at that. You heard Campbell say it appeared to him that it had been used to wipe up blood and then washed out. Somebody'd wrung it out. Mr. Lindville doesn't process in their tent in here, and doesn't look in the shower for evidence, doesn't look in the garage for evidence. He does not go to any other unit looking for evidence. Doesn't go out here in this field where they threw the gun, crowbar[,] and piece of plastic, and look for evidence. They don't bother to go interview these folks along the road here. And he kept saying the one word over and over. I assumed it was done. I assume this[,] and I assume that. My grandfather told me a long time [ago] never assume anything because it makes an ass out of you and me. That's pretty good advice.

What do we do when we arrive on the crime scene and we want to make sure that we've got all of the evidence that will point to the true killer or killers. You throw away available source[s] of evidence. You look at the footprints. You go to the garbage. You can learn more about somebody looking at their garbage than any other item in a criminal investigation. The thread in the—in the gag used on the three little girls. Look at it. It's green thread. Now where did the thread come from? The Girl Scout clothes are green. Sid Wise couldn't investigate a dog fight.[291]

"Sid Wise couldn't investigate a dog fight" is one of the memorable phrases from this trial. One would have thought the two prosecutors would have jumped to their feet and vigorously objected. Neither one did. Thus, the jury was left with the impression that it was true. Mr. Fallis did not defend Mr. Wise in his closing. Mr. Wise was listening to the closing arguments through an intercom in the Court Clerk's Office. When Isaacs made the "dogfight" statement, Wise said someone should put Isaacs "in jail."

You know he's out there giving orders to law enforcement officers. Pete Weaver hates Gene Hart worse than Christ hates sin. He's out there giving orders. The investigators, the technical investigators for the medical examiner's office, they only use the iodine vapor on the exposed areas of the bodies. Listen, whoever was in that tent was banging those little girls around something fierce to get them tied up and they were thrown all over the place. You can look at the blood on the floor. Those girls had fingerprints on them from somebody. But we don't know the—they decided they'd only do the exposed areas. Where are they?

The State of Oklahoma could never get around the fact that there were *no* fingerprints of Hart at Camp Scott. A jury can understand fingerprints. They could not understand the prosecutor's hair and sperm evidence.

> Could've solved this case with an Atom bomb, neutron activation. Did they use that? No. You heard them actually tell you that neuron activation will pick up trace elements in your hair. And by running those on a scan you can have a much more accurate reading than by a visual examination of hair in making a determination that hair is similar.

> Chris and everybody else wants the good citizens of the State to think that Gene Hart is an animal. I know him, and he's not.[292]

Mr. Isaacs gave his personal opinion on Mr. Hart. An attorney is not supposed to do that at a trial. Yet, there was no objection from the prosecutors.

> They want you to think he is a Mayes County Tarzan, and he goes out there and swings from tree to tree on grapevines and that he is a mad dog wildman that lives out there in the jungle with the apes, and he's not. They want you to think that he's the Mayes County Houdini, he can outrun the damndest dogs you've ever seen and they shouldn't catch him if they had a head start on him, but he's not. He's a human being just like you and me and everybody else.

One thing that Gene Hart has that I envy, he has a good family. He's got a lot of friends. Not all of us have a family like his. Not all of us have that many friends. You can bet your boots [if] those people didn't know beyond any doubt Gene Hart was an innocent man[,] they wouldn't support him in a minute.[293] His family suffered so many indignities that surround this investigation that it makes me emotion[al] to even talk about it, it infuriates me.[294]

Mr. Isaacs was building up Mr. Hart's credibility and reputation based on conjecture. There was no objection by the prosecutors. The prosecutors sat silently and did not object to the statements about the "indignities" suffered by Hart's family.

The man on the creek with the Khakis, where is he? Like to get our hands on him.[295]

Bill Stevens, where's he? State makes a record [regarding] Bill Stevens. Mr. Stevens, where were you on June thirteenth, 1977? Mr. Isaacs begins an argument where he portrays himself asking the questions he would have asked if Bill Stevens had been called to the stand. This is a very effective technique.

Mr. Stevens, isn't it true you were at Camp Scott, tent number eight? And Mr. Stevens, were you on your hands and knees like a mad dog. Did you have your flashlight with you, Mr. Stevens?

Do you know, Mr. Stevens, that Ms. Payne and her two sons have been here and they've told us all about your flashlight. Is that right? Well, Mr. Stevens, why didn't you just tell us how it came to be that your fingerprint appears on the flashlight?"

At that point, Mr. Fallis objected. "If it please the court, we'll object to that statement. It's totally outside the scope of any evidence." Finally, an objection.

What occurred thereafter was probably one of the most heated interplays between opposing counsel in an Oklahoma jury trial. At one point during the argument over the objection, Mr. Isaacs stated, "Your Honor, that's a lie, and you know it." The following transcript excerpt shows the competitiveness of the two lawyers, Mr. Fallis and Mr. Isaacs:

> THE COURT: Gentlemen—
>
> MR. FALLIS: Sir, you are certainly using that word for a man—
>
> THE COURT: Gentlemen! Approach the bench.
>
> MR. FALLIS: Your Honor, we object to him totally going outside—
>
> MR. ISAACS: That's my—
>
> MR. FALLIS:—totally outside the record—
>
> THE COURT: My memory is going in both that—
>
> MR. FALLIS: I understand, Your Honor. I apologize to the court.
>
> THE COURT: I want to admonish both of you for sort of losing your cool.
>
> MR. FALLIS: I understand.
>
> THE COURT: I'm afraid you are making a very bad play for the bar here in front of all of those jurors
>
> MR. FALLIS: I apologize to the court

THE COURT: I want to admonish both of you. Now the first objection was the statement there is no evidence. The statement—

MR. ISAACS: That's right

THE COURT: The court has ruled before that—

MR. FALLIS: Well, it's—Your Honor, yeah, I wonder if counsel would acknowledge to the court that he understood your ruling on that?

MR. ISAACS: I've been honest [with] this court ever since I've been here. You're the one that's misleading everybody and withholding evidence and technical reports[,] and you know that.

MR FALLIS: No, Your Honor.

MR. ISAACS: Judge, I am not going to be intimidated by Mr. Fallis jumping up in an argument and making a scene here in front of the jury.

THE COURT: Well, you're going to change your course unless the case is—

MR. ISAACS: The facts are what was said there's a fingerprint on that flashlight that I know—

MR. FALLIS: But nobody knows whose it is.

MR. ISAACS: No

MR. FALLIS: All right. Your Honor—

MR. ISAACS: It's a proper part of cross-examination for me.

Mr. Isaacs continued his closing argument:

Look me in the eye, Mr. Stevens, don't look at Mr. Fallis so he can help you.

Now, Mr. Stevens, is it not correct you were in Locust Grove on the night of the homicide. And, Mr. Stevens, isn't it true that you had this red flashlight with you when that occurred, otherwise, we wouldn't have witnesses who put you in the area, would we? And isn't it correct, Mr. Stevens, that after you'd murdered the three little girls[,] you went to a café in Chouteau and you were nervous and you kept looking at your boots [because] they had blood on 'em?

Mr. Isaacs acted like he was cross-examining Stevens as if Stevens were there. Such is an effective technique.

If Mr. Stevens were on trial and I was the prosecutor, I would call Joyce Payne and her son[,] and I'd let them testify about seeing him on the morning of the fourteenth with all of those scratches all over him. You heard one of the boys say he had them up on his neck. During the struggle in that tent you know that those little girls were scratching for all they were worth in that death struggle.

And by golly when you consider that and you consider the fact that man has been seen in Chouteau, Oklahoma, consider the fact that one of the little girls in that Scout camp saw him a couple of weeks before this all happened, and you consider the fact that another little girl saw somebody, saw the back of their head. And I ask you why? Had to have been the death of little girls. I tell you why. Because it's all a part of the grand design, Hart's in the area. Hart's the one that did it. Hart's mother lives down here. Focus on him. If we convict an innocent man, probably would be the loneliest feeling in the world. In this business sometimes you meet the people who you can't describe it. To convict an innocent man of murder, a crime he didn't do, is to say you can find no worth as a human being. Leaves him out there alone by himself in the whole world. Let ['em] talk to you about the—we can talk about the flashlight."

Hey, I learned a new way to take the Fifth Amendment during this trial. Janice Davis was on the witness stand, ["]I refuse to answer upon the grounds my answers would be what I learned from Dr. John Macleod.["] She said it twenty times. It kind of reminded me of the McCarthy hearings back when I was a kid and they had them on TV and everybody was taking the Fifth, taking the Fifth Amendment. We all learn from what other people teach.

Qualified as an expert, yet she's got to put—put her guard up and shield herself from any question that might in some way throw some light on all of these tests that an 800-year-old man performed. I thought it was unusual when I read the report. You heard Dr. McLeod testify that he had 40,000 cases. The State of Oklahoma paid sixty-five hundred dollars, okay? If they paid at the same rate as the patients did, that comes out to two hundred and sixty million dollars.

I suggest we all quit work, let Mr. McLeod do his thing, and retire the national debt. If he did the same tests that he did on Gene's undershorts and spermatazoa submitted to him in the slides, the reports indicates that there was about ten days work involved. If there were ten days work involved with 40,000 patients, he'd be 1,076 years old. If it took him seven days to perform all of those experiments, he'd be 767 years old, so we'd call him an 800-year-old man.

Interestingly, the prosecutors never offered an explanation as to why what Isaacs is saying is not true.

> But the point I want to make here is he's never performed these types of tests before. You heard him say he's out of his field, that this is a forensic case, he deals in male infertility. The man told you he doesn't know what effect [certain things] has on spermatozoa, he doesn't know what effect bacteria has upon spermatozoa, doesn't know what effect weather conditions would have on spermatozoa, didn't know what effect agent of Y would have on spermatozoa found in a body cavity.
>
> The basis for his test is that he's had samples of spermatozoa taken from a living person. In this case we don't have spermatozoa from a living person and we don't have the list of samples. You know John Wilkerson, the policeman at Kansas City that came down here, he told us there's a big difference between working on dried seminal stains and working on the liquid form. You can make a better slide. And often times the morphology of the shape of these sperm are damaged by the stain, by transportation, by friction, but you don't recall that long hypothetical that I asked Mr. Maxey about transporting these slides.
>
> You gonna recall those slides that were damaged. And I asked Maxey what effect that would have on the spermatozoa[,] and Mr. Maxey told you it was going to break the tails of them. Dr. McLeod in his report which Mr. Wilson testified about, told us that the elongated and tapering form, the elongated and tapering forms, these two right here, were— could have been misshaped, or misshapened by the fact that they came from a dry specimen. You're going to recall that, I hope.

Now the testimony of Wilson was about the validity of his test. And you've got to remember when I
asked Wilson whether or not that test would be valid
and he said, in so many words, well, he didn't think
so because that particular doctor was used to using
liquefied samples and not dry samples. In other
words, the man is out of his field. If a dried sample
causes a spermatozoa to be tapered and elongated,
it's going to throw your whole test out of whack[,]
and there is not going to be a good basis for it. And
when you throw these two out you come up with
a normal average of oval spermatozoa. Wilson told
you that about 75 percent[,] and he told you that—
use the report. It was made on—test was made on
Mr. Hart and his were normal. He also told you
that spermatozoa can appear abnormal by decom-
position and by performance.

We don't have any photographs of all this stuff.
I think that would shed some light on it. Ms.
Matthews told about the costs of some of this
equipment that the State has at their disposal. It
shows about the nuclear reactor. It costs $400,000.
No telling how much the microscope cost.

The same thing in the hair area. We don't have
any pictures of the hair to show us the microscopic
characteristics. I've seen pictures of them in books.
Where are they? Maxey told you they look similar.
He's telling you one characteristic. They appear the
same. He told you to know the other characteristics
we could perform certain tests. They weren't done.

Here, the prosecutors were criticized and rightfully so
that they did not present any enlarged photographs of the
hair samples. The witness could have shown how the hair
"matched." Reliance on the expert's word alone obviously

was not enough. The point that there were other tests that could have been done and were not was excellent. Why were the tests not done? Defense counsel makes it appear that law enforcement was not trying to be thorough in their investigation. This case was the biggest in Oklahoma history and the additional testing should have been done.

> Both Dr. McLeod and—Dr. McLeod told you that you couldn't identify anybody by this test that he ran. Ann Reed told you she couldn't identify anybody. She said she couldn't exclude Gene Leroy Hart from those total number of persons. I submit to you she could. And John Wilson told us why. To be thorough in a criminal investigation, all of the hairs from the crime scene have to be compared. Now he didn't do that. Now we didn't do that. If there is a range of hair in every head, and there is an inconsistency in that range, that inconsistency or dissimilarity can exclude that person from that particular group of persons who would follow into that category of suspects. But nobody did that. We can't do it because they got all the hair, they got all the equipment, and believe me, as Gene Hart said, somebody must be watching over us because we started out with nothing and we're right here and I don't—I don't know how it happened. It must have been some divine revelation. We know that Clayton Potts, the guy on the creek was an Indian person. We know that Espinaldo, one of the lab testing agents, didn't have a hat on[,] and he was in there sweeping hair up in the tent. You heard Dr. Moore tell you about the racial characteristics of the population and how many persons of different racial mixtures was found in Mayes County, Locust Grove, the State of Oklahoma.

Ann Reed. Ann Reed does her job, and she does it well. She wants to please her peers. She has been promoted. Ann Reed gets stronger every time she testifies. She started out saying they were similar in characteristics. Then she said they could have come from the same source. Then she said they are microscopic—they have the same source as the hair of Gene Leroy Hart, or someone else whose hair is microscopically consistent in ever characteristic, except the only characteristic she talked about what she saw under the circumstances.

The only footlocker which didn't go with the little girls home was Karen Mitchell's footlocker. We don't know how the footlocker got from Camp Scott to the Locust Grove Police Station. We don't know how the pipe and the mirror got to Mr. Pigeon's house. Mr. Pigeon didn't see it. Bolton didn't see it. We didn't see it. Croslin Smith didn't see it. The State here is saying that Sam Pigeon is going to come here and try to pull a fast one on you, hoodwink you by using an interpreter. Well a lot of you are older than I am[,] and you've lived in this area longer than I have[,] and you know that those people who speak in the native tongue don't always communicate well with persons in English because of their comprehension level is low.

When you talk to Sam Pigeon and you want to be sure that what you're talking to him about and that he understands what you say and you understand what he says, you are going to have to have somebody there to talk to him. He doesn't understand something. But in a court of law, lawyers are going to ask him questions which suggest the answer[,] and if you ask him in English, maybe just the rhythm of the questions, isn't it true Mr. Jones, you name is Jake, you went to the eighth grade at the Locust Grove Elementary, didn't you? You worked at the American Airline plant. You live in Tulsa, don't you? Just that rhythm will tell the guy sometimes the answer that is expected of him. That type of mirror nobody is going to carry a type of mirror all over the State of Oklahoma that came out of the [G]irl [S]cout camp that did the murders of the three little girls. He's going to get rid of the evidence. He's going to ditch it. He's going to dig a hole. He's going to throw it in the trash someplace. He is not going to carry it around any more. We've got a girl scout, Kim Lewis, who identified feet. We've [got] Dean Boyd, the waitress identifying the feet. You want to remember when the Lunderman girl got on[,] she testified that she's been talking about her testimony to Mr. Fallis during the noon hour. You know the results that backed up[,] and she said yeah, she couldn't tell whether it was a man or a woman. I want to point something else out to you. When the OSBI agent went down there to talk to the little Brooks girl, they didn't want her mother and dad there. They wanted to talk to her. When you go talk to a child, if you're going to be fair and square, you'd better have their mother and dad there. You heard the little Brooks girl get on there and say that they were similar shoes to Gene's but that they had four eyelets in them. And they showed her pictures of them, didn't show her the shoes.

The reward, $8000 paid to one man. What's he get if Hart is convicted? The reward is one times $50,000, you know that, you read [it] in the paper. Who was that—what does he know about the corncob pipe and the mirror? We don't know that because they didn't bring him here. Back on *voir dire*[,] we talked about the circumstantial evidence instruction. That instruction reads, in part, all of the facts and circumstances proved to not only be consistent with the guilt of the accused but consistent with any other reasonable hypothesis or conclusion than that of reasonable doubt. I told you the judge is going to tell you in so many words beware the—where you can make more than one inference from the evidence that you have to find in favor of the defendant. There's a ton of evidence there. Some of it points to the guilt[,] and some of it points to innocence. You have to resolve that out to the defendant's favor.

Earlier I mentioned one of the big facts that a defendant has going for him in a criminal case is that the law says every citizen accused is entitled to the presumption of innocence, the burden of proof, and promise of the jurors. Now you're going to think about this case many, many times during the course of your life. You're going to retry this case in your own mind many, many times. Some morning when you wake up[,] you're going to think about it.

Some day while you're eating lunch you're going to think about it. The next thought that will pass through your mind is, *Boy, am I glad I did the right thing, and I did justice and [passed the test].*

A common argument made to jurors is to talk about the future and what they will later think about their verdict.

Now Mr. Hart and I cannot look into your minds and your hearts. When we examined you as jurors[,] I asked you and you told me that you wouldn't base [your decision] on what might look like suspicious circumstances or hunches or intuition. We believed you. You're going to retire, are you not, and when you were asked whether or not you would hold the prosecutorial team to that burden of proof of every element of the offense, you said you would, you promised you would and we believed you.

You are going to recall, are you not, when you're asked to follow the circumstantial evidence instruction, that where more than one inference can be made, the law requires you to find that inference consistent with innocence. You promised you'll do that. Gene Hart and I believed you. When you promised you wouldn't take the word of a law officer over that of any witnesses merely because he's a law officer, you promised you wouldn't. So when you go to your home tonight[,] you all will have done justice.

Mr. Isaac made a great argument here as he nears the end of his closing. The State of Oklahoma's case was built on circumstantial evidence. He referred the jury to the actual instruction and explains it. Mr. Fallis did not tell the jury in his closing how the requirements of the State of Oklahoma has satisfied the legal requirements of obtaining a conviction on circumstantial evidence. Finally Isaac draws to a close: "The prosecution has not proven Mr. Hart guilty beyond a reasonable doubt, and, therefore, I say to you, your verdict must be not guilty. Thank you very much."

Defense lawyers should always end a closing argument with a reference to "beyond a reasonable doubt."

Later that day, Garvin Isaacs would tell his co-counsel that he thought he had given a bad closing argument. John Zelbst, the law student, who was watching his first trial ever, told him he thought it was good. Years later, Zelbst would state he, due to his inexperience, did not really know a good closing from a bad one. One thing is certain: the argument was good enough.

the state's rebuttal closing argument

Mr. Fallis gave the State's final closing argument, "Ladies and gentlemen, I do want to thank you for your time and patience. I want to apologize to you.[296] A moment ago it was necessary for the State, myself, to make an objection. The objection is [Mr. Isaacs's saying "liar, liar, liar]."

Mr. Isaacs jumped up and objected: "I said it and I meant it and I object to it again." At that point, the spectators applauded and reacted to the objection.

> Mr. Fallis should have been more concerned with the facts of the case and convincing the jury he had proven Hart guilty beyond a reasonable. Instead, he opens the biggest argument of his life by complaining about Isaacs.

The judge declared: "If the court hears any reaction in the courtroom again, I may clear the courtroom." Mr. Fallis then returned to his argument:

> The objection was prompted, however, by what counsel did several times in his statements in his opening and they is he has been employed as Gene

over and over again. That is record's show to be low as the attempt of, you know, when he badly discounts the State. Now, like Mr. Isaacs says, I will repeat if I misstate what the evidence is, and you remember it not as I say it, because during the course of the trial that's been of this duration, and always are involved in the representative sides, and to bring the system is nothing you say is evidence. But it's unusual that you might say a—what—remember as you remember it, not as how I necessarily said it. If I misstate anything, I assure you it be through inadvertence on my part.

I would like to call one other thing to your attention. That is that this ploy concerning the smoke screen as the State was referred to was very dramatically illustrated before you a moment ago. Dr. McLeod, that man is probably just about as qualified as any man that I've ever seen in this field.[297] Yes, he's the same as any lawyer [or] doctor during this trial.

Mr. Fallis improperly vouched for his witness. Defense counsel should have objected.

You know I recall he was generous on the witness stand and his demeanor on the witness stand and the judge had told you that you are to use your own judgment as to his demeanor. That Irish stuff showing, that's what it was. It had to be didn't he? I think so. He was kind and courteous to counsel for the defense. He was kind and courteous to counsel for the State. And so what did he receive in return for his honest statements, his honest testimony? He received the same type of titillating little make up, 800-year-old man. Old man. Do you believe that's appropriate? No, you could say right away he'd

Gloyd McCoy

have to say no. Well, I don't know the answer to smear that gentlemen, but it [is] conduct that you observed in court during this, who really is speaking the truth here. The man just spends 40 years of his life [in] research, he can come here and testify, he was seeking the truth and I think you can judge his competency of the people in this courtroom, not just today but for the last four weeks and say who's speaking the truth.

Mr. Fallis spent a lot of time standing up for Dr. McLeod. Yet, he does not give the jury any reason to doubt Mr. Isaac's statements and calculations.

The cheering section and these people giggling and laughing after you [had] the experience of looking at these excruciatingly horrible pictures of the little girls mutilated. Now that isn't funny. Who wants to punish? That's what we are here for. Am I asking him where their talking cheating about I've never seen the demonstration that I've seen in this court-room. When we deal with a serious matter, when there is something like this, and then talks about all of this junk. What was he referring to?

Well, let's look at this junk! Here's some of that junk Mr. Isaacs talked about. That's belonged to Michele Guse, Lori Farmer. That's junk, he says.

At that point, Mr. Isaacs objected. "I wasn't talking about the books, I was talking about some of that other stuff." The objection was overruled.

Mr. Fallis continued:

You will recall his remarks. This is junk. [The little girl] took this book from the public library. Well, you know what? It's overdue. She was supposed to return [the book] on the tenth of July. She didn't do that.

Lori Farmer, her items intermingled with the items Doris Denise Milner's things. Didn't return her books before Gene Hart got under the tent, tied her up and gagged her and murdered her.

There's another book entitled *Ragged Ann and Andy*. Junk. Here are some items. Junk, as counsel called it, Lori Farmer. *Every Girl Scout Learns Like Every Boy Scout, Be Prepared.*

Be prepared, Lori, so when you're in camp you're glad to be there, when you go to camp you can pick put a band-aid on. There is no way to [protect] a child from the assault of this defendant. What do you put in your bag of goodies to take to camp to prevent Gene Leroy Hart, [a man who] will mutilate little children and then have his counsel stand before you and laugh and giggle.

Mr. Isaacs objected. Mr. Fallis attempted to continue his argument. Mr. Fallis took a shot at Mr. Isaacs when he said, "He objects because it hurts him." The judge called for a bench conference.

"Mr. Isaacs, you are getting hoarse," the judge said.

Mr. Isaacs responded, "I may get hoarser."

The judge then said to Mr. Isaacs, "I am going to order you out of here shortly. As of this moment you can prepare yourself to be [held in contempt]."

Mr. Isaacs said, "I apologize to the court at this time. I objected three times and at no time did Mr. Fallis stop."

"All right. Take it easy. You don't know how emotionally your outbursts are affecting the jury," said the judge.

"I'd like it if it did," said Mr. Isaacs. Mr. Isaac's objection was overruled. Mr. Fallis continued his argument:

> Ladies and gentlemen, I believe this book here is called *The Light Princess* published in 1977. *The Light Princess* by George McDonald. You've seen this front page. They get to camp, the first night at camp. Some of the evidence hear what happened. The very first night at camp. Somebody says, what? No children? Where are the children? They're gone. I just can't believe it. We'd better look.
>
> They find them. What little angels.

The question must be asked, "Why was Mr. Fallis talking about the books found in the tent?" The books pertained to no important factual issue. He wasted his time.

> Mr. Isaacs told you, and he's exactly correct. Sure we want to make sure the kids are—the defendant here gets every right he's entitled to. That's not a—that's the way it should be. [For] God's sake, [I hope] it never changes. But let's also think about three little persons who can't sit here and look at you, who can't sit here and say to you, My God, speak for us, do something about this, because that's what it's about.
> 298

The comment that the victims would say "do something about this" is improper and could have been objected to as overly sympathetic if nothing else.

> You know counsel has interfered to you and taking inventory is just a whole—the whole thing. Oh, thank God, you can take the form and your—your oath and do it. If he were right you would feel guilty

for doing right? You would feel guilty for following your oath as jurors. No. If you were the other party and saying rise that protest is wrong.

Render unto him according to his work and according to the people's needs and unto him according to his work and according to the people's needs and unto this evidence the human needs of this man. He's made it abundantly clear. No more "say" it "will." Don't work when you say to Lori and you say to Michelle, it's awful, you two had your day in court and you, too, will to examine this evidence—examine it. [L]ook over it, you know that any man and woman brings into this world a child. And you were asked during you much in process as this jury if you knew can your members of the families of Lori Farmer and Michelle Guse are just the final source of. [I]f else protests in her too, that's the crying anger of these little children are here sending this horror of the little charms they forward in this evidence.

It's that simple. Counsel has misstated his evidence several times and so it's necessary that I tell you again, as Mr. Shaffer did. Statements concerning that evidence. First he reminds us look on the scene. The center of the camp. How quiet it was, it must have been this individual. It's quiet. But that scene at that camp bore with it on the morning of that grizzly [day].

The newspaper in that lantern ties that to the cellar/cave. And of course tied them to it because of the glasses. And the glasses, counsel put those on, and you know those are unusual. I would have to agree with him. Every one of his witnesses, every one of our witnesses, say look, he wore the glasses, and they're bent. It's a combination. I wonder what our game is. Said he was wearing them. Counsel does take some dispute with—by the way that intrigues me. He took some dispute with the testimony of Mr. Stanford. In any event, Mr. Hart's tied to the cellar/cave. That man. There's no question Mr. Hart's lied to Sam Pigeon's and there's no question that the pipe and the mirror were found at Sam Pigeon's. You heard when he testified yesterday and believe me, I have respect for Mr. Sam Pigeon. I have every respect for the man who was the interpreter for Sam Pigeon. I don't think there is anything I said or did to those gentlemen would cause you to think otherwise.

They just said they went there. They didn't see him. We didn't hear [they] were conducting some kind of search. Counsel overlooked the fact they just state they looked for him.

Remember Mr. Christo from the OSBI? He said, "Hey! I remember seeing the little pipe and he got the mirrors and—or the mirror and got the picture," and all of that's when the counsel said to get it stricken, weren't any pictures.

Well, I'm sorry we didn't live up to his expectations but after all whatever Gene Hart likes or dislikes are it is—that we are, he's the one who put those in Mr. Pigeon's house. Why he is confused by such pictures as these I have no idea. They may not be of interest to counsel and they may not live up to his expectations of what he'd hoped to see, but I know that there's three little young girls, dressed in majorette costumes. I notice all types of pictures, young girls that you have seen and we passed among you. Surely you can see somebody who apparently has access to newspapers and magazines, cutting such things out and saving them. Oh, no, he wouldn't do that, would he. Counsel told you that people wouldn't return to their boyhood haunts if they—

when he described. Why not? What was the testimony about this boyhood haunt to the cellar/cave? Very obscure. The men who were hunting squirrels told you. Hey, you know that thing's hard to get to, hard to see. That's what the troopers [who went there] say, hard to get there, hard to see. Didn't even know it was there.

One man said, "I've lived there a long time, I didn't know it was back there." What about Sam Pigeon? Would you read this stuff? You wouldn't because you wouldn't be murdering little girls. You [wouldn't] because you create life. You don't take life. You wouldn't because you are logical in your thinking because you are honest people doing a day's work. You're not running the hills, running from the law, escaping from jail. So keep in mind that you can't judge the conduct of Gene Leroy Hart by that which is lawful, that which is logical. You've got to judge it with the knowledge that you have in common with other people. Counsel's production to give a demonstration, oh, it's Mr. Stevens. Let me ask you this, let me ask you if the imaginary witness chair, Mr. Stevens wasn't there, was he? Mr. Stevens, ah, the man they tell you they wouldn't check out. He was checked out. Counsel says it's impossible to report how he was checked out.

Dr. MacLeod talked about how he checked him out on the sperm. Ann Reed. Ann Reed talked about how he was checked out on the hair.

And this whole testimony, keep this in mind, you remember the—the two boys and the common law wife of the twenty-some year old inmate up there…[A]n interesting woman, a rather interesting woman. At any rate, they took 'em, come and get those boots. They were Dingo boots, had metal rings across them. Their witness, the little Cox girl,

Gloyd McCoy

too. She's up on the stand, looked like these pictures. Counsel didn't want those pictures. Counsel didn't want those picture, if you will recall. I am going to be honest with you. Remember when Kathy Christian said a moment ago, oh, little children remember better than anybody. The little child. Their witness. Outside the bunch to be on.

She and mama Buckskin's testimony puts Gene Leroy Hart's shoes there at that scene at the latrine at eleven thirty at night when she and her little partner are going down, flagging the light like they're taught to do in the Girl Scouts, watch out for snakes and watch out for danger where you might fall, they got light down there. Now they will say, "Wait a minute. Is there three or four eyelets?" She said she saw three or four.

Can you imagine this little girl walking down the dark path, seeing it was night, shining a light, she's shaking, she sees some legs. Can you imagine her saying, well, let's see, one, two, three, four, five, six, she's not there, count the eyes.

Everything but the eyelets in the boots. Right now. We've got him for only four weeks. You can tell I've worn this suit many days now. You remember the color of it, and what tie I wore in the last week, if you were asked that. That little girl was honest. Something else that's intriguing, too. He [Mr. Isaac's] blustered over this lantern. Oh, Mr. Stevens, tell us about this little lantern you had. This lantern, ladies and gentlemen, is a most intriguing piece of evidence. It's intriguing because of the way Gene Hart had this evidence prepared to do this dastardly deed. He fixed it also because he was apparently scared off either by the alarm of that clock, could not have time to retrieve this lantern, which ties [him] to the cellar/cave," It's intriguing also for another reason. That this woman, the common law wife of a twenty-some year old man in the Creek Penitentiary in Kansas, who was thoroughly checked out, thoroughly checked out, by law enforcement.[299]

Counsel made the remark he wasn't checked out. He was. Counsel was aware of that. But it's intriguing for another reason. He wasn't identified. And you men on the jury, perhaps more than women, I don't know, but I'm not—ladies, I don't mean to indicate ladies aren't intelligent. I'm just saying that men just not—try this on, the ladies to try to stop them, you notice, oh, I identify it by the nick.

There were six women on the jury. Mr. Fallis gets flustered because he thinks he has insulted them.

Any of you own a lantern like that? Many of them are manufactured just like that. In fact that night at the tent there's a lantern there. They identified it too because he said he put some plastic in there, lots of tape, and I had him demonstrate, he tape holding the microphone—holding the microphone down. The agent when he took it apart he found no tape at all. No tape in there. Intriguing, isn't it? Must not be the same lantern. Oh, yes, there's scratches on the outside. Scratches on the outside? Intriguing, there's a number of scratches that's identification, but there's no tape on there. I put some gray tape around there and I put some gray tape around there. Why? To repair it. If you been— owned a lantern like that you'd tell me what was broken about it. That's not broken. This part connects on to the battery, has a little screw top, goes on there. But remember the young lady said I didn't buy a battery for it. Okay. He tells you about a—

he tells you about a coat, doesn't he? This is their witness. Throw it on the tags. 095446. He said he meant the department. This meant the counter. This meant the forty-fourth week, and he said that was October. And this meant the year 1976. That's when the battery went on the shelf at Walmart, according to their witness. What's the average life of a battery on the shelf? How long do they stay there? The question was first asked by Mr. Isaacs. Now he would—oh, it should be a month, or it should be longer? Yeah, it could be longer. Well, let's give them the benefit of eight weeks, okay? Let's give them the benefit of twelve weeks. If we talk about October of '76, November, December, January, February, March, April, May—1, 2, 3, 4, 5, 6, 7 months or better. And she said, "Oh, I bought that battery, the one I had last year. When my son gave it to me and there wasn't a battery in it." You know that's another interesting thing. Can you imagine a guy who gets up there and claims that he repaired the battery but he never, I mean—excuse me, he said he repaired the light but he never put a battery in it. How did he know he repaired it, huh? You go down to have your sewing machine repaired ladies, or you gentlemen go down to have your car repaired, you go in and say would you repair this, sir? And he just says to you that—that's it, will be five dollars. Wouldn't you want him to plug it in, see if there's power to run that motor a little bit?

When her son repaired but he didn't put a battery in it. He said he had to put wire or tape there, he said. Intriguing. Little inconsistent. Again, I don't want to in any way imply those folks aren't trying to be honest. I would imply [sic] where from. Knowing that the judge's—here. That boogie man. Didn't get checked out. He's in prison in Kansas. On this lantern you, upon the fact that their boots—description of those boots compared to the little Brooks girl of that camp doesn't match. Oh, yes, we had the—

At that point, Mr. Isaacs objected, "Judge, I object. That's a misstatement. Mr. Potts said the guy on the creek had those boots too."[300]

The judge at that point made the following ruling:

Ladies and gentlemen, you are the judges of the credibility of the witnesses. You are also the judges of the evidence that has been presented. The court has rather consistently overruled both sides in their objections to statements by counsel. It's been a long trial. You are going to have to rely on your memory of what happened and what is said. The objection is overruled. You may continue.[301]

Mr. Fallis resumed his closing argument:

You did have the lady from the Midway Café. Mr. Isaacs said he received a call from her, I think he asked her the question and she…You remember that she…She said that he said to her in question that remember you just called me yesterday. He put her on yesterday, so that would have been the day before.

Wham! You see a picture on channel eight. And the picture on channel eight said she said is a picture that she saw that appeared nervous. Do you know something about her identifying that man, she couldn't make up her mind whether he had a mustache or he didn't have a moustache.

Her description doesn't match that of the family that came up here with flashlight and all said oh, there's claw marks all over his face. She hadn't mentioned any claw marks all over his face. She hadn't mentioned any claw marks on his face, did she?

And can you imagine this, counsel says how preposterous that Gene Leroy Hart would go back to his boyhood haunt to hide. Well, my God, if that's preposterous, how preposterous would it be for a man who would presumably under their theory or hunch, guesswork and speculation, and that's what their asking you to do, committed these crimes we drive twelve miles down the road, walked in a well-lighted restaurant, sits there by the window, just immediately after doing it. Amazing. Then make it all the way back to Henrietta in time to be there at eight-thirty. According to one of the young man's testimony up here.

My point is this. That is a straw man. If you can get a jury to thinking about something else out there, they will forget about the evidence against our client. Counsel said something else, and I think it's extremely important here. Counsel used an expression here, and I wrote it down because it is important, a matter of law. He said Gene Hart says we started without anything but we got here. That's what he said Gene Hart said. When did he say that? I didn't hear him say it, did you?[302] Hurry, Mr. Stevens, let me cross-examine you. Let me ask you these questions.[303]

Much—it's speculation and guesswork. Counsel asked you not to do that and do the same. Ladies and gentlemen, to insult your intelligence, stand before you and hash and rehash this evidence, but please understand it is so critically—so critically important you folks to do the right thing, that you understand the connection of the cellar/cave to Gene—the defendant. That you understand the connection of the cellar cave to Gene Hart. That you understand the connection of Gene Hart to Sam Pigeon where he was arrested. And that you understand the completion of the circle back to where Gene Hart used Sam Pigeon attached to the scene of the camp were the little mirror and the little pipe. By the way, that's intriguing also. Counsel in his innuendos, insisted on the pranks some day he must argue by all sources that are in his statement, railroad, I guess Pete Weaver can do it, would frame Mr. Hart in that matter, in this case. Can you imagine why they would want to do that?[304]

Why would you go to an area outside of the Kiowa Camp and catch all of this gory stuff, we had all the skilled knowledge that was there. All the resources and stuff. Try law enforcement. Try Mr. Wise. Try—try anybody, but please don't try Gene Hart. That's what they are saying. Well, you're here to try Gene Leroy Hart, not somebody else. Not the little victims. Not me. Not anybody else. But in desperation—always a last desperation is and that's perhaps we—we'll see some type of results that will encourage people who make up the politics of this state to have chocolates in a system of jury trials to know when the juries can assume their responsibilities, that's the politics of it. You are the politics. There are ambitions involved in this case, believe me. Ambitions. Not mine. Not Mr. Weaver, the sheriff of this county.[305]

Mr. Fallis should not have been talking about ambitions involved in the case. No one knows what he is talking about. Any ambitions of anyone in the case are not relevant.

You know counsel states, oh, what a slipshod investigation. And, you know, there [could have been more done]. That would be more—in your work, I never thought building your homes and your labors, you say the same thing. You know, I mean, you'd like to do more, and yet he had the audacity to stand before you and say just give me Mr. Maxey and By God we'll find the killer here.

He belittles Dr. MacLeod and demeans Mr. Maxey. I think he is a well-meaning person. I think he is an honorable man. My point is, though, he's the guy that spent ten minutes at looking at the hair. He's the guy that spent twenty minutes looking at the sperm. Counsel wanted to resurrect dead ones.

Then again, you remember the evidence, don't you? Ladies and gentlemen, that circle goes from camp, cellar/cave, Sam Pigeon's, and back to the camp is complete with this evidence. In the middle of that circle you have an arrow. The arrow you call hair and call sperm, and it points to Gene Leroy Hart. The complete circle, sufficient in and of itself, before above that we have the hair, and we have the sperm. And what about the hair? Not one hair, not two hairs, we have as many as six and possibly nine, and Janet—excuse me, Ann Reed told you, she said this is very important. She said she got a broader spectrum of exemplar hairs from—from somebody in that tent. It makes your identification more conclusive.

Their expert, Mr. Wilson, said the same thing. As their expert, Mr. Wilson, seems to be in conference with counsel, said they have solved this case with the atomic bomb. They put John Wilson on, a hired man for him to say the laboratory there, law enforcement laboratory, and remember what he said? He said I recognize factors. And you draw that conclusion that now the test is no longer worthy, the FBI accepts the fact it's no longer worthy.[306]

The man said it's not being used for testing, it's not being used. That was their witness. And he said something else, he said in reference to Dr. John MacLeod, he said that he had read Dr. MacLeod's report. Apparently he gave it more perusal than did Mr. Maxey. He said that he didn't see much chance for perusal.

At that point, Mr. Isaacs objected, "I object to that because we didn't get them until after Dr. McLeod had been on the witness stand and testified."

The judge then asked counsel to approach the bench. "In order to avoid being removed from this courtroom, you are going to have to watch your conduct," the judge told Mr. Isaacs.

"Judge, I'm objecting on two grounds[:] he is stating facts to the jury. He is representing to the jury that we had those reports. And Your Honor knows we didn't get them until the witness testified."

The court responded, "Well, I don't believe he's testified [to] that."

"Well, he said evidently I read them, and Mr. Wilson has read them, and if that was true, Mr. Maxey had," said Mr. Isaacs.

At that point, Mr. Isaacs moved for a mistrial. The motion for mistrial was denied. Mr. Fallis resumed his closing argument.

Dr. MacLeod didn't just work, by the way, I don't know if he [was] ever a doctor. Whether they have a problem with infertility and were having difficulty having children, people do that. It's a fact of life.

Gloyd McCoy

They call John the so-called infertility [specialist]. He's not involved in an examination to determine, you now, only is there sperm or any other sperm. Are there sperm capable of fertilizing the egg, and so on. But interestingly people go to these kinds of doctors for consultation. That's what Dr. McLeod stated. And he stated he works in a very broad field, you heard him, he's done the research and so on. Well, now although Mr. Maxey has not had any, you know, no idea as to the validity of McLeod's— Dr. McLeod's work because he even admitted it. He said I don't know anything about that when it came down to that.

In any event, the intriguing thing about this is that Mr. Wheeler—Will—is he only appropriate— independent. Do you remember what he says on redirect exam—recross exam—cross-examination, I'm sorry. I said now, well, you've read Dr. MacLeod before and he said, yes, sir. There is no question in my mind because he pointed out that Mr. McLeod, in answering my question, took into consideration in his work, this is Dr. McLeod said this, took into consideration any type of problem that the sperm that's made on the side will—from the undershorts, would have encountered and maybe have distorted it. And when I asked him that question he said yes. He said he took that into consideration and in Dr. McLeod's report, and according to Dr. MacLeod.

And I said, "And you just tried to pursue that?"

And he said, "Oh, yes, sir."

I said, "Dr. McLeod, do you recognize him as expert?"

"Most definitely."

Okay. So, therefore, Dr. MacLeod pointed to their own witness and Dr. McLeod himself stated he took all these factors into consideration. Intriguing.

He came up with the average in his tests. Now the so called tapering, and you've heard tapering, tapering form of sperm, the morphology of the sperm that he referred to, as 3.8 percent in his study, the average.

What do the families of Doris, Michele and Lori have here. Because of a brutal act of Gene Leroy Hart for the trouble of guilt is now slain he screams through his lawyer, oh, let me go! Find out it's a straw man. Well, now there's a boogie boo here somewhere. Front of this jury that you may not be able to face yourself in that mirror. Well, that road that started back on June the twenty-third of 1977 there, that road of evidence and the work and the effort because of the tragedy of the three little lives gone. What acts?

The brutalizing acts of a man who counsel says I object to them calling him an animal. Well, I'm not going to call him an animal. You judge the evidence and tell us what he is. He is a guilty man by this evidence.

Mr. Fallis was name-calling which is improper. He also gave his personal opinion of guilt.

And when that road started, that road began June the thirteenth, 1977, and those three little lives that have been lost, and that road continues by the efforts made by the agents. Long tedious effort the prospect hits you with. It's a long tedious effort to get to this point and when we stop here those lawmen, those witnesses, those counselors, those people that did all they could.[307] No, it's not up the—meet up to the standards of counsel. It's the standards that we will provide. They bring them to you. They lead you right here at this time. And if you're in that jury box you must act with what has been presented to you. Counsel said can you look Gene Leroy Hart in the eye and say I can be honest. We know you're honest people. Can you turn your back on three little tots? Can you turn your back on the evidence? It's up to you. Can you take and assume your responsibility that you said you would, according to the law and the evidence, so help us God, it's yours.

Act upon this evidence. It's that what you must do. That's what the duty and responsibility of a juror is. At the start of this trial I said nobody—nobody would say this is a happy occasion. It's not. It's not worthy of any mirth. It's a sad occasion. But you know when good people get enough, then good people they will act and we'll all hear you. For every faucet that is allowed to drip without being repaired becomes a flood."

You have a chance. You have an opportunity to speak according to the evidence in this case, coupled with the law as given by Your Honor. So speak loudly to Gene Leroy Hart, the type of conduct, that action cannot be and will not be and must not be tolerated.

And you say to Lori, you say to Denise, and you say to Michele, yes, your death is not in vain in one sense, and we'll set it right. You've gone away, but you're coming back. That's right. Now, as a matter of fact, right is the hardest thing here. Right is the hardest thing here. Right is the hardest thing to own up to. To be right. You have an obligation. The families have given you the responsibility to charge your knowledge every day, you have got to exercise that risk.

Ladies and gentlemen of the jury, I have every confidence that you will analyze this and think of the little girls and if you will return the appropriate [verdict] that will find him guilty.

Closing arguments were over. The case of *State of Oklahoma v. Gene Leroy Hart* would now be submitted to the jury.[308]

the deliberations
and the verdict

The closing arguments ended at 11:55 a.m. The judge gave the jurors the following instructions:

> Ladies and gentlemen, it is now ten minutes after twelve. Up until this point I have been the dictator and told you when you would go eat and when you won't. At this point you get to take over. While you are deliberating you can decide when you decide when you will go eat and you may make that decision right now, in whatever way you do find appropriate.

The judge concluded his remarks to the jury by saying the following:

> I do want to make this observation. Of course it's very obvious that this is a very important and very lengthy case. You will decide this case at your leisure. If you decide that it's time you stop your deliberation for the evening, and that decision should be made at whatever hour, you may do so, go back to the motel, put your mind on something else, and

come back to it refreshed tomorrow, if that's what you decide to do.

The jury then retired to deliberate. The jury eventually left for the night without reaching a verdict. As in any case, the action of the jury in going to bed for the night caused speculation on what was going on. Such actions by the jury, however, say little about what is going on.[309]

Garvin Isaacs was confident of victory. He told reporters, "I'm feeling optimistic. I really can't say why. I just have it on feelings."

The next morning the jury resumed deliberations. On that day, a verdict was reached.

John Zelbst and Barry Cousins had just returned from the jail. Zelbst watched from the law library window as Hart was escorted back into the courthouse wearing his favorite blue blazer. Hart could tell Zelbst was anxious about the forthcoming verdict.

Hart told Zelbst, "Don't worry, the Cherokees have a saying that when it rains it's a sign that God has answered your prayers. And he will answer ours today."[310]

Whenever it is announced a jury has reached a verdict, people act frantically. In this case, even more so. In a big case with lots of people involved, the announcement is like the start of the Kentucky Derby.

Most observers thought the jury would be out longer than they were. Richard Guse just made it back in time to hear the jury. He was able to squeeze himself into the crowded courtroom. Millie Littledove, Hart's sister, was across the street sweeping the floor at the Hart Hotel. She had to scramble to get across the street and into the courtroom.

Gloyd McCoy

Hart's mother had returned to her home in Locust Grove. She would miss the verdict announcement.

Court was called to order.

Three small pieces of paper were passed from the bailiff to the judge.

Displaying no expression, Judge Whistler looked at the verdicts. He then passed the verdict forms to Court Clerk Eloise Gist, who read them aloud[311]: "We the jury, duly impaneled and sworn to try the above, entitled cause, upon our oath find the defendant, Gene Leroy Hart, not guilty."

The verdict of "not guilty" was read three times. One for each dead Girl Scout. It was like the tolling of a bell three times. One reporter would later describe the verdicts as being like a "thunderbolt."[312]

As the words *not guilty* were announced, screams of both joy and anguish cut through the silence. A "thunderous cheer" broke out from the relatives and supporters of Hart.[313]

Garvin Isaacs pounded his fist onto the table. Hart and his lawyers embraced.

Prosecutor Ron Shaffer, who was seated alone at the prosecution table, dropped his head into his hands. Fallis, based on his long-standing policy, was not present when the verdict was announced. He had stayed at the motel.

Judge Whistler ordered the courtroom cleared. Sheriff Weaver, red-faced with anger, jumped up and yelled at his deputies. "Get them out of here! Get them out of here!" Approximately, thirty people were removed from the courtroom.

Betty Milner remained composed until she left the courtroom. She then broke into tears.

"It's not over," Richard Guse would later say from his Broken Arrow home. He did not explain what he meant.[314]

After the initial reaction subsided, Judge Whistler made the following remarks to the jury:

> Ladies and gentlemen, I think there are very few times, there is only one I know of[,] when the State calls upon a citizen to do more than you have been called upon to do in this case. Of course that's obviously military service. I want to commend you. I know you have worked hard. You have been conscientious. There were some who said that this defendant could not receive a fair trial in Mayes County. I think that's been demonstrated to the contrary. I want to commend you for your valiant efforts in this case, and you are at this time discharged. Thank you very much.

At the conclusion of the judge's remarks, Gene Leroy Hart stood and started to ask if he could thank the jury. "Your Honor, may I be permitted to—" Judge Whistler immediately said, "You may not. You may sit down, Mr. Hart." However, as the jurors walked out of the courtroom, Hart was able to comment to several of them, even calling some of them by name.[315]

Judge Whistler made remarks to Mr. Isaacs about his behavior:

> This is very distasteful to me personally, but there are two instances that occurred during the course of this trial that I feel go way beyond the scope of legitimate advocacy. And those two instances that the court has in mind were the instance where you, while addressing the jury, after the court had made a ruling, said words to the effect "have you ever been

Gloyd McCoy

in a situation where two people ganged up you," referring to myself and the prosecutor. The second instance was yesterday when you in a very loud voice cried, "Liar." The court found your conduct to be contemptuous and juvenile at best. I expect you to be prepared to answer these two charges that the court is preferring [sic] against you today at one o'clock.

Mr. Isaacs, ever the advocate, said: "At this time I move that the court disqualify itself from my contempt charge. I move that I be granted an O.R. Bond and that I have time to retain attorneys to represent me."

Judge Whistler replied, "I will take the matter under advisement. In regard to bond, all I want is your personal assurances that you will be in attendance upon this court at one o'clock." The matter was eventually postponed. Mr. Isaacs eventually apologized to the judge per the advice of noted Oklahoma City attorney D.C. Thomas, who had agreed to represent Isaacs.[316]

Thomas agreed to represent Isaacs on one condition, "That he shut up." Reporter Dick Rouse said Judge Whistler told him he was shocked to see D.C. Thomas show up. He said the contempt situation was "not that big of a deal." Apparently, all the judge wanted to do was scare Isaacs.[317]

Isaac's zealousness may have irritated the judge and opposing counsel but obviously had a positive effect on the jury. Trial lawyers virtually unanimously agree that some-times jurors make a decision, in part, on the basis of which lawyer(s) they like best.

Following the courthouse celebration, another victory celebration was held at the Hart Hotel. At that celebration, Hart's mother, Ella May Buckskin, arrived from Locust

Grove. Upon her arrival, when she saw Garvin Isaacs, she began to cry. She asked him if she would be able to see her son. Isaacs told her he had already been taken back to the prison.

Buckskin hugged Isaacs and sobbed, "God is going to bring my boy home to me." At the time, she did not know her son would, indeed, be coming home for good.

reaction to the verdict

Gene Leroy Hart cried when the verdict was read. He had also cried during defense counsel's closing argument.[318] He was emotional about what had occurred.

In June of 1979, he was interviewed by reporters from the *Cherokee Advocate*, the newspaper for the Cherokee Nation. He was interviewed at the Oklahoma State Penitentiary. He was present with his two defense lawyers. Hart gave the following remarks about his reaction to the jury's verdict:

> Relief. Relief in the sense that I felt the world had been lifted from my shoulders and relief in knowing that it was all over...all three at one time...all over. I didn't have to go through it two more times. Just knowing that it was all over and justice had been served. The jury voted right. There is no question in my mind that they voted right.

Hart later responded to a letter from a reporter who asked him for an interview. Hart wrote: "The record has been set straight as far as I am concerned—the jury voted right when they voted 'not guilty,' and my family and supporters knew the entire process was a sham."

In the letter, Hart complained that the prosecutors and news media attempted to convict him unjustly. Hart wrote:

"I and my friends and relatives will never forget or forgive such an injustice. Most of the media did their best to see that I was convicted unjustly of a crime that I had absolutely nothing to do with."[319]

The day after the verdict, the *Daily Oklahoman* described the "tomblike" atmosphere at the Mayes County Sheriff's Office. The article said, "Hart's pursuers, investigators and prosecutors were dumbstruck with bitter disappointment."

The disappointment was obviously compounded when it was reported that one juror had commented that the jury had basically made up its mind with regard to Hart's innocence within five minutes of beginning deliberations.[320]

"The evidence was pitiful," one woman juror was quoted as saying. "All they had was circumstantial evidence."[321]

After the verdict announcement, prosecutor Ron Shaffer exited the courtroom and declined to make any comment. Prosecutor Fallis had not been present at the verdict announcement. The new Mayes County district attorney said he planned to leave it entirely up to Sheriff Pete Weaver as to whether to reopen the investigation

A bitter Sheriff Pete Weaver told the press, "I do not intend to reopen any investigation. We had the man we were after." Weaver told one reporter, "I don't have anything to say that's printable."

Ted Lemke, OSBI director, echoed Weaver's attitude, saying "Why should we [reopen the investigation]? We had the right man."

A Hart supporter, Rudy Leach, said he hoped the OSBI would find the real killer. "Maybe this will get these lazy OSBI agents off their seats and they'll do something."[322]

Today, on the official OSBI website, the OSBI discusses its role in the Hart case and says Hart was acquitted by a "local" jury. Of course, all juries are local. The OSBI, how-ever, meant "biased" jury.

On the same website, the agency discusses its role in the Jack Burris matter, another Mayes County matter not solved by the OSBI. Jack Burris was the only prosecutor in Oklahoma history to be assassinated.

Mayes County Undersheriff Al Boyer vented his disap-pointment on a television reporter in the hallway following the announcement of the verdict. "You boys get in every-body's way," Boyer said as he pushed the newsman against the wall.[323]

On another occasion during trial, Boyer and Garvin Isaacs almost came to blows. After the jury was selected, the judge had told Catherine Bennett she could not sit at coun-sel table anymore. During a recess, she had wanted to tell Isaacs good-bye as she was leaving. Boyer blocked her way. Isaacs took offense. Bennett began to cry over the incident.

"It's just not worth it," she said.

Boyer also expressed his displeasure with the jury's ver-dict to a *Washington Post* reporter: "It's just Mayes County justice. I think it was an easy way out for them. I think that the fact the families of the victims live in Tulsa and that the jurors won't have to face them like they will the Hart fam-ily—that's what happened.[324]

OSBI Agent Don Sharp espoused that, despite the fact they had exhausted 10,000 manhours and approximately $100,000 in their investigation, the agency was not demor-alized by the "not guilty" verdict. Sharp said the OSBI was "confident" that it had found the killer—whether or not the jury believed it—and said he considered the case to be closed.

"I don't think anybody here, that I know of, feels Gene Hart did not committed the crime…I have no doubt in my mind that we had the right man," said Sharp.

"You don't have to be demoralized about it—you don't cry in your beer. We work about 175 to 200 homicides a year. We've got them waiting in line." Sharp denied any despondency over the verdict. "You can't really feel that way about it," he said. "You have to divorce yourself from any personal impact about it. Otherwise, you'd be on a psychological roller coaster."

The press reported comments from the jury.

One juror, who asked to remain anonymous, said the panel had its mind made up five minutes after beginning deliberations. The juror asked not to be identified "because we're already in trouble."

In brief remarks to the press, jury foreman George Kelley praised his fellow panel members as hard working and expressed gratitude to the court officials for their kindness. Kelley said the jurors had agreed unanimously not to say anything about the case.

Despite this so-called pact not to say anything about the verdict, Juror Joan Littlefield was quoted as saying, "We looked at every piece of evidence one at a time…we were very thorough."[325] Juror Littlefield said the jurors began their deliberations with open minds. "There was no one who was way over here for guilty and no one way over there for innocent," she said.[326]

On the twenty-fifth anniversary of the murders, some of the jurors were persuaded to talk about their verdict.[327] "We didn't have any choice but to acquit him," said Juror Lela Ramsey. "The judge gave us twelve different things we had to connect before we found him guilty. Given the testimony, we did not even find two of those things."

Ramsey, a Pryor housewife for over fifty-six years said, "Things just didn't add up."[328] She said there was definitely some reasonable doubt. Ramsey said, "I'll never forget those little girls—or Gene Leroy Hart."

Juror Ed Shipp told how he was visited afterward by Sheriff Pete Weaver. He was questioned by Weaver as to why he had voted the way he did. Weaver told him the State had other evidence they could have put on but prevented from doing so by the judge. Weaver was trying to both intimidate the juror and trying to make the juror feel guilty.

Weaver was referring to evidence of Hart's rape convictions. The evidence was not admissible. In America, the general rule is that a person should be convicted only of what he has been charged and not based on a crime he may have committed. There are limited exceptions. However, the prior convictions here were not relevant to show common scheme or plan, motive or identity.

Juror Shipp was not convinced by the State's assertion that Hart had acted alone. He said, "[The jury] talked about the possibility of there being more than one person involved. I've always said that if he did it, he wasn't alone. There was too much going on."

Jeanna Kelly, wife of jury foreman George Kelly, said her late husband agreed with the assessment that Hart could not have acted alone. "Deep down inside, I think George thought there were too many agencies involved to present a good case against Hart. Things were botched, and a lot of jurors didn't think it was possible for more than one man to do all that they say he did."

The jury did not buy the State of Oklahoma's circumstantial case. Except for speculative forensics, no direct evidence ever put Hart at the crime scene. The jurors could not understand how Hart could have committed the murders by himself.[329]

As one headline proclaimed, "[The] Prosecuting Evidence Seemed 'Mixed Up'"[330]

Several of the jurors said they were followed in the days and weeks after the trial. Some received threatening telephone calls.

The day after the verdict, the local Pryor newspaper ran a banner headline, "Hart Not Guilty." The article about the verdict ended with the question that remains today: "With Gene Leroy Hart found innocent, who is responsible for the brutal slayings of those young girls, and where is that person today?"[331]

The *Tulsa World* editorialized about the verdict and concluded by stating: "But whatever dispute may linger after the verdict, it is unlikely that anyone will argue that a minority defendant cannot get a fair trial in Pryor, Oklahoma or that widespread publicity about the crime automatically convicts the accused."[332]

In July 1979, Buddy Fallis spoke to the Downtown Rotary Club in Tulsa. Fallis told the group that, since there were so many questions about the case, the investigation should continue. However, Fallis made it clear his opinion of who the perpetrator was had not changed.

"Quite frankly, in my mind, there is no question about the man's guilt." Fallis also said, "But I think the investigation will and shall continue because I'm satisfied there had to be many people hiding him, there had to be many people concealing evidence, and there had to be many people who have knowledge of the crime."

Fallis further stated, "There could be more than one person involved." Fallis did not elaborate as to who the other person or person might be. Fallis received a standing ovation.

A future Oklahoma governor, Frank Keating, expressed his opinion that the case should remain open. Keating, then a state senator, wrote a letter to OSBI director, Tom Kennedy, asking the OSBI to keep the case open.[333]

Was the media surprised at the verdict? Mildly. Most of the media was. One reporter commented years later, "Remember at one end of the spectrum, the OSBI was absolutely rock solid in their statements to the media, (based on the record and in informal chats while setting up for a story) that they had the perpetrator. I have no question they knew in their 'heart of hearts' that they had the right guy and had the forensics to back it up with the 'deformed sperm.'" [334]

At the time of the apprehension of Gene Leroy Hart, many thought he was a victim of a witch hunt. At the conclusion of the ordeal, many of the "witch hunters" thought they were the ones bewitched.

god returns gene leroy hart home

Prior to the announcement of the verdict, it has been said Sheriff Weaver and a Cherokee medicine man met outside the courthouse. The medicine man performed a ceremony that involved the burning of tobacco on the ground. The medicine man said that if Hart was guilty the Great Spirit would rise up and strike him down.[335]

On June 4, 1979, just weeks after his legal triumph, Gene Leroy Hart died. He collapsed while jogging in the exercise yard of the Oklahoma State Penitentiary. He was rushed by ambulance to the McAlester Regional Hospital where he was pronounced dead.[336]

Oklahoma Department of Corrections' spokesperson, Nancy Nunnally, reported the doctors worked on Hart for twenty minutes but to no avail.[337] Dr. Blake Berry, chief of emergency medicine at the hospital, said his examination of Hart indicated arrhythmia. "Basically, this is just a heart that doesn't pump any blood."

Dr. Berry believed that Hart was probably dead by the time he reached the hospital. Dr. Berry said, "We attempted vigorously to revive him but were not able to get [any] signs of life at all." Berry said there were no marks on Hart's body.

"I'm really sorry about the ol' fellow," said Berry. "You know we didn't actually know who he was until after we pronounced him dead."

Hart's life at the prison, except for a trip back to Pryor on May 22, 1979, to plead guilty to escape charges, had been uneventful.[338] His life appeared to be settling into a routine. At his own request, he had been placed in the general population.[339]

The day after his death, an autopsy was conducted. The autopsy was done by Dr. A. Jay Chapman of the Oklahoma Medical Examiners Office. According to Dr. Chapman, Hart had died of "a plain, simple heart attack." Chapman elaborated on the subject by saying, "Only a tiny pinpoint of blood was going through to his heart."[340]

Arterial sclerosis or hardening of the arteries was found in two of the three main arteries. Hart had apparently also suffered a prior heart attack within the past three months. One artery was 80 to 85 percent closed and another 98 percent closed.

Dr. Chapman said the heart attack "probably caused Hart to suddenly collapse and be unconscious." Chapman suggested that immediate resuscitation attempts might have revived him. Chapman also surmised the physical activity—Hart had been lifting weights prior to jogging—could have brought on the heart attack.

According to Chapman, Hart probably felt little pain. Dr. Chapman refused to speculate as to whether the ordeal of the trial contributed to Hart's death.[341]

Many people doubted that Hart died of a heart attack.[342] The main rumor that circulated was Hart had been poisoned by other inmates. Actually, since he had been returned to prison, Hart had gotten along fine with inmates.

He was interviewed by reporters from the *Cherokee Advocate* with his lawyers present only a few days before his death. If he was having any kind of problem in prison, it is obvious he would have told the reporters and his lawyers.

In 2007, Jimmie Don Bunch claimed Hart had not died in prison of a heart attack. Bunch stated, "As you know, soon after that Hart was release back into the general population, he was killed (poisoned) by some inmates."[343]

Bunch also said, "At the time I could have probably warned Hart that there was a good possibility that his life would be in jeopardy if he went back into general population. However, I felt the same way the majority of the inmate population felt about the crimes Hart allegedly committed. I had lost what compassion I once had for Hart, and back then I felt Hart should pay the supreme price for what he had done to them little girls."[344]

Bunch swore, "I had received word from friends of mine in the general population that they planned to kill Hart when he was released from the maximum security unit on Death Row. Thereafter, I must confess that I knew that Hart was to be killed, and I did nothing to warn him or try and prevent his death."[345]

Bunch's statements about Hart being murder are beyond belief. The autopsy did not reveal any poison in Hart's system. The only drug found in his system was lidocaine, which was administered by medical personnel to control his heartbeat. Additionally, if there had been any basis that Hart was murdered, his trial lawyers would have pounced on that fact, and it would have been first-page news and the subject of a lawsuit.

Unknown to most people, an independent pathologist was hired by Hart's lawyers. The independent pathologist agreed with the medical examiner's autopsy report. Hart had died of a heart attack.

Hart's physical condition was not monitored by prison officials. Medical care for prisoners was not a top concern in Oklahoma. Since his return to prison, Hart had gone to the infirmary one time. He needed medication for a skin rash.

Following Hart's death, one inmate, Jesse E. Cochran, tried to convince the Oklahoma Pardon and Parole Board he should be released from prison because he had discovered poison, some of which had been used against Hart and turned it in to prison officials.[346] Cochran asked the Board to release him "to take the heat off me" from possible vengeful convicts still incensed that he had collaborated with prison officials.

Despite the autopsy findings, many inmates still believed that Hart had been poisoned. According to Cochran, when rumors began circulating that there "was enough poison to kill everyone in McAlester" he was asked by the Warden's staff to find the powdery substance and bring it to them.

Cochran said supposedly told he was told he would receive assistance in securing a parole if he helped. However, Prison officials denied they offered any suggestion of assistance. "This man is walking with death at his shoulder constantly, with what he has done to better this institution," declared his attorney Ed Edmondson.[347] "I don't think there is any question he's put himself in danger for what he's done," Edmondson said.

The Oklahoma Pardon and Parole Board unanimously denied Cochran's plea for release. The board members cited the fact Cochran had used illegal drugs during his incarceration. Also a protest had been received from Oklahoma

City law enforcement authorities who described Cochran as a "serious threat to society."

The *Tulsa World* summed up Hart's life as follows: "Hart started out a winner, a hero of his high school football team. Then he became a convicted criminal, finally charged with capital crimes. When he was acquitted, his supporters made him out to be a martyr, a victim himself of a miscarriage of justice."[348]

On the editorial page, the same newspaper pontificated on the subject of Hart's death:

> Those convinced of his innocence see his death as a tragedy perhaps brought on by the trauma of a long manhunt and legal fight. He is being portrayed as a good, even religious man who was setting out on a life of service in prison. Whatever the facts of Hart's innocence in the Girl Scout deaths, his life was a genuine waste and a tragedy. Those contending his innocence should not be allowed to forget he was after all serving a long sentence for crimes of kidnap, rape, burglary, and escape he had admitted. But aside from the Hart family, understandably believing in his innocence, few will mourn his passing.[349]

The *Tulsa World* would conclude its editorial by saying: "The unfortunate life of Gene Leroy Hart has ended in premature death. It is time that society closed the book on the tragedies that were part of that life."[350]

Interestingly, the *Tulsa World*, although saying the books should be closed on Hart's life, continued to publish stories about his funeral and burial. Apparently, sometimes cases that should be closed are too interesting to actually be closed.

Sheriff Pete Weaver assumed Hart had been murdered in prison. He said, "I was not surprised. Even convicts have their code of honor."[351]

Sid Wise reflected on Hart's death and said, "It reaffirms my belief that justice will prevail, even if you have to go higher than men and women sitting on a jury. The hand of fate or the Almighty steps in when the system fails."[352]

It is always interesting and sometimes humorous when one presumes to speak for "the Almighty." Like generals in the Civil War, prosecutors and defense attorneys alike always presume that God is on their side. Mr. Fallis commented, he "did not rejoice in the death of any individual." However, "to be candid and fair, though, I would have to say it is not the same feeling of sorrow I had at the announcement of the death of those three little girls."[353]

The Oklahoma State Prison has a prison museum. Visitors can see all types of prison memorabilia. In 1984, one of the highlights of a tour of the museum was the opportunity to see what prison officials claimed to be a set of prison blues (clothes) worn by Gene Leroy Hart on the night he died of a heart attack. [354]

may he rest in peace

The funeral of Gene Leroy Hart was the largest in Locust Grove history. It was held in the Locust Grove High School gymnasium, the place where he had played basketball for the Locust Grove Pirates. Locust Grove Superintendent Leonard Yarbrough agreed to let the family use the gym. Hart was "a good fellow while he was in high school here."

Folks in Hart's hometown of Locust Grove mourned. "Like a rag doll held up by many strangers too many times, this Mayes County town ha[d] become frayed at the edges."[355]

Hart's sister, Millie Littledove, said, "I think he's been cheated. I don't think it should have been him. I think it should have been Pete Weaver, Buddy Fallis, or Sid Wise. I think they killed him. I think they wanted him dead, and they got their way."[356]

Hart's mother, Ms. Buckskin, said, "He [Gene] always told me 'I'm living proof you can beat the system.' But he still didn't beat them. They killed them."

Ms. Buckskin had just received a letter from her son who had told her, "I just got saved." He would have a place in heaven amongst the angels.

An estimated 1,300 people attended the funeral. The population of Locust Grove at the time was estimated at 1,090. Three hundred people waited outside the facility during the funeral service. Among the attendees were Hart's defense team and the chief of the Cherokee Nation, Ross Swimmer.

The vast majority of the mourners were non-celebrity individuals. Many of the women wore simple print dresses while men wore blue jeans, western shirts, and boots. Hart's son was not in attendance. Lela Ramsey, one of Hart's jurors, was in attendance. Years later, Garvin Isaacs would say, "I'll never forget the kindness his family showed me at his funeral. They're the most generous people I've ever met."[357]

The crowd was so large the employees of the Jones Wilson Cunningham Funeral Home ran out of programs. On the cover of the funeral program was a drawing of a Cherokee warrior in full Indian dress. The drawing was by Gene Leroy Hart himself. Inside the program were the words of Locust Grove English teacher, Mary Bell: "Our God has come and picked a rose out of the garden of life to brighten the city which we are all looking toward. Always remember that in death our loss is Heaven's gain."

Sam Pigeon wore a brand new pair of overalls for the funeral of "Drum," the man he harbored during one of Oklahoma's most intensive manhunts.[358] Floral arrangements stretched for more than forty feet on either side of the bluish-gray coffin that held the body of Hart. The body was attired in a dark blue three-piece suit Hart favored during his trial.

Shortly before the arrival of the family, Bob Kashiuay, a friend of Hart's, wearing soiled jeans, a t-shirt, and a blue-

and-white headband, startled the crowd. He walked to the front of the casket. He boldly spoke to Hart's body in the native Cherokee language. He said, "Brother, it has been a long time since we have been together. It's a damn pitiful shame I have to see you this way." After his remarks, he went and stood silently in the corner of the gymnasium.

During the service, one of the ministers spoke of a beckoning God who called his servant home. "Son, you trusted me, and you've been through enough. Come live with me." Rev. Bill Grass, pastor of the Spavinaw Freewill Baptist Church, spoke of Hart's life. "He had a terrible time getting a start on this earth. It was a struggle for him to get shelter and food." According to the minister, Hart "began to have a little trouble running into man's laws after his high school football star days."

Glass said Hart's prison sentences were too long and called his death an act of God. Glass also said, "God stepped in with his mighty works and power and called Gene home. [H]ad he had a square chance he wouldn't [be] in the place he is now." Glass referred to "jail food and jail cells and jail life." Such had taken its toll on Hart, and that when "life was not up to standard, God would provide."

After Rev. Glass spoke, another minister spoke. He spoke to the crowd in the native Cherokee language.

The chief of police of Lone Grove, Kenneth Demps, said the funeral was the largest he had seen in Locust Grove. "There won't ever be another one like it." He was right. Since then, there has not been one of that magnitude.

Following the one-hour service, it took another hour for all the people to file past the open coffin. A three-mile procession of cars drove to the cemetery. At the grave more words were said. Prayers were given. Mourners tossed handfuls of dirt, symbolic of handshakes upon the coffin. The coffin was then lowered into the ground. Hart was buried at the Ballou Cemetery near Locust Grove. His grave has a granite marker.[359] He is buried within two miles of the Camp Scott location.[360] Speculation about his innocence "followed him to his grave."[361]

the civil suit

The families of two of the murdered girls filed a civil lawsuit. The Guse family did not choose to participate in the lawsuit.[362]

The case was tried in March of 1985.[363] The lawsuit was filed against the Girl Scout organization and the Hartford Accident and Indemnity Company. The camp operators were accused of failing to provide sufficient security measures at Camp Scott. Hartford Accident and Indemnity Company was accused of negligence in failing to tell camp operators of the security needs following a 1976 inspection. A settlement could not be reached. The case was tried in the District Court of Tulsa County. The lawsuit was filed on September 22, 1977, before Hart was even captured. The presiding judge was The Honorable William R. Beasley, Associate District Judge.

Dan Rogers, attorney for the Magic Empire Council, told the jury in his opening statement that no amount of security could have deterred whoever killed the girls. He said lighting and fencing, two measures, which the dead girl's parents claimed the camp operators negligently failed to provide, would have been of no use. "There's not anything you're going to do that would discourage somebody like that," he said. "He had to be crazy." Rogers said, "I submit to you that the kind of deterrence they're talking about might discourage a reasonable person, but there's not anything you can do to discourage a person like this."[364]

During the civil trial, plaintiffs called Pete Weaver to testify. Weaver told the jury that, shortly before the murders, he had stepped up his search for Gene Leroy Hart. Hart had recently been sighted near his mother's house, which was just a mile from the camp. On occasion, according to Weaver, Hart had been sighted within two and a half miles of the camp. According to Weaver's testimony, on the day the girls had arrived at Camp Scott, he was dutifully investigating a second-degree burglary of a farmhouse, a half-mile away from the camp. Weaver suspected that Hart was the perpetrator of that burglary. Weaver was critical of the security at Camp Scott. Specifically, he said tent number eight was not visible from the camp counselor's tent. The tent was shielded from view by foliage.[365]

Weaver said he did not know Camp Scott was being utilized on June 12, 1977. He would have warned the camp officials that Hart was believed to be in the area if he had known there were campers present. "I don't know if I could have prevented them from coming in, but I certainly would have warned them," Weaver testified.

Weaver was questioned about his lack of knowledge of operations at Camp Scott. Weaver did not know the camp was operated year-round. During the summer, the camp was almost continuously occupied. Weaver said he had visited the forty-nine-year-old camp on one occasion. That visit had taken place before he became sheriff.

"That's the only time you ever went out there, and you were sheriff for ten years?" Weaver was asked.

Gloyd McCoy

"I had no occasion to," Weaver replied. "We never had any occasion to visit the camp, in an official capacity or otherwise."

Weaver's testimony was incredible. Hart had been on the loose for four years prior to the deaths of the girls. He had been spotted in the area several times. He was a convicted rapist. Yet Weaver did not see the necessity of going to Camp Scott and warn the officials to take precautions.

At trial, plaintiffs' counsel presented evidence and argument the Magic Empire Council should have taken certain precautions such as secure fences, outdoor lighting, and better communications between the counselors and the director of the camp. It was also argued the camp should have had armed security patrols at night.

Marriliea Turner, eighteen, and Johana Wright, eighteen, who had attended the camp at the time of the murders when they were ten, testified regarding strangers at the camp. Both said they saw strangers at the camp the day before the bodies were found.[366]

Evidence was presented to show the torment of the two families had suffered. Dr. Mark Kelly, a psychiatrist who treated Sheri Farmer, mother of Lori, during the trial of Gene Leroy Hart testified Mrs. Farmer was bitterly disappointed when Hart was acquitted of the murders. "She had a feeling that she had a terrible loss and no one was held accountable."[367] Psychological profiles of the parents showed they were spinning in a "wheel of pain." During closing argument, Plaintiff lawyer Jack Gaither evoked the grief and anguish of the murdered girls' families. He also emphasized the pain and horror the girls must have suffered in their last moments of life. Defense counsel Rogers told the jury a verdict for the plaintiffs would destroy the Girl

Scout organization. "You can destroy camping. You can absolutely destroy camping," he argued.

Rogers pleaded to the jury, "This is a case that the Girl Scouts have got to win. You're the only ones that can preserve what we've got, what we've had for so long." During closing, Rogers told the jury that no reasonable security could have deterred the killer. The jury was told both sides believed that Gene Leroy Hart was the killer. Normal security measures could not have deterred Hart, Rogers said. Rogers emphasized the fact that, for over ten months, Hart had eluded one of the most intensive and extensive manhunts in Oklahoma history.

The supernatural was discussed during the defense's closing argument. Hart's spirit was mentioned. "I think his spirit is here today," Rogers said, "wanting somebody, wanting you, the jury to assume responsibility for the death of these girls." Rogers also said, "I don't want to give that man [Hart] the satisfaction of knowing that he's destroyed the Girl Scout movement with what he did that night."

Rogers agreed the deaths of the girls was tragic. He also, probably improperly, argued that the filing of the lawsuit was also a tragedy. "His words," Rogers said, nodding toward defense counsel, Gaithers. "Callous, uncaring, indifferent. That's one of the tragedies of this lawsuit. All these people are going to have to live with that accusation. It's been said only to turn you against the Girl Scouts."

The contentiousness of the lawyers, as in the criminal case, was apparent. Gaither countered Rogers' arguments with vigor. He argued the evidence showed that Magic Empire officials had engaged in a cover-up prior to the murders. According to Gaither, Magic Empire officials deliberately suppressed reports of repeated intrusion onto the camp grounds, thefts, and burglaries at the camp in the years before the murders. Gaither argued, if the public had known about these incidents, "Camp Scott would have been out of business years ago." Gaither argued the incidents were evidence that the man who killed the girls played a "game of death" for years inside the camp.[368]

The jury retired to deliberate. Once again, the vote did not go the way desired by the girls' families. By a nine to three vote, the six-man, six-woman civil jury[369] found in favor of the defendants.[370] The jury deliberated five hours before arriving at the defense verdict. Afterward, none of the jurors made any comment on their verdict. Attorney Dan Rogers told the media he had been confident of victory. He was quoted as follows: "The jury had to hear it, and I think they [the slain girls' families] had to tell their story, and we understand that, and we feel for them."

Plaintiffs' lawyer Gary Gaither immediately said an appeal would be filed. He was "shocked" by the verdict. "[We] still believe that [we] were right, and the Magic Empire Council of Girl Scouts was negligent." He added, "If nine of twelve people disagreed with us, all I can say is the Girl Scouts were lucky to have that nine on the jury." An appeal was filed. No appellate relief was granted.

In 2002, Sheri Farmer told a reporter she was still angry and bitter at the Girl Scout organization. She said officials from the organization had always treated her as an adversary rather than as a parent who had lost a child.

"It would have meant a great deal to us if they had treated us just like a mom and dad," she said. "They did absolutely nothing to be comforting to us." Desperate to get any information about her daughter's last hours, Farmer recalled trying to find out what her daughter had for dinner. The organization would not tell her.[371]

life goes on

Camp Scott closed on the day of the murders. The land was subsequently sold. Today, the deeply rutted dirt road—once called the "Cookie Trail"—drifts into the dense woods and ends at the ghostly remains of the camp lodge. Screenless, wood-framed doors flap in the wind at the lodge entrances where excited girls once found refuge from a thunderstorm on the first day of camp in 1977. A lone picnic table sits in the shadow of a blackened stone fireplace, perhaps just as it did thirty years ago. Outside, weeds have overtaken the now empty cement pool. And if pieces of the wooden tent platforms remain, they have long been swallowed by the dense overgrowth of the woods. The laughter of children, heard for nearly fifty years, is gone. Quiet relents only for the wind.[372]

The Magic Empire Council is now known as Eastern Oklahoma Girl Scouts and has a campground in Osage County. The place is called Camp Tallchief. There, the atmosphere is much different. The scouts sleep in raised cabins rather than tents. There are fewer trees. A large fence with barbed wire at the top surrounds the area.[373]

The courthouse where Oklahoma's "trial of the century" took place has been demolished. A new $9.4 million dollar courthouse has taken its place.[374] The new courthouse is across town one block off of Graham Avenue, the town's main street. The courthouse sits on a square and even has a gazebo, along with benches and various memorials. The Mayes County Courthouse is the finest courthouse in Oklahoma.

Law enforcement continued to criticize the jury's verdict in *State of Oklahoma v. Hart.*[375] Sheriff Pete Weaver was quoted in 1985 saying: "There wasn't a lawman who helped work the case from the OSBI and the FBI to the Tulsa police Department, who doubted that Hart was guilty."[376] Members of the jury can take comfort that all juries are criticized usually by the losing party.[377]

Twenty years after the murders, Buddy Fallis said he "respects the jury's verdict but can't help wondering what the outcome would have been if the trial had been held outside of Mayes County."[378]

As for the events of 1977, speculation still exists as to who committed the crimes. "Web forums are crammed with rumors and theories as to who committed the murders. In some cases, full names of those suspected of being involved are even listed. Books have been written and documentaries produced."[379]

dna fails to solve the mystery

In 2008, attempts were made to obtain a conclusion to the Girl Scout murder case by submitting certain DNA evidence for testing. The testing became possible when the OSBI obtained a federal grant that permitted private laboratories to examine DNA evidence in cold cases. In April 2008, the OSBI, with approval of the then district attorney of Mayes County, Gene Haynes, had tests done on semen stains from pillow cases and a swab taken from one of the victims. Haynes agreed to the tests even though the tests would exhaust the evidence from the swab and prevent any future tests.[380]

The test results did not identify a killer. In fact, the results muddied up the perception of what had occurred on that fateful night. The tests revealed a partial female DNA profile. The tests raised the possibility of a female attacker. Sheri Farmer, Lori's mother said, "I've always felt in my gut that there was a girl present. So when I saw the DNA results, that was a concern with me."[381]

Was a female involved? Who was it? There was never an allegation that a female ever alone or in tandem with anyone had committed the murders.

"Anytime you play with evidence long enough, you run the risk of things becoming cloudier," said Buddy Fallis. "It would be nice if we had pristine DNA samples from all parties involved, but we don't. Now the case becomes murkier, and that's real sad. The more this is played out, the more the lore of public speculation grows. Of course, this doesn't change my belief. I've always believed we charged the right guy in Gene Leroy Hart."[382]

The *Tulsa World*, on the editorial page, expressed disappointment that science could not give a conclusion to the matter: "As much progress as science has made the last thirty years, it still has its limits. That became clear this week when DNA testing in the murder of three Girl Scouts near Locust Grove thirty years ago found no conclusive evidence."[383]

Defense lawyer Garvin Isaacs remains steadfast in defending Gene Leroy Hart. "I feel badly for the families of those little girls who were murdered," he said. "But Gene Leroy Hart was an innocent man."[384]

If the events of the case occurred today, the matter of guilt would be solved through the DNA evidence. The semen evidence discovered at the scene would have been compared with samples from Hart. If they matched, the only question would be whether or not Gene Leroy Hart would get the death penalty. If they did not match, he would, even if charged, have an opportunity for acquittal.

the o.j. simpson connection

Years after the death of the Oklahoma Scouts, America became obsessed with the Los Angeles murder case involving O.J. Simpson.[385] The Hart case provided a spooky premonition of many of the elements of the Simpson case: the us-against-them cultural clash of victims families and law enforcement authorities against racial and cultural supporters of the defendant, many of whom believed investigators had fabricated evidence against them.

Coincidently, both O.J. Simpson and Gene Leroy Hart were former football players. Of course, Hart never came close to the level of football success as Simpson. Other similarities between the two cases include the following: Nicole Simpson and Ronald Goldman were murdered on the same date that the bodies of the dead Girl Scouts were found, June 13.

The juries in both cases did not take long to reach their verdicts. Hart's jury deliberated only five hours over two days before acquitting him. Simpson's jury took less than four hours to find him guilty. As in the Hart case, many believed strongly the jury's verdict was wrong.[386]

Unfortunately for the disbelievers in both cases, the vote by the jury in both cases will last forever. There are no second chances for prosecutors. As Garvin Isaacs said, twenty years after the murders, "The jurors heard all of the evidence and came back with a not guilty verdict. That's the decision they made, and it should be respected."[387]

In both cases, unknown people would rise to prominence. To some it was a boon, to others a burden. None, however, really had a choice. Their lives were touched forever.[388]

what happened to ...?

Ella Maye Buckskin, Gene Leroy Hart's mother, died on May 31, 1993. Before her death, she survived a bout with cancer, her son's trial, and several heart attacks, which her doctors say were stressed induced. She was buried beside her son.

Garvin Isaacs made little money representing Hart. However, the publicity of the case made him a much sought-after lawyer.

Years later one of the reporters who covered the Hart trial, said of Isaacs, "At the other end of the spectrum was this upstart kid no one had ever heard of, sleeping on a mattress over a dentist's office and putting up one hell of a fight with no apparent budget. He was fighting an uphill battle and getting cited for contempt."[389]

After the Hart trial, Garvin Isaacs was no longer an "upstart kid." He was a lawyer to be reckoned with from then on. He has handled numerous high-profile criminal and civil cases.[390]

Because of the publicity of the victory in the Hart case, his continuous success and his numerous continuing legal education presentations on trial practice throughout the State of Oklahoma and the nation, Isaacs became a very popular lawyer. His place in Oklahoma legal lore is firmly established.

Creekmore Wallace, II, a long-time Oklahoma criminal defense lawyer from Sapulpa, said of Garvin Isaacs:[391]

> Garvin, though inexperienced at the time, came out with an incredible result in a over-publicized trial. At the time I was envious, but that was before we met and became friends. I believe Garvin's Apache heritage drove him and continues to drive him in many cases. In my office, you will note almost all of the artwork was done by my wife, who is an incredible and imaginative woman. The major exception is a photograph that Garvin took at the Geronimo gravesite with both a black and white soldier in full gear preparing to go to war. We all remember Pat Williams's[392] description of the difference between an attorney and a lawyer. I would add that some of us are warriors. That's how I think of Garvin.[393]

Co-defense counsel, Gary Pitchlynn opened a law practice in Norman, Oklahoma. Pitchlynn devotes a substantial part of his law practice to providing legal counsel to Indian tribes.

Barry Cousins has retired from the practice of law. He lives today in Lawton, Oklahoma.

John Zelbst, the law student who helped the defense team, has practiced law in Lawton for many years, He holds the Oklahoma record for largest civil jury verdict in state court, $24 million, and the largest verdict in an Oklahoma federal court verdict, $7 million. He has also obtained not guilty verdicts in over twenty murder cases. In 2009, he obtained a not guilty verdict in a highly publicized case in Mississippi. A Mississippi state trooper had been accused of fondling a young boy.[394]

S.M. "Buddy" Fallis, Jr., remained Tulsa County district attorney until 1981. He then joined a civil law firm. He remained a vigorous advocate for crime victims.

In 1994, Fallis was inducted into the prestigious American College of Trial Lawyers. The organization includes trial lawyers from the United States and Canada and accepts only the top 1 percent of lawyers from Oklahoma.[395]

Ron Shaffer, prosecutorial co-counsel with Fallis, served a total of twelve years as chief prosecutor for Tulsa County. In May of 1981, he was appointed special judge. In 1982, he won election as a district judge. He served Tulsa County as judge until 2006 when he retired.[396]

Former Mayes County District Attorney Sid Wise was widely criticized both before and after the trial. Critics said he had tried to use the publicity to obtain higher office. He came in last in the Democratic primary race for Attorney General. He tried to come up with a plan to get a book published about the case. No book was written by Wise. Wise eventually settled in Mesa, Arizona where he served for ten years as a Municipal Judge. [397]

Sheriff Pete Weaver lost his bid for re-election in 1980. He lost a run-off election to Paul Smith. Smith had challenged Weaver in 1976 but had lost the election. Weaver died in 1991 at the age of 71.[398]

The sheriff who replaced Weaver, Paul Smith, added to the mystery of who committed the murders of Lori, Denise, and Michele. In May 1984, Smith announced he had three suspects in the case. Smith would not reveal their names, saying they were Locust Grove natives. He then made a plea for a key witness to come forward.

According to Smith, the unnamed witness had fled Mayes County because of death threats.[399] Smith, a former

Locust Grove policeman, said he had seen the three suspects in a car near Camp Scott the day of the slayings.[400]

Smith claimed to possess the murder weapon—a roofing hammer. He had divers search Lake Fort Gibson for the car he believed the suspects drove the night of the murders. The diver came up empty-handed. The hammer was inconsistent with the injuries of the victims.[401] Smith refused to tell who the suspects were in the case.[402]

Smith turned his information over to the OSBI. The OSBI officials termed the evidence insubstantial. A 250-page report was supposedly prepared but never released to the public. It was reported that a woman who had originally implicated Paul Smith's three suspects had lied.

Smith lost his bid for reelection. He was defeated by H.W. "Chief" Jordan. Two days after the civil case verdict, Jordan announced he was following a new lead in the case.[403]

On July 16, 1984, the headline of the *Daily Oklahoman* read, "Answers About Scout Murders Die with Stabbed Inmate." William A. Stevens, the Kansas prison inmate who defense counsel argued was the actual perpetrator of the Camp Scott murders, was found stabbed to death in his prison cell. The lead paragraph of the article asked the question of whether Stevens "really had something to do" with the murders "[o]r was the former Okmulgee man was a victim himself of a bizarre scheme designed to win freedom for his co-defendant and cellmate?" The answer to the question was, "The answers died with Stevens."

Cathy Bennett, who aided the defense in picking a jury, died June 9, 1992, of breast cancer at the age of forty-one.[404] At the time of her untimely death, she was the leading jury consultant in America. She was the only non-lawyer to receive the "Lifetime Achievement Award" presented by the National Association of Criminal Defense Lawyers.[405] Bennett had a long-history of assisting in high-profile cases.[406]

Jimmie Don Bunch, the witness at the preliminary hearing who switched his story, was incarcerated at the Lawton Correctional Facility in Lawton, Oklahoma, inmate number 88449, when he sent an affidavit to Tulsa attorney David Riggs in 2007. Bunch told Riggs he could use the affidavit as he saw fit.[407] Riggs saw fit to give the affidavit to the author.

The information contained in Bunch's affidavit "concerns my association with Gene LeRoy [sic] Hart during the past thirty-five years, and any knowledge I have about his involvement in the murder and the rape of the [three] girlscouts [sic] in Mayes County[,] Oklahoma."[408] Bunch claimed to be "a friend and associate of Gene Hart since approximately 1968." He met Hart at the Arena Club in Tulsa, Oklahoma and they became "drinking buddies during the following year."[409]

Bunch described Hart as having a "hidden personality that very few people were aware." According to Bunch, Hart was able to "manipulate people with his qualities such as his clean[-]cut, [A]11-American look, his polite manners and his high IQ." He described Hart as being "very intelligent" with a "good educational background."[410]

Bunch said, "People did not realize that Gene Hart could be very antisocial when he was drinking alcohol or using drugs." Hart, according to Bunch, could become "very aggressive with people around him—especially women."[411]

In the affidavit, Bunch told of incriminating statements Hart made to him.[412] Bunch swore to the following:

> It was at that point that [I] asked Hart point blank
> if he had anything to do with the death of them

three girlscouts? [sic] When I asked Hart that question he was standing in front of my cell talking to me. Hart replied, and I quote…"Jimmie, please try to understand that I had been drinking wine and smoking weed for a week and hadn't slept in two days. I remember very little about what actually transpired that night; all I know is when I regained conscious I was in a cave not far from where the girlscouts [sic] were camped out. I had a terrible headache, and I can't recall what I actually did. I know I would never have hurt them little girls if I had been in my right mind and thinking clearly."[413]

Bunch said that when Hart made the preceding remarks, he reached a conclusion. "[I] realized that I was talking to the man who actually raped and murdered them three little girls."[414]

Bunch was trying to use the affidavit to stir up interest in a long-over case. He wanted out of prison. His affidavit was of no interest to anyone.

Bunch's veracity as a witness for the State of Oklahoma was lost when he switched his testimony at the preliminary hearing. A less scrupulous prosecutor probably would have called Bunch as a witness at the trial. Bunch could have testified about what he says Hart told him. That would have provided the link the jury said they needed. Of course, Bunch would have been subject to intense cross-examination. It would have been up to the jury to decide if he was telling the truth. If Bunch had been smarter, he would have told the prosecutors about the supposed incriminating statements made by Hart. If he had not tried to trick Isaacs, his testimony would have been more credible. He could have testified for the State, and his testimony would have placed Hart in the confines of Camp Scott. Perhaps the jury

Gloyd McCoy

would have convicted Hart if they had evidence, even from a convict, that placed Hart at Camp Scott. This testimony might even have enhanced the confusing forensic evidence presented by the State.

Richard Guse, the father of Michele Guse, helped form the Oklahoma Chapter of Parents with Murdered Children. He was also the first chairman of the Oklahoma Victim's Compensation Board. That board was established to provide compensation to the victims and families of victims of crimes.

In 1985, Guse was given the Fred Lazarus, Jr., Award by the National Retail Merchants Association. The award is given by that association to a member who, on his own time, has done important community service work.

Walter Milner, the father of Denise, died at the age of fifty-three. Milner was a veteran of thirty-one years with the Tulsa Police Department. He died of a heart attack. He is buried next to his daughter.

His wife said he never learned how to deal with Denise's death. She told how his hair had quickly turned gray after her murder.[415] During his tenure as a police officer, Milner worked primarily as a patrolman. He was awarded the medal of valor by the Oklahoma Association of Chiefs of Police for his action in a gunfight following a bank robbery. Bettye Milner, Denise's mother, on the thirtieth anniversary of the murders, told a reporter she has never been able to bring herself to visit her daughter's grave. "I can't take it," she said. "I've been to the cemetery and tried to psyche myself up to see it, but I cannot face going to the grave."[416]

Sadness is the word that sums up the events described here. Let us hope that nothing like this ever happens again.

bibliography

Case Law

Batson v. Kentucky, 475 U.S. 79 (1986).

Furman v. Georgia, 408 U.S. 238 (1972).

Gibson v. State, 1972 OK CR 249, 561 P.2d

Hart v. State, 1971 OK CR 471, 490 P.2d 140.

Romero v. Lynaugh, 884 F.2d 871 (5th Cir. 1989).

State v. Poole, 489 N.W.2d 537 (Minn. App. 1992).

Williamson v. Reynolds, 904 F.Supp. 1520 (E.D. Okla. 1995).

Internet

"Infamous Girl Scout Murders May Go Unsolved Forever." www.kjrh.com

"Late Lawyer D. C. Thomas 'Absolutely Lived His Work.'" www.newsok.com, April 3, 2009.

"Timeline of Marcia Trimble's Case." www.msmv.com

Wood, E. Thomas, "Nashville Now and Then." www.nashvillepost.com

Wood. E. Thomas, "Trimble Murder Trial: Mother Describes Her Ordeal." www.nashvillecitypaper.com (July 15, 2009)

Law Review Articles

Armour, Marilyn Peterson & Mark Umbrecht, "The Ultimate Penal Sanction and 'Closure' for Survivors of Homicide Victims." 91 *Marq. L. Rev.* 381 (2007)

Burstein, Brian, "Religious Appeals in Closing Arguments: Impermissible Impact or Benign Banter." 29 *L. & Psych. Rev.* 29 (2005).

Findley, Keith and Michael S. Scott, "The Multiple Dimensions of Tunnel Vision in Criminal Cases." 2006 *Wisc. L. Rev.* 291 (2006).

Jones, Stephen, "A Lawyer's Ethical Duty To Represent The Unpopular Client." 1 *Chapman L. Rev.* 105 (1998).

Jones, Stephen and Jennifer Gideon, "U.S. v. McVeigh: Defending The Most Hated Man in America." 51 *Okla. L. Rev.* 617 (1998).

Koehler, Jonathan, "The Individualization Fallacy of Forensic Evidence." 61 *Vand. L. Rev.* 199 (2008).

Miller, Monica and Brian Burstein, " Religious Appeals in Closing Argument or Benign Banter." 29 *Law & Psych. Rev.* 29 (2005)

Nelson, Robert B., "The Curious Case of Terry Lynn Nichols: Are Television Cameras Really Banned From Oklahoma Court Proceedings." 3 *Vand. Ent. L. & Prac.* 4 (2000)

Note, "Thou Shalt Not Quote The Bible: Determining the Propriety of Attorney Religious Philosophy and Themes in Oral Argument, 33 *Ga. L. Rev.* 1113 (1999)

Note, "Guilty Until Presumed Innocent: Leonard Peltier and the Sublegal System." 34 *B.C.L. Rev.* 901 (1993).

Pitts, Wayne, David Giacopesi and K.B. Turner, 10 *Loy. J.P. Int. J.* 199 (2009)

Sellers, David, "The Circus Comes To Town: The Media and High Profile Trials." 71 *Law & Contemp. Probs,* 181

Smith, Clive Stafford and Patrick Goodman, "Forensic Hair Comparison Analysis: Nineteenth Century Science or Twentieth Century Snake Oil?" 27 *Colum. Hum. Rts. L. Rev.* 227 (1996).

Strickland, Rennard, "The Genocidal Promise Native American Law and Policy: Exorcising Aboriginal Ghosts." 1 *J. Gender Race & Just.* 325 (1998).

Symposium, "Is There A Higher Law? Does It Matter?" 36 *Pepp. L. Rev.* 463–665 ( )

Weaver, Russell, "The Perils of Being Poor:Indigent Defense and Effective Asssistance of Counsel." 42 *Brandeis L.J.* 435 (2003–04).

Newspaper Articles/Periodicals

"400 Attend Dinner To Help Raise Money." *Daily Times,* June 1, 1978.

"2 County Scouts at Camp Scott." *Claremore Daily Progress,* June 14, 1977.

"2 Win Runoffs Despite Problems With the Law." *Daily Oklahoman,* September 16, 1970.2

"4-H District Selects Chiefs; 4 Snare Trips." *The Oklahoman,* May 31, 1962 (Internet Archive).

"AIM Claims Family Harassed." *The Oklahoman,* August 16, 1977 (Internet Archive).

Allen, Robert B., "Judge Declares Mistrial in Perjury Case." *Daily Oklahoman,* May 2, 1980 (Internet Archive).

Allen, Robert B., "Hart Defense Fund Victim of Intense Split in Hometown." *The Oklahoman,* April 9, 1979 (Internet Archive).

Allen, Robert B., "Hart Declared Armed By Sheriff, Witness Said." *The Oklahoman,* March 27, 1979 (Internet Archive)

Allen, Robert B., "Completion of Hart Jury, Not in Sight." *The Oklahoman,* March 10, 1979 (Internet Archive)

Allen, Robert B., "Five Excused in Fourth Day of Jury Selection." *The Oklahoman,* March 8, 1979 (Internet Archive)

Allen, Robert B., "Judge Orders Hart Held For Death." *Daily Oklahoman,* July 7, 1978.

Allen, Robert B., "Writing Analyst Sees Hart Link." *Saturday Oklahoman & Times,* July 1, 1978.

Allen, Robert B., "Girls' Camp Strangers Reported." *Daily Oklahoman,* June 27, 1978.

Allen, Robert B., "Witness Abruptly Switches Story, Implicates Hart." *Saturday Oklahoman & Times,* June 17, 1978.

Allen, Robert B., "Hair on Girl's Body, Hart's Matched." *Daily Oklahoman,* June 14, 1978.

Allen, Robert B., "Death Scene Tied to Hart's Hideout." *Daily Oklahoman,* June 13, 1978.

Allen, Robert B., "Evidence Rarely Mentions Hart." *Sunday Oklahoman,* June 11, 1978.

Allen, Robert B., "Fingerprints Fail to Link Gene Hart." *Saturday Oklahoman & Times,* June 10, 1978.

Allen, Robert B., "Camp Trouble Signs Preceded Killings." *Daily Oklahoman,* June 9, 1978.

Allen, Robert B., "Counselor Tells of 3 Slain Girls." *Daily Oklahoma,* June 8, 1978.

Allen, Robert B., "Witness Admits Lie: Teen Cites Bounty Hope for Story." *Daily Oklahoman,* July 4, 1978.

Allen, Robert B., "Gene Leroy Hart Eludes Hunters." *Daily Oklahoman,* December 11, 1977.

Allen, Robert B., "$100,000 Drug Ring Suspended." *The Oklahoman,* December 8, 1977 (Internet Archive).

Allen, Robert B., "Dogs Hunt Clues in Scout Killing." *Oklahoma City Times,* June 16, 1977.

Allen, Robert B., "Suspect Held in Girl Scout Slayings." *Oklahoma City Times,* June 15, 1977.

Allen, Robert B., "Three Tulsa Girls Slain." *Tulsa Tribune,* June 13, 1977.

Allen, Robert B., "Officers Grope For Clues in Three Girls' Murders, *Oklahoma City Times,* June 14, 1977.

"Annual Graduation Scheduled At Locust Grove on Friday." *Pryor Jeffersonian,* May 16, 1963.

"Attorneys, Judge Reportedly Work Out Agreement on Contempt Citation." *Daily Oklahoman,* April 18, 1979.

"Baccalaurette Services Set Sunday For Locust [Grove] School Grads." *Pryor Jeffersonian,* May 9, 1963.

Barber, Brian, "20 Years Later, Slayings at Camp Still Shock, Horrify." *Tulsa World,* June 9, 1977.

Barron, Robert, "Multiple Murders Shocks Residents." *Woodward Daily Press,* September 4, 1974.

Baxter, Debby, "Tent Prison Idea Pushed." *The Oklahoman,* June 9, 1977.

Baxter, Ruth, "Father Recounts Missing Slain Daughter." *Tulsa Tribune,* March 22, 1985.

Baxter, Ruth, "Violence Rare at Camps, Scout Official Testifies." *Tulsa World,* March 25, 1985.

Baxter, Ruth, "Mother Testifies in Second Trial." *The Tulsa World,* March 19, 1985.

Baxter, Ruth, "Slain Scout's Mother Vows To Learn of Killing." *Daily Oklahoman,* June 9, 1978.

Baxter, Ruth, "First Televised Trial in State Glues Spectators to Chairs." *Daily Oklahoman,*

Berry, Janis, "Teen Quizzed in 4 Woodward Killings." *Daily Oklahoman,* September 17, 1974.

"Boren Aides Denies Parole Offered to Convicted Thief," *Daily Times,* July 9, 1978.

Bradshaw, Jim, "Gene Leroy Hart is Found Innocent in Sex Slayings of Three Girl Scouts." *Washington Post,* March 31, 19179.

Bradshaw, Jim, "Girl Scout Slaying Goes to Jury in Oklahoma Case." *Washington Post,* March 30, 1979.

"Camp Director Begins Testimony Tuesday." *Daily Times,* June 8, 1978.

Carter, Tom, "Gene Hart Collapses, Dies." *Tulsa World,* June 5, 1979.

Chavez, Jan, "Sheriff Better After Seizure." *The Oklahoman,* August 29, 1978 (Internet Archive).

"Clanton, Prosecutor Tell Isaac to Hurry." *Daily Times,* June 30, 1978.

"Continuance Granted For Hart Preliminary." *Daily Times,* May 3, 1978.

Curry, Bill, "Cherokee Goes on Trial in Slaying of Girl Scouts." *Washington Post,* March 20, 1979 (Lexus-Nexus)

"DA Required Monthly Gift, Ex-Aide Says in Campaign." Daily Oklahoman, August 24, 1974.

Decker, Cathlen and Sherry Stalberg, "Half of America Disagrees With Verdict." *Los Angeles Times,* October 4, 1995.

"Does Hart Fit Pattern of Child Killer." *The Paper,* July 24, 2002.

Early, E. N. and Ralph Marsh, "Fugitive Named in Girl Scout Murder." *Tulsa Tribune,* June 23, 1977.

Editorial, "Hart Hearing Far Too Long." *Daily Oklahoman,* July 8, 1978.

Erwin, Chuck, "Heart Disease Took Hart." *Tulsa World,* June 6, 1979.

Etter, Jim, "Sheriff Bans Future Hunts for Suspects." *Daily Oklahoman,* August 13, 1977 (Internet Archive).

"Ex-Camper Recalls Screams Near Death Sites." *Tulsa Tribune,* March 20, 1985.

"Family of Four Found Murdered." *Woodward Daily Press,* September 5, 1974.

"Football Star to Escapee, Running the Story of Hart's Life." *Sunday Oklahoman,* April 10, 1978 (Internet Archive).

"Former DA Inducted Into Lawyer Group." *Tulsa World.* December 13, 1994.

Fossett, Judy, "Ex-OSBI Agent Brothers Sell Book About Girl Scout Killing." *The Oklahoman,* August 20, 1980 (Internet Archive).

Fossett, Judy, "Lawyer Loses Count of Murder Acquittals." *The Oklahoman,* May 14, 1979 (Internet Archive).

Fossett, Judy, "Mistrial Pretty Close." *The Oklahoman,* March 20, 1979 (Internet Archive)

Fossett, Judy, "Hart Replaces 'Bogeyman' For Scared Little Girls." *Daily Oklahoman,* June 20, 1978.

Fossett, Judy, "Hart Lawyers Lose Bid for Protection." *Sunday Oklahoman,* June 18, 1978.

Fossett, Judy, "Teen Reports Threat to Hart Link." *Daily Oklahoman,* June 16, 1978.

Fossett, Judy, "Sisters Rip Boren Role," *Saturday Oklahoman & Times,* June 10, 1978.

Fossett, Judy, "Hart Legal Team Splits." *Daily Oklahoman, June 7, 1978.*

Fossett, Judy, "Gospel Sing Pulls Hart Supporters Together." *Saturday Oklahoman & Times,* June 5, 1978.

Fossett, Judy, "Money Raised For Hart Stolen." *Daily Oklahoman,* April 15, 1978.

Fossett, Judy, "Two Jailers Suspended." *The Oklahoman,* August 17, 1976 (Internet Archive).

"Funeral Services Set For Thrasher Family." *Woodward Daily Press,* September 6, 1974.

"Guardsmen Aid in Manhunt." *Oklahoma City Times,* June 21, 1977.

"Gene Hart to Face Escape Trial." *The Oklahoman,* May 5, 1979 (Internet Archive).

"Gene Hart Jury Motions Overruled." *Daily Times,* January 28, 1979.

"Gene Leroy Hart Dies After Heart Attack in Prison." *Washington Post,* June 5, 1979 (Lexus-Nexus).

"Giant Manhunt Launched for Suspect." *Oklahoma City Times,* June 24, 1977.

Gipson, Jim, "Gene Hart Found Innocent." *Tulsa Tribune,* March 30, 1979.

"Govenor Swapped Parole for Hart Information." *The Paper,* June 17, 2002.

Gorov, Lynda, "10 Million Estimated for McVeigh's Defense, Paid By Taxpayers." *Boston Globe,* June 1, 1997.

Gustafson, David, "Remembering Denise: Tulsa Girl Didn't Like Camp: Wanted to Go Home." *The Paper,* July 1, 2002.

Gustafson, David, "Thousands Attended Camp Scott Before…" *The Paper,* June 24, 2002.

Gustafson, David, "Hart Defense Attorney Knows The Truth." *The Paper,* June 24, 2002.

Gustafson, David, "Remembering Michele." *The Paper*, June 24, 2002.

Gustafson, David, "Remembering Lori: Tulsa Girl Was Youngest Girl at Camp Scott." *The Paper*, June 17, 2002.

Gustafson, David, "She Never Quit Believing." *The Paper*, June 17, 2002.

Gustafson, David, "Hart Jurors Say 'Things' Didn't Add Up.'" *The Paper*, June 10, 2002.

Gustafson, David, "A Crime That Shocked The Nation: Anniversary of Camp Scott Murders This Week." *The Paper*, June 10, 2002,

Hale, Cindy, "Hart Not Guilty." *Daily News*, March 30, 1979.

Hale, Cindy, "Closing Statements Made: Jury Deliberating." *Daily Times*, March 29, 1979.

Hale, Cindy, "Defense Reopens With Surprise Witness." *Daily Times*, March 28, 1979.

Hale, Cindy, Hair Samples Could Be Damaging." *Daily Times*, March 22, 1979.

Hale, Cindy, "Autopsy Testimony Presented." *Daily Times*, March 21, 1979.

Hale, Cindy, "Hart Denied Self Defense." *Daily Times*, March 20, 1979.

Hale, Cindy, "Testimony in Hart Case to Begin on Monday." *Daily Times*, March 18, 1979.

Hale, Cindy, "Hart Jury Selected; Trial to Begin Monday." *Daily Times*, March 16, 1979.

Hale, Cindy, "State Expects to Start Hart Trial Monday." *Daily Times*, March 9, 1979.

Hale, Cindy, "Whistler Wants Jury By Friday." *Daily Times*, March 8 1979

Hampton, Joy, "She Shot Him Through His Cheatin' Heart…The Murder Case of Zoella Mae Dorland." *Claremore Daily Progress,* November 5, 2009 (Internet).

"Hart Assigned to General Inmate Section." *Claremore Daily Progress,* April 5, 1979.

"Hart Motions Resume Monday." *Daily Times,* January 28, 1979.

"Hart Preliminary Dragging Into Tenth Day." *Daily Times,* June 27, 1978.

"Hart Preliminary Hearing Underway Tuesday." *Daily Times,* June 7, 1978.

"Hart Defense Fund Swells." *The Oklahoman,* June 6, 1978 (Internet Archive).

"Hart Defense Denied Continuance." *Daily Times,* Jun 4, 1978.

"Hart Sisters Ask For Help." *Daily Times,* June 1, 1978.

"Hart Fair Trial Hurt?" *Daily Times,* April 23, 1978.

"Hart Fund Organized." *Daily Times,* April 12, 1978.

"Hart, Dry Back in Jail After 2-Weeks Absence." *Daily Times,* June 1, 1973.

"Hart, Dry, Third Man Break Jail Here Sunday." *Daily Times,* September 17, 1973.

"Hart's Sister Asks For Help." *Daily Times,* June 1, 1978.

"Harboring Charges Filed Against Pigeon and Smith in Tahlequah." *Daily News,* April 12, 1978.

Harper, David, "Mom Keeps Low Profiles on Girls' Anniversary." *Tulsa World,* June 13, 2007.

Hicks, Douglas, "1, 000 Mourners Pack Locust Grove Gym for Hart's Funeral." *Tulsa World,* June 9, 1979.

Hicks, Doug, "Prosecution Rests Case in Hart Trial." *Tulsa World,* March 25, 10779.

Hicks, Douglas, "Hart Jury Visit Desolate Slaying Site." *Tulsa World,* March 23, 1979.

Hicks, Douglas, "Hart Trial Scheduled to Start Today." *Tulsa World,* March 19, 1979.

Hobbs, Cathy, "'It's a Nightmare,' Twin Sister Says." *Daily Oklahoman.* September 5, 1974.

Hutchison, Mark A., "Bid To Reopen Probe of 1977 Girl Scout Slaying Stall," *The Oklahoman,* June 22, 1997.

"Inmates Tell About Dying Man's Pleas." *Daily Oklahoma,* June 12, 1976.

"Investigators Checking Burglary in Scout Tent." *Claremore Daily Progress,* June 16, 1977.

"Isaacs Mad Over Sketch." *Daily Times,* February 4, 1979.

"Isaacs Accuses Wise of Lying Under Oath." *Daily Times,* January 31, 1979.

Jackson, Jim, "Ouster Petition Aims at Mayes County Sheriff." *Daily Oklahoman,* April 9, 1970.

Jackson, Ken, "Wanna Start Something? Start Asking Why the Book Was Pulled?" *Tulsa World,* June 11, 1989.

Jackson, Ron, "Murder Case's Lore, Mystery Keep Growing." *The Oklahoman,* June 29, 2008.

Jackson, Ron, "DNA Tests Bring More Questions." *The Oklahoman,* June 25, 2008.

Jackson, Ron, "In 1977, Three Girl Scouts Went Into The Woods, Never to Return." *The Oklahoman,* June 10, 2007.

Jackson, Ron, "Memories of a Manhunt." *The Oklahoman,* June 29, 2008.

Jayro, Walt, "Things Just Kind of Went Downhill: From Star Athlete to Fugitive." *Daily Oklahoma,* July 10, 1977 (Internet Archive)

Johnson, James, "Burglary Began Week of Fear for Slaying Victims." *Daily Oklahoman,* September 6, 1974.

Johnson, James, "Killings Baffle Woodward Sheriff." *Daily Oklahoman,* September 5, 1974.

"Jurors Names To Remain Silent." *Daily Oklahoman,* February 4, 1979.

"Jury's Time Out Means Little Experts Say." *The Oklahoman,* December 23, 1997.

Kelley, Ed, "Inmate Claims Hart Death Made Him A Target for Revenge." *Daily Oklahoman,* December 15, 1980.

Lambert, Bruce, "Cindy E. Bennett, Who Pioneered Jury Selection Method, Dies at 41." New York Times, June 12, 1992 (Internet).

"Law Officers Threatened." *The Oklahoman,* July 6, 1978 (Internet Archive)

"Letter Arrived Monday." *Claremore Daily Progress,* June 6, 1979.

Manley, Dan, "Six Deaths The Worst in State History." *The Oklahoman,* July 18, 1978.

Martindale, Bob, *"Hart Called Himself Religious, Sympathetic to Girls' Families."* Tulsa World, March 21, 1979.

McCarthy, Tom, "Break Made in Woodward Slaying Case." *Daily Oklahoman,* September 15, 1974.

"Medicine Man Pleads Not Guilty in Harboring Charges." *Daily Times,* April 14, 1978.

Medley, Robert, "Prosecutor Remembers Former Cases." *The Oklahoman,* June 3, 2006, 2006 WLNR 276622.

"Minister's Strange Tale Renews Interest in Scouts' Murders." *Wichita Eagle,* August 26, 1990.

"Missing and Murdered Children." *Tulsa World,* June 15, 2008, 2008 WLNR 113072.

Morgan, Rhett, "Pieces of Pryor History Going On Sale." *Tulsa World*, January 27, 2006, 2008 WLNR 151317.

Margolick, David, "Simpson Tells Why He Didn't Testify; As Two Sides Rest Case." *New York Times*, September 25, 1995.

Ninnger, Victoria, "Law Officer, Lawmaker Don Mentzer Dies." *Tulsa World*, September 11, 1990.

"No DNA Clues." *Tulsa World*, June 26, 2008, 208 WLNR 1200,

"Not Offended By $1 Million Story." *Daily Times*, March 11, 1979.

"Official's Whereabouts Still Mystery." *Daily Oklahoma*, February 29, 1972 (Internet Archive).

Olson, Pam, "Shadow of Doubt." *Tulsa World*, June 9, 2002.

"Oklahoma Search Abandoned." *Washington Post*, June 29, 1977.

"Our Opinion: Innocent Until Proven Guilty." *Daily Times*, April 7, 1978.

Palmer, Griff, "Sheriff Checking 'Lead' in Girl Scout Slayings." *The Oklahoman*, March 29, 1985 (Internet Archive).

"Petite Jailer 'Safe for Inmates.'" *The Oklahoman*, September 19, 1979 (Internet Archive).

"Posse Hunts Suspects in Scout Murders." *Tulsa World*, June 24, 1977.

Powell, Judy, "Hart Attorney Says He's Sorry." *Daily Oklahoman*, April 24, 1979 (Internet Archive).

Pratt, Tim, "Trooper Found Not Guilty of Fondling Teen." *The Dispatch*, February 6, 1979.

Price, Marie, "Oklahoma American Indian Artist Uses His Craft to Catch Criminals." *Journal Record*, December 3, 2008 (Internet).

"Pugh Informant Asks for Protection." *The Oklahoman,* June 9, 1977 (Internet Archive)

Roloff, Scott, "Surprise Defense Testimony Slashes Hart." *Daily Times,* June 18, 1978.

Roloff, Scott, "Judge Overrules Dismissal of Hart Case." *Daily Times,* June 16, 1978.

Roloff, Scott, "Preliminary Finished: Hart May Go To Trial." *Daily Times,* June 14, 1978.

Roloff, Scott, "Hart Link to Murder Not Yet Established." *Daily Times,* June 13, 1978.

Roloff, Scott, "Hart Developed Pictures Found Near Camp." *Daily Times,* June 11, 1978.

Roloff, Scott, "Hart Pleads Not Guilty: Will Stay in County." *Daily Times,* April 12, 1978.

Roloff. Scott, "Relief, Hope Voiced." *Daily Times,* April 7, 1978.

Sasser, Charles, "He Couldn't Forget: Sheriff Weaver Was Haunted by Camp Scott Murders." *The Paper,* July 1, 2002.

Schoch, Phil, "Rape Motive Out in Deaths at Woodward." *Daily Oklahoman,* September 7, 1974.

Shanker, Thom, "Gene Leroy Hart Summarizes His Life." *Daily Oklahoman,* June 5, 1979 (Internet Archive)

"Sheriff Races Won't Be The Same." *The Daily Times,* October 13, 1991.

Soldan, David, "Fugitive Rapist Being Charged in Murders of 3 Girl Scouts." *Oklahoma City Times,* June 23, 1977.

"Stipe 'Surprised" By FBI Probe." *Daily Oklahoman,* June 1, 1978.

Stott, Kim, "Quality of Justice Better for Wealthy Than Poor, City Attorneys Agree." *The Oklahoman,* June 10, 1983 (Internet Archive).

Taylor, Jack, "Stipe's First Love, The Law, Practiced With Passion." *Daily Oklahoman,* June 12, 1978.

Taylor, Jack, "Gene Stipe—Just Who or What, Is He?" *Sunday Oklahoman,* June 11, 1978.

"The Hart Interview." *The Paper,* July 29, 2002.

"Teens Recall Seeing Strangers at Scout Camp." *Dallas Morning News,* March 21, 1985.

"This is That Pryor County Justice." *Daily Times,* June 14, 1978.

Thomas, Susan, "City Lost Its Innocence With Marcia Trimble's Murder." *The Tennessean,* February 25, 2001 (Internet)

"Three Girls Are Slain in An Oklahoma Girl Scout Camp." *New York Times,* June 14, 1977.

"Three Tulsa Girls Slain." *Tulsa Tribune,* June 13, 1977.

"Tragedy or Divine Justice." *Tulsa World,* June 6, 1979.

Trammel, Robby, "Sheriff Vows To Continue Girl Scout Murder Investigation." *The Oklahoman,* June 13, 1984 (Internet Archive).

"Trial to Boost Economy." *Daily Times,* March 4, 1979.

"Two Men Flee Jail on Sunday." *Daily Times,* May 21, 1973.

"Two Week Guess on Hart Trial." *Daily Times,* January 28, 1979.

"Veteran Prosecutor Ben Baker Dead at 79." *Tulsa World,* November 16, 1993.

West, Gary, "A Historical Leap: A Special Group of Players Changed TCU Basketball 40 Years Ago." *Fort Worth Star Telegram,* February 24, 2008.

Wheat, Michael, "Comment." *The Paper,* June 17, 2002.

Williams, Larry, "Judge Overrules Trial Delay Attempt." *Daily Times,* March 4, 1979.

Witt, Susan, "Hart Rejected in Bid to Be Own Lawyer."
    Tulsa Tribune, March 19, 1979.

Witt, Susan, "Hart Jury Completed." *Tulsa Tribune,* March
    16, 1979.

Witt, Susan, "Juror Blames 'Guilty' Feeling on Attorney."
    Tulsa Tribune, March 13, 1979.

Witt, Susan, "A Mixed Blessing, Storm Muffled Killer's
    Moves, But May Have Saved Girl's Life." *Tulsa Tribune,*
    June, 1977

On a warm summer day in 1977, the State of Oklahoma was shaken by the heinous and vulgar murder of three Girl Scouts in *Tent Number Eight* at Camp Scott near Locust Grove, Oklahoma. The investigation of their murders and the subsequent trial of the Native American man accused of those murders will forever be marked as one of the most historical in Oklahoma history.

Author Gloyd McCoy dissects the investigation of the Girl Scout murders as well as *The State of Oklahoma vs. Gene Leroy Hart* from the vantage point of the families, the law enforcement, the news reporters, the lawyers, the judges, and the jury. He provides background information on all the parties involved and explanations regarding why certain decisions were made, including the acquittal of the accused murderer, and what might have happened if the lawyers on both sides had made different decisions and modern technology were available.

Tent Number Eight will enlighten you on the court proceedings and cultural influences of 1977 and preserve this piece of history in your mind forever. Follow the overgrowth of history back to the site of the crime. Step into *Tent Number Eight* and witness the events of the murders and trial first hand.

Gloyd McCoy was a criminal defense lawyer for over twenty-five years. He has represented many notable criminal defendants and has won the release of one man wrongfully convicted of murder. In 2006, he was awarded the Thurgood Marshall Award for outstanding appellate advocacy by the Oklahoma Criminal Defense Lawyers Association. He currently lives in Noble, Oklahoma, with his wife, Penny, and their three children. *Tent Number Eight* is his first book.

endnotes

1   Brian Barber, "20 Years Later, Slayings at Camp
     Scott Still Shock Horrify." *Tulsa World,* June 9, 1997
     (Internet).

2   Ruth Baxter, "Violence Rare at Camps, Scout Official
     Testifies." *Tulsa Tribune,* March 25, 1985, at B1.

3   Robert B. Allen, "Dogs Hunt Clues in Scout Killing."
     Oklahoma City Times, June 16, 1977, at 2.

4   *Claremore Daily Progress,* June 14, 1977, at 3 ("No
     arrest was made in the case and one Colorado deputy
     said he heard that the man believed responsible has
     since died")

5   Susan Thomas, "City Lost Its Innocence with Marcia
     Trimble's Murder." *The Tennessean,* February 25,
     2001 (Internet)

6   "Timeline of Marcia Trimble's Case." www.wsmv.
     com; E. Thomas Wood, "Trimble Murder Trial:
     Mother Describes Her Ordeal." www.nashvillecitypa-
     per.com, July 15, 2009; E. Thomas Wood, "Nashville
     Now and Then." www.nashvillepost.com,, December
     7, 2007.

7   Ron Jackson, "Murder Case's Lore, Mystery Keep Growing." *The Oklahoman,* June 29, 2008, at 2A.

8   "Infamous Girl Scout Murders May Go Unsolved Forever." www.kjrh.com.

9   David Gustafson, "Thousands Attended Camp Before..." *The Paper,* June 24, 2002, at 10.

10   "Hart's Fund Gets $12,500," *The Oklahoman,* October 16, 1978, at 33 (Internet Archive)

11   Ron Jackson, "Memories of a Manhunt," *The Oklahoman,* June 29, 2008, at 19A.

12   Robert B. Allen, "Officers Grope For Clues in Three Girls' Murders." *Oklahoma City Times,* June 14, 1977, at 2.

13   "Ex-Camper Recalls Screams Near Death Site," *Tulsa Tribune,* March 20, 1985, at E1.

14   David Gustafson, "Remembering Michele," *The Paper,* June 24, 2002, at 8.

15   David Gustafson, "Remembering Lori: Tulsa Girl Was Youngest Scout at Camp Scott." *The Paper,* June 17, 2002, at 8.

16   Ron Jackson, "In 1977, Three Girl Scouts Went Into The Woods, Never to Return." *The Oklahoman,* June 10, 2007, at. A6.

17   Pam Olson, "Shadow of Doubt." *Tulsa World,* June 9, 2002, at 1. *See also* Ruth Baxter, "Mother Testifies in Scout Trial." *Tulsa Tribune,* March 19, 1985, at C1.

18   Ruth Baxter, "Mother Testifies in Scout Trial." *Tulsa Tribune,* March 19, 1985, at C1.

19   David Gustafson, "Remembering Denise: Tulsa Girl Didn't Like Camp; Wanted To Go Home," *The Paper,* July 1, 2002, at 11.

20 Ruth Baxter, "Father Recounts Missing Slain Daughter." *Tulsa Tribune,* March 22, 1985, at F1.

21 Ron Jackson, "In 1977, Three Girl Scouts Went Into The Woods, Never To Return." *The Oklahoman,* June 10, 2007, at A1 ("The joy and laughter at Camp Scott ended 30 years ago. All that remains now are a few gutted buildings ravaged by time and heavily wooded trails haunted by the memory of three stolen souls").

22 "Oklahoma Girl Scout Murders." http://en.allexperts.com

23 *Id.*

24 Charles Sasser, "He Couldn't' Forget: Sheriff Weaver Was Haunted By Camp Scott Murders." *The Paper,* July 1, 2002, at 10.

25 Testimony of Trooper Harold Berry in trial of Gene Leroy Hart, quoted in Cindy Hale, "Hart Denied Self-Defense," *Daily Times,* March 20, 1979, at 1.

26 "2 Win Runoffs Despite Problems With the Law," *Daily Oklahoman,* September 16, 1970, at 43 (Weaver was defeated by Doyle W. 'Hokey' Freeman, a former United States Marshall. Weaver had 2566 votes and Freeman had 2809) The article shows that two Sheriffs won their elections despite legal trouble. Weaver was not so fortunate. For more details on Weaver's alleged law violation, *see* Jim Jackson, Ouster Petition Aims At Mayes County Sheriff." *Daily Oklahoman*, April 9, 1970, at 157. The article discloses a petition was filed with the Oklahoma Attorney General. The petition was signed by seven Mayes County residents and alleged Weaver was drunk in a public place on New Year's Eve. Some of the OSBI agents who investigated

Weaver's alleged misconduct also investigated the murder of the girl scouts.

27   "Inmates Tell About Dying Man's Pleas," *Daily Oklahoman,* June 12, 1976, at 53.

28   Judy Fossett, "Two Jailers Suspended," *The Oklahoman,* August 17, 1976, at 103 (Internet Archive)

29   "Petite Jailer 'Safe' for Inmates." *The Oklahoman,* September 19, 1979, at 3 (Internet Archive)

30   Bill Curry, "Cherokee Goes on Trial in Slaying of Girl Scouts," *Washington Post,* March 20, 1979 (Lexus-Nexus)

31   Jon Chavez, "Sheriff Better After Seizure." *The Oklahoman,* August 29, 1978, at 56 (Internet Archive)

32   Debby Baxter, "Tent Prison Idea Pushed." *The Oklahoman,* June 9, 1977, at 65 (Internet Archive)

33   Robert B. Allen, "$100,000 Drug Ring Smashed." *The Oklahoman,* December 8, 1977, at 85 (Internet Archive)

34   Cindy Hale, "Hart Denied Self Defense." *Daily Times,* May 20, 1979, at 1.

35   "Official's Whereabouts Still Mystery." *Daily Oklahoman,* February 29, 1972, at 29 ("The where-abouts of former Assistant District Attorney Sid Wise, who suddenly resigned last week, remained a mystery Monday. District Attorney Robert J. Vinzant, Claremore, was in Pryor Monday but said he had not seen or heard from Wise."). The article stated all Vinzant knew about Wise resigning was "what he had read in the papers."

36   "DA Required Monthly Gift, Ex-Aide Says in Campaign," *Daily Oklahoman*, August 24, 1974, at 57.

37   Bill Curry, "Cherokee Goes on Trial in Slayings of Girl Scouts." *Washington Post*, March 20, 1979 (Lexus-Nexus).

38   "Investigators Checking Burglary in Scout Tent." *Claremore Daily Progress,* June 16, 1977 at 3; The Claremore Daily Progress, June 17, 1977, at 1 (describing Wise as a "pistol packing district attorney").

39   Email from Pam Henry, February 12, 2011.

40   *Id.*

41   For the story of Vera Evans, an x-ray technician at the Claremore Indian Hospital, and her trip to Camp Scott to find out if her daughter, Connie Sue, was alive and her description of the "hysterical" parents who waited at the gate, *see* "2 County Scouts at Camp Scott." *Claremore Daily Progress*, June 14, 1977, at 1.

42   Michael Wheat, "Comment," *The Paper,* June 17, 2002, at 8.

43   James Johnson, "'Killings Baffle Woodward Sheriff." Daily Oklahoman, September, 5, 1974, at 1. ("Woodward County Sheriff A. C. Gaston confessed Wednesday that he is apparently up against a stone wall in his probe of the death of the Thresha family. 'All I have as evidence is a handful of spent cartridges and four bodies,' the sheriff said at the end of a long day of investigation. The quadruple slaying has badly shaken the community the sheriff said"). *See also* Cathy Hobbs, "'It's A Nightmare,' Twin Sister Says." *Daily Oklahoman,* September 5, 1974, at. 1.

44   "Family of Four Found Murdered," *Woodward Daily Press,* Sept. 4, 1974, at 1

45   *See* Tom McCarthy, "Break Made in Woodward Slaying Case." *Daily Oklahoman,* September, 15, 1974, at 1 ("A 19-year-old Woodward laborer was arrested Saturday night and charged with burglary of the Melvin Thrasher home, the first major break in the macabre Sept. 3 slaying of Thrasher, his wife and children"); Janis Berry, "Teen Quizzed in 4 Woodward Killings." *Daily Oklahoman,* September 17, 1974, at 12.

46   James Johnson, "Burglary Began Week of Fear for Slaying Victims." *Daily Oklahoman,* September 6, 1974, at 1.

47   *Furman v. Georgia,* 408 U.S.238 (1972).

48   *See* Stephen Jones and Jennifer Gideon, "U.S. v. McVeigh: Defending The Most Hated Man in America." 51 *Okla. L. Rev.* 617 (1998); Stephen Jones, "A Lawyer's Ethical Duty to Represent The Unpopular Client." 1 *Chapman L. Rev.* 105 (1998).

49   Dan Manley, "Six Deaths The Worst in Statehood," *The Oklahoman,* July 18, 1978, at 60. ("In the infamous history of multiple killings in Oklahoma, the execution Sunday night of six employees of the southwest Oklahoma City steakhouse is the worst single event recorded since statehood").

50   Newspapers across Oklahoma covered the story. At the time, Oklahoma City had a morning and evening paper, The *Daily Oklahoman* and The *Oklahoma City Times.* The two newspapers published by the same company, The Oklahoma Publishing Company, were later merged into one morning paper, *The*

Oklahoman. Tulsa also had two papers, the *Tulsa World* and *Tulsa Tribune.* The *Tribune,* an evening paper, is no longer published. Pryor, Oklahoma, the county seat of Mayes County had a daily newspaper, still published today, called The *Daily News.* Another newspaper from Pryor is *The Paper.* All these newspapers are cited extensively herein.

51   "Three Girls Are Slain in An Oklahoma Girl Scout Camp." *The New York Times,* June 14, 1977, at 20.

52   David Gustafson, "A Crime That Shocked The Nation: Anniversary of Camp Scout Murders This Week." *The Paper,* June 10, 2002, at 7 ("For more than a month in the summer of 1977, CBS news anchor Walter Cronkite read the names of three little girls every night on the evening news while law enforcement officers combined the hills of Mayes County for the killer").

53   Paul Wenske, "Dogs Sniff for Killing Clues." *The Oklahoman,* August 6, 1977, at 1 (Internet Archive)

54   *Daily Oklahoman,* July 14, 1977, at 1. *See* Brian Barber, "20 Years Later, Slayings At Camp Still Shock, Horrify." *Tulsa World,* June 9, 1997, at A1 ("It was on a stormy night 20 years ago in the dense woods of Camp Scott near Locust Grove that a monster crept into the tent of the three sleeping Girl Scouts, brutally raped and murdered them and vanished into the darkness").

55   Robert B. Allen, "Officers Grope For Clues in Three Girls' Murders." *Oklahoma City Times,* June 14, 1977, at 1.

56   Dr. Phillips' speech was analyzed in "Does Hart Fit Pattern of Child Killer.'" *The Paper*, July 24, 2002, at 8, an article printed twenty-five years later.

57

58   Robert B. Allen, "Officers Grope For Clues in Three Girls' Murders." *Oklahoma City Times*, June 14, 1977, at 1.

59   "Three Tulsa Girls Slain." *Tulsa Tribune*, June 13, 1977, at 1.

60   Robert B. Allen, "Suspect Held in Girl Scout Slayings." *Oklahoma City Times*, June 15, 1977, at 1.

61   *Id.*

62   Robert B. Allen, "Dogs Hunt Clues in Scout Killings." Oklahoma City Times, June 16, 1977, at 2.

63   "Guardsmen Aid in Manhunt." *Oklahoma City Times*, June 21, 1977 at 1.

64   *Id.*

65   The precise moment that Weaver mentioned Gene Leroy Hart as a suspect is not known. The second day of the investigation appears to be the consensus. The FBI reported Hart also used the aliases of "Gene Leroy Sullatesky" and "Ralph Yellowfeather." *See* "Hart Sketch is Released." *Daily Oklahoman*, January 31, 1978 at 30 (Internet Archive)

66   Robert B. Allen, The Oklahoman, January 1, 1978, at 24 (Internet Archive)

67   E. N. Early, Ralph Marsh, "Fugitive Named in Girl Scout Murder," *Tulsa Tribune*, June 23, 1977, p. 1; David Soldan, "Fugitive Rapist Being Charged in Murder of 3 Girl Scouts." *Oklahoma City Times*, June 23, 1977, at 1.

68 "She Never Quit Believing," *The Paper*, June 17, 2002, at 9.

69 Chuck Erwin, "Heart Disease Took Hart," *Tulsa World*, June 6, 1979, at 1.

70 *See* Walt Jayro, "'Things Just Kind of Went Downhill'; From Star Athlete to Fugitive." *Daily Oklahoman*, July 10, 1977, at 204 (Internet Archive)

71 Walt Jayro, *Id.*

72 In 1962, in a game against Westville, won by the Pirates 22–14, Hart scored a two-point conversion. *The Oklahoman,*, October 27, 1962, at 35 (Internet Archive) This was the only coverage of Hart's football career that could be found in *The Oklahoman*.

73 *The Oklahoman*, August 26, 2007, at 27S.

74 *See generally* Note, *Guilty Until Proven Innocent: Leonard Peltier and The Sublegal System*, 34 b.c. L Rev. 901 (1993). *See also* Rennard Strickland, *The Genocidal Premise in Native American Law and Policy: Exorcising Aboriginal Ghosts*, 1 J. Gender, Race & Just. 325, 325–326 (1998)("American Indian Leonard Peltier was imprisoned on federal murder charges. You know it must be bad when George Bush is so offended by the FBI's conduct in the case that he urges Peltier's release. There seems to be general agreement about the facts of the case. Anyone who carefully examines the evidence in this case would believe that Peltier is a political prisoner, or at least, he was imprisoned as a result of perjury")

75 Rennard Strickland, *The Genocidal Premise in Native American Law and Policy: Exorcising Aboriginal Ghosts*, 1 J. Gender, Race & Justice 325, 325 (1998) (footnotes omitted).

76 *See* "Baccalaurette Services Set Sunday for Locust [Grove] High School Grads." *Pryor Jeffersonian*, May 9, 1963, at 8; "Annual Graduation Scheduled At Locust Grove on Friday." *Pryor Jeffersonian*, May 16, 1963, at p. 12. A photograph of the class is on page 12 of the *Pryor Jeffersonian* article on the graduation. The class photograph lists Hart as "Gene Hart."

77 Robert B. Allen, "Hart's Attorneys Try to Lift 1966 Penalty." *The Oklahoman*, July 8, 1978, at 49 (Internet Archive)

78 Judy Fessell, "Gospel Sing Pulls Hart Supporters Together." *Saturday Oklahoman & Times*, June 5, 1978, at 1.

79 Affidavit of Jimmie Don Bunch, May 2, 2007, at 2–3.

80 Bob Martindale, "Hart Calls Himself Religious, Sympathetic to Girls' Families." *Tulsa World*, March 21, 1979, at 1.

81 "Two Men Flee Jail on Sunday," *Daily Times*, May 21, 1973, at 1 ("Two men being held in the Mayes County [Jail] escaped Sunday after sawing through the bars of the cells to gain freedom").

82 "Hart, Dry Back in Jail After 2-Weeks Absence." *Daily Times*, June 1, 1973, at 1.

83 "Hart, Dry, Third Man Break Jail Here Sunday." *Daily Times*, September 17, 1973 at 1 ("Gene Hart and Larry Dry, who may have been in and out of the Mayes County Jail more than any other prisoner, especially during the post few months, escaped from the jail a second time sometime early Sunday morning. This time the notorious pair took along a third man, Adam Rice").

84   *Id.* ("None of the three men had been allowed visitors since the day they were jailed. How the men apparently obtained a hacksaw blade…has not been determined")

85   Charles Sasser, "He Couldn't Forget: Sheriff Weaver Was Haunted By Camp Scott Murders, *The Paper*, July 1, 2002, at 10. (reprint from Tulsa World, November 1985).

86   Email from Dick Rouse, September 17, 2009.

87   *See* Judy Fessell, "Gospel Sing Pulls Hart Backers Together." *Saturday Oklahoman & Times,* June 5, 1978, at. 1 ("[Hart backers] are equally convinced that Hart, a fugitive at the time, was an easy mark for law enforcement officials to blame").

88   Judy Fessell, *Id.* at 2.

89   Bill Curry, "Cherokee Goes On Trial in Slayings of Three Girl Scouts, *Washington Post,* March 20, 1979 (Lexus Nexus)

90   Bill Curry, *id.*

91   "Governor Swapped Parole for Hart Info," *The Paper,* June 17, 2002, at 7.

92   Ron Jackson, "Memories of A Manhunt," *The Oklahoman,* June 29, 2008, at 19A; "Giant Manhunt Launched for Suspect," *Oklahoma City Times,* June 24, 1977, at 1.

93   Ron Jackson, *The Oklahoman*, June 10, 2007 at 7A ("One of the largest manhunts in state history follows involving more than 400 law enforcement agents"). James "Jake" Wilson, currently a lawyer in Lawton, Oklahoma, was at the time working for the Alfalfa County Sheriff, Willson said, he was "chomping at the bit" to get sent to the area to help in the search.

Email from James "Jake" Willson, August 21, 2009. Many Oklahomans wanted to do what they could to help.

94   Bill Curry, "Cherokee Goes on Trial in Slayings of Three Girl Scouts." *Washington Post,* March 20, 1979 (Lexus-Nexus)

95   David Smith, a Norman, Oklahoma lawyer, said, "I remember the news coverage. In particular when Hart was on the run, interviews with locals in that area. Uniformly they said things like 'we don't need no jury or trial. We just need to run him down and hang him.' Then when he was acquitted, it was a different story. 'I knew all along he didn't do it'" Email from David Smith, August 20, 2009.

96   *See* "Posse Hunts Suspect in Scout Murders." *Tulsa Tribune,* June 24, 1977, at 1.

97   Interestingly, these same tracking dogs from Pennsylvania had, two years earlier, been taken to Nashville to assist in the Trimble case. In neither case did the dogs contribute much in the way of success.

98   A documentary, *Some Cry for the Children*, presented the theory that the two dogs had died as a result of a curse imposed upon them by a Cherokee Medicine Man. The film and the book of the same name discuss the "medicine" of the Indians and how it played a part in the failure to eventually convict Hart.

99   Judy Fossett, "Hart Replaces 'Bogeyman' For Scared Little Girls." *Daily Oklahoman,* June 20, 1978, at 1.

100 "Oklahoma Search Abandoned," *Washington Post,* June 29, 1977, at A3.

101   Jim Etter, "Sheriff Bans Future Hunts for Suspect."
       Daily Oklahoman, August 13, 1977, at 48 (Internet
       Archive)

102   Robert B. Allen, "Gene Leroy Hart Eludes Hunters."
       Daily Oklahoman, December 11, 1977, at 14.

103   Robert B. Allen, *id.* .

104   Robert B. Allen, *id.*

105   Robert B. Allen, *id.*

106   "AIM Claims Family Harassed," *The Oklahoman,*
       August 16, 1977, at 1 (Internet Archive)

107   Robert B. Allen, *id.*

108   Robert B. Allen, *id.*

109   *See* "Harboring Charges Filed Against Pigeon and
       Smith." *Daily Times,* April 12, 1978. at 1. William Lee
       Smith, of rural Vian, Oklahoma, who allegedly had
       introduced Hart to Pigeon, was also charged. Both
       men were released on $5000 bond. Pigeon's bond was
       secured by his nephew, Richard Holcolm. Pigeon was
       represented by attorney John Ghostbear of Tahlequah,
       Oklahoma. Smith was arraigned a day after Pigeon.
       He was flown in a plane from Arkansas where he was
       on-the-job for the Kansas City Southern Railroad.
       The use of the plane was provided by the Cherokee
       Nation through Chief Ross Swimmer. There were
       rumors that the Oklahoma Highway Patrol were wait-
       ing at the Arkansas border to arrest Smith. By flying,
       Smith was able to avoid being arrested and was able
       to be processed at his convenience. Smith was rep-
       resented by lawyer Jack Bliss. *See* "Pigeon 'Says' Not
       Guilty." *Daily Times,* April 13, 1978, at 1; "Medicine
       Man Pleads Not Guilty to Harboring Charges." *Daily
       Times,* April 14, 1978, at 1. *See* Rennard Strickland,

supra at 332. *See* Jo Layne Keble, "Dissertation: The Leadership of Ross O. Swimmer 1975–1985: A Case of A Modern Cherokee Chief (2008)(Quoting Ross O. Swimmer, "[I] asked our pilot to go to Ft. Smith and bring William [Smith] back, instead of having him arrested and put in shackles").

110 Rennard Strickland, "Law and Policy: The Genocidal Premise in Native American Law and Policy: Exorcising Aboriginal Ghosts." 1 *J. Gender Race Just.* 325, 332–33 (1998)(footnote omitted),.

111 Cindy Hale, "Defense Reopens With Surprise Witness." *Daily Times,* March 28, 1979, at 1.

112 Ron Jackson, "Memories of A Manhunt," *The Oklahoman,* June 29, 2008, at 20A. For further information on Harvey Pratt, *see* Marie Price, Oklahoma American Indian Artist Uses His Craft to Catch Criminals." *Journal Record,* December 3, 2008 (Internet). *See also* www.harveypratt.com.

113 Debby Baxter, "Walk Silent to Death Row," *The Oklahoman,* April 7, 1978, at 4 (Internet Archive)

114 Nick Hinton, "Chains, Media Draw Fire." *The Oklahoman,* April 8, 1978, at 7 (Internet Archive)

115 Judy Fossett, "Sisters Rip Boren Role." *Saturday Oklahoman & Times,* June 10, 1978, at 1; "Boren Aide Denies Parole Offered To Convicted Thief." *Daily Times,* June 9, 1978, at 1.

116 Jim Etter, *The Oklahoman,* August 3, 1979, at 104 (Internet Archive)

117 *Id.*

118 *Id.*

119 *Id.*

120 "Football Star to Escapee, Running the Story of Hart's Life." *The Sunday Oklahoman,* April 10, 1978, at 3 (Internet Archive)

121 "Hart Arraignment Set for Tuesday." *Daily Times,* April 7, 1978, at 1.

122 Scott Roloff, "Hart Pleads Not Guilty: Will Stay in County." *Daily Times,* April 12, 1978, at 1.

123 "Our Opinion, Innocent Until Proven Guilty," *Daily Times,* April 11, 1978, at 1.

124 Scott Roloff, "Relief, Hope Voiced," *Daily Times,* April 7, 1978, at 1.

125 Scott Roloff, *id.* at 2.

126 Russell Weaver, "The Perils of Being Poor: Indigent Defense and Effective Assistance of Counsel." 42 *Brandeis L.J.* . 435 (2003–04).

127 Kim Stott, "Quality of Justice Better for Wealthy Than Poor, City Attorneys Agree." *The Oklahoman,* June 12, 1983, at 27 (Internet Archive)

128 *Tulsa World,* March 21, 1979, at C8.

129 Judy Fossett, "Lawyer Loses Count of Murder Acquittals," *Daily Oklahoman,* May 14, 1979, at 9 ("Tony Jack Lyons isn't sure whether its 58, 61 or 62. 'But it's at least somewhere in the 50s, he says with some modesty'")

130 Charles T. Jones, "Still No Justice After 20 Years: Slain Girl Scout Parents Haunted By Murders." www.newsok.com, June 1998.

131 Charles T. Jones, *id.*

132 Judy Fossett, "Hart Legal Team Splits," *Daily Oklahoman,* June 7, 1978, at 2.

133 Affidavit of Jimmie Don Bunch, May 2, 2007, at 4.

134 David Gustufson, "Hart Defense Attorney Knows the Truth." *The Paper,* June 24, 2002, at 7 (The article mentions that Isaacs was thirty-three at the time he defended Hart. "But I had lots of miles on me," Isaacs was quoted as saying. "A lot of miles indeed")

135 Ironically, a former Chief of the Choctaw Nation was named "Isaac Garvin." The small-town of Garvin, Oklahoma in McCurtain County is named for this chief.

136 "Alternate List," *Daily Oklahoman*, March 24, 1963, at 112 (Internet Archive)

137 *The Oklahoman*, February 20, 1963, at 16 (Internet Archive)

138 "4-H District Select Chiefs; 4 Snare Trips," *The Oklahoman,* May 31, 1962, at 19.

139 Gary West, "A Historic Leap: A Special Group of Players Changed TCU Basketball 40 Years Ago." *Fort Worth Star Telegram,* February 24, 2008, at C1.

140 Hart granted an interview to reporters from The Cherokee Advocate, the newspaper of the Cherokee Nation. Present with Hart were Garvin Isaacs and Gary Pitchlynn. The interview was published in a series of articles in 2002 in *The Paper. See* "The Hart Interview." *The Paper,* July 29, 2002.

141 " For an article on Stipe's various exploits during this time period, *see* Jack Taylor, "Gene Stipe—Just Who or What, Is He?" *Sunday Oklahoman,* June 11, 1978, at 1; Jack Taylor, "Stipe's First Love, The Law, Practiced With Passion." *Daily Oklahoman,* June 12, 1978, at 1 ("With an easy-going, gregarious manner, a down-home county style and a courtroom skill unmatched by many peers in Oklahoma, state Sen.

Gene Stipe has built a lucrative law practice known for its big name clients, sizeable judgments and legal fees").

142   Judy Fossett, "Hart Lawyer Loses Bid for Protection." *Sunday Oklahoman,* June 18, 1978, at 1.

143   Robert B. Allen, "Indictments Set Fire to Tulsa Campaign." *The Oklahoman,* October 17, 1966, at 13 (Internet Archive)

144   "Pugh Informant Asks for Protection," *The Oklahoma*, June 9, 1977, at 78 (Internet Archive)

145   Joyce Peterson, "Tulsa D.A. Eyes Blasphemy Laws." *The Oklahoman*, October 24, 1979, at 57 (Internet Archive)

146   "Jail Criticism Boomerangs, Tulsa Prosecutor Discovers." *The Oklahoman,* December 18, 1980, at 4 (Internet Archives)

147   "Tulsa Man Guilty of Drug Charge." *The Oklahoman,* September 29, 1971, at 43(Internet Archive)

148   Bob Williams, "1,700-Year Term in Assault on Nun." *The Oklahoman,* May 17, 1980, at 1 (Internet Archive)

149   Julie Del Cuor, "The Enforcer: Former DA Knows What Faces Newcomer." Tulsa World, June 14, 1998 (Lexus-Nexus)

150   "Friends of Hall Opposing Fallis." *The Oklahoman,* December 22, 1969, at 54 (Internet Archive)

151   *See, e.g.,* "DA Requests No Clemency for Convict." *The Oklahoman,* March 24, 1969, at 39 (Internet Archive); "Boren Denies Parole For Embezzler Padgett." *The Oklahoman,* December 22, 1977, at 35 (Internet Archive)(Pardon and Parole Board recommended by 4–1 vote that prisoner receive parole.

Fallis protested. Governor declined to grant probation parole.)

152 Ron Grimsley, "Tulsan Joins Prosecution of Hart.," *The Oklahoman,* June 1, 1978, at 11 (Internet Archive)

153 Jim Etter, "Wise Leaves Hart Case Prosecution." *Daily Oklahoman,* November 23, 1978, at 55 (Internet Archive)

154 Dick Fricker, "Case in Tulsa Goes To Jury." *The Oklahoman,* September 28, 1971, at 19 (Internet Archive)

155 "Hart's Sister Asks for Help," *Daily Times,,* June 1, 1978, at1.

156 "400 Attend Dinner to Help Raise Money." *Daily Times,* June 4, 1978, at 1. Several years ago, an Oklahoma City attorney was contacted about representing a young man charged with participating in a drive-by shooting. He quoted the family a very large fee. They told the lawyer they could pay it. Days passed and the lawyer had not received his promised fee. He contacted the father of the youth about the fee which was over six figures. The father told him they were working on it and planned to have their first bake sale on Saturday. The youth ended up being represented by the public defender.

157 Judy Fossett, "Gospel Sing Pulls Hart Backers Together." *Saturday Oklahoman & Times,* 5, 1978, at 1. ("They knew Gene Hart when he was a little boy. They remember he was a football stand out. And some of them may have hidden him from authorities")

158 *Id.*

159 *Id.*

160   "Hart Defense Funds Swells," *The Oklahoman,* June 6, 1978, at 62 (Internet Archive)

161   Robert B. Allen, "$2-A-Plate Fry Boosts Hart's Defense Fund." *The Oklahoman,* July 2, 1978, at 22 (Internet Archive)

162   *Minutes of the Cherokee Council Meeting,* October 14, 1978, Book 1, p.82.

163   Lynda Gorov, "$10 Million Estimated for McVeigh's Defense, Paid By Taxpayers." *Boston Globe,* June 1, 1997, at A34.

164   Lynda Gorov, "Taxpayers Buy McVeigh A High Powered Defense," *Austin American-Statesman,* June 1, 1997, at A8.

165   Judy Fossett, "Money Raised for Hart Stolen." *Daily Oklahoman,* April 15, 1978 at 47 (Internet Archive)

166   Robert B. Allen, "Hart Defense Fund Victim of Intense Split in Hometown." *The Oklahoman,* April 9, 1979, at 295 (Internet Archive)

167   Robert B. Allen, Widow Aids Guests, Home Open to Hart Family, *Daily Oklahoman,* June 7, 1978 at 1.

168   "Hart Preliminary Dragging Into Tenth Day." *Daily Times,* June 27, 1978, at 1.

169   Robert B. Allen, "Girls' Camp Strangers Reported." *Daily Oklahoman,* June 27, 1978 at 57 ("Defense lawyers for Gene Leroy Hart Monday sought to show that strangers were in the Camp Scott area less than 24-hours before three Girl Scouts were found slain outside their tent last June"). This article reported, "Former camp counselor Celia Elaine Stall, testified two Girl Scouts became frightened when two mysterious men came near their tent shortly before the June 1977 murders, and the husband of the camp director

told of coming face to face with a tall stranger near a creek on the day before the killings."

170 "Continuance Granted for Hart Preliminary." *Daily Times*, May 3, 1978, at 1.

171 "Hart Defense Denied Continuance." *Daily Times*, June 4, 1979, at 1.

172 Debby Baxter, "Slain Scout's Mother Vows To Learn of Killing," *Daily Oklahoma*, June 9, 1978, at 1.

173 Debby Baxter, "Slain Scout's Mother Vows to Learn of Killing." *Daily Oklahoman*, June 9, 1978, at 1–2.

174 Debby Baxter, "First Televised Trial in State Glues Spectators to Chairs." *Daily Oklahoman*, June 8, 1978, at 1. For an update on the status of court proceedings in Oklahoma, *see* Robert B. Nelson, "The Curious Case of Terry Lynn Nichols: Are Television Cameras Really Banned From Oklahoma Criminal Proceedings?" 3 *Vand. J. Ent. L. & Prac.* . 4 (2000) (The article mentions that three individuals charged with capital crimes had previously consented to have their case proceedings televised. The individuals were Roger Dale Stafford, Glen Burton Ake and Gene Leroy Hart)

175 Robert B. Allen, "Evidence Rarely Mentions Hart," *Sunday Oklahoman*, June 11, 1978, at 2.

176 "Camp Director Begins Testimony Tuesday." *Daily Times*,, June 8, 1978, at 1.

177 Robert B. Allen, "Counselor Talks of 3 Slain Girls." *Daily Oklahoman*, June 8, 1978, at 2.

178 *Id.*

179 Robert B. Allen, "Camp Trouble Signs Preceded Killings," *Daily Oklahoman*, June 9, 1978, at 1. The article disclosed that Mrs. Darrell Hoffman "in a

televised interview from her Owasso home, said her 16 year old daughter, found the note in April 1977 and gave it to the camp director, Mrs. Day. "It's my understanding," said Mrs. Hughes that the note was thought to be a prank by one of the girls and it was simply thrown away" *Id.* at 2.

180   Robert B. Allen, id. at 1.

181   Robert B. Allen, *id.* at 2.

182   Robert B. Allen, "Fingerprints Fail to Link Gene Hart," *Saturday Oklahoman & Times,* June 10, 1978, at 1.

183   *See* Robert B. Allen, "Evidence Rarely Mentions Hart." *Sunday Oklahoman,* June 11, 1978, at 1. *See also* Scott Roloff, "Hart Link to Murder Not Yet Established." *Daily Times,* June 13, 1978, at. 1.

184   Robert B. Allen, "Counselor Tells of 3 Slain Girls." *Daily Oklahoman,* June 8, 1998, at 2.

185   Robert B. Allen, "Evidence Rarely Mentions Hart." *Sunday Oklahoman,* June 11, 1978, at 2.

186   Robert Allen, "Death Scene Tied To Hart's Hideout." *Daily Oklahoman,* June 13, 1978, at1; Scott Roloff, "Hart Developed Pictures Found Near Camp." *Daily Times,* June 11, 1978, at 11.

187   Robert B. Allen, "Hair on Girl's Body, Hart's Matched." *Daily Oklahoman,* June 14, 1978, a 1.

188   Robert B. Allen, "Hair on Girl's Body, Hart's Match." *Daily Oklahoman,* June 14, 1978, at 1.

189   "This is That Pryor County Justice." *Daily Times,* June 14, 1978, at 1.

190   Scott Roloff, "Judge Overrules Dismissal of Hart Case." *Daily Times,* June 16, 1978, at 1; Scott Roloff,

" Preliminary Finished: Hart May Go To Trial." *Daily Times,* June 14, 1978, at 1.

191 Judy Fossett, "Teen Reports Threat in Hart Link Try." *Daily Oklahoman,* June 16, 1978, at 1.

192 Clanton, "Prosecutor Tell Isaacs to Hurry," *Daily Times,* June 30, 1978, at 1.

193 Robert B. Allen, "Witness Admits Hart Visit Lie: Teen Cites Bounty Hope for Story." *Daily Oklahoman,* July 4, 1978, at 1.

194 Robert B. Allen, *Id.*

195 Scott Roloff, "Surprise Defense Testimony Slashes Hart." *Daily Times,* June 18, 1978, p. 1. *See also* Robert B. Allen, "Witness Abruptly Switches Story Implicates Hart." *Saturday Oklahoman & Times,,* June 17, 1978, at 1.

196 Robert B. Allen, "Hart Legal Team Mapping Strategy," *The Oklahoman,* June 18, 1978, at 234 (Internet Archive)

197 "Hart Trial Dramatics Intensify," *The Oklahoman,* June 17, 1978, at 25 (Internet Archive)

198 Robert B. Allen, "Judge Orders Hart Held for Death Trial." *Daily Oklahoman,* July 7, 1978, at 1.

199 Robert B. Allen, *Id.*

200 Robert B. Allen, "Writing Analyst Sees Hart Link," *Saturday Oklahoman & Times,* July 1, 1978, at 2. Sheriff Weaver did not disclose what were the "certain activities" that prompted a change in security. The article also reported, "For the first time since the preliminary hearing began early this month Hart elected not to leave the courthouse at noon for lunch and requested his meal be sent in." Hart's mother made him a home-cooked meal for lunch every day.

201   Editorial, "Hart Hearing Far Too Long," *Daily Oklahoman,* July 8, 1978, at 10.

202   Neither side requested a change of venue. It is doubt-ful that the State would have standing to request a change of venue. *See* Robert B. Allen, "Judge Orders Hart Held for Death Trial." *Daily Oklahoman,* July 7, 1978, at 2 ("Fallis, who is Tulsa County district attorney, said there were no provisions in which the state could seek to move the trial elsewhere in the state.") However, at least one court has approved a trial judge's changing venue on its own volition. *See State v. Poole,* 489 N. W. 2d 537 (Minn. App. 1992) (Change of venue on court's own volition over defen-dant's objection did not violate defendant's right to be tried by impartial jury of county or district wherein crime had been committed).

203   "Law Officers Threatened." *The Oklahoman,* July 6, 1978, at 73 (Internet Archive)

204   "Hart Motions Resume Monday." *Daily Times,* January 28, 1979, at 1; "Gene Hart Jury Motions Overruled." *Daily Times,* January 28, 1979, at 1.

205   "Hart Fair Trial Hurt?" *Daily Times,* April 23, 1978, at 1. ("The attorney for Gene Leroy Hart says Hart's chances for a fair trial is being threatened by pros-ecution reports that Hart might attempt to break out of [the] Mayes County Jail"). The motion was four pages long. The motion accused Sid Wise, Pete Weaver and the OSBI of "having released rumors" to the press for the alleged purpose of denying Hart a fair trial and the effective assistance of counsel. A review of the newspapers of the time does not reveal that any of the rumors were published. Ironically,

once the motion was filed, the rumors were reported to the public indirectly.

206 "Isaacs Mad Over Sketch," *Daily Times*, February 4, 1979, p. 1.

207 Larry Williams, "Judge Overrules Hart Trial Delay Attempt." *Daily Times*, March 4, 1979, at 1.

208 The presented facts of this case come from a well-written article in the Claremore Daily Progress. *See* Joy Hampton, "She Shot Him Through His Cheatin' Heart: The Murder Case of Zoella Mae Dorland," *Claremore Daily Progress,* November 5, 2009 (Internet).

209 Judy Fossett, "Mistrial 'Pretty Close." *The Oklahoman,* March 30, 1979, at 103 (Internet Archive)

210 Thom Shanker, "Gene Leroy Hart Summarizes His Life," *Daily Oklahoma,* June 5, 1979, at 10.

211 *Daily Oklahoma* March 5, 1979. *See also* "Trial to Boost Economy" *Daily Times*, March 4, 1979, at 1.

212 *See* "Trial to Boost Economy." *Daily Times*, March 4, 1979, at 1.

213 *See* "Not Offended By $1 Million Story," *Daily Times,* March 11, 1979, p. 1.

214 *Id.*

215 Debby Baxter, "Hart Hearing No Business Boom for Pryor." *The Oklahoman,* June 8, 1978, at 7 (Internet Archive)

216 Debby Baxter, "Hart Hearing No Business Boom for Pryor Entrepreneurs." *The Oklahoman,* June 8, 1978, at 9 (Internet Archive)

217 David A. Sellers, "The Circus Comes to Town: The Media and High Profile Trials." 71 *Law & Contemp. Probs.* 181 (2008). *See* David MacKenzie, "Gene

Leroy Hart's Life of Jail Cells Ends Peculiarly." *Tulsa World,* June 5, 1979, at B1.

218 *Daily Times,* March 2, 1979 at 1.

219 "Hart Prosecutors Aren't Disqualified," *Daily Oklahoman,* March 1, 1979.

220 Larry Williams, "Judge Overrules Hart Trial Delay Attempt." *Daily Times,* March 4, 1979, at 1.

221 Larry Williams, *id.* at 1.

222 Brian Barber, "Elusive Truth: Speculation Still Rampant 20 Years After Slayings" *Tulsa World,* June 9, 1999 (Lexus-Nexus)

223 Douglas Hicks, "Hart Trial Scheduled to Start Today." *Tulsa World,* March 19, 1979, 2A.

224 Robert B. Allen, "Completion of Hart Jury Not in Sight, Judge Says." *The Oklahoman,* March 10, 1979, at 25 (Archive Internet)

225 Douglas Hicks, "Hart Trial Scheduled to Start Today." *Tulsa World,* March 19, 1979.

226 "Two Weeks Quest on Hart Trial." *Daily Times,* January 28, 1979, at 1.

227 *Romero v. Lynaugh,* 884 F.2d 871, 878 (5th Cir. 1989).

228 *Daily Times.* March 6, 1979, at 1.

229 Cindy Hale, "Whistler Wants Jury By Friday." *Daily Times,* March 8, 1979, at 1.

230 Susan Witt, Juror Blames 'Guilty' Feeling on Attorney." *Tulsa Tribune,* March, 13, 1979, at 1.

231 Susan Witt, "Hart Jury Completed,," *Tulsa Tribune,* March 16, 1979, at 4A.

232 *Batson v. Kentucky,* 475 U. S. 79 (1986).

233 *Daily Oklahoman,* March 12, 1979.

234 Cindy Hale, "State Expects to Start Trial Monday." *Daily Times,* March 9, 1979, at 1.

235   Robert B. Allen, "Five Excused in Fourth Day of Hart Jury Selection." *The Oklahoman,* March 8, 1979, at 9 (Archive Internet)

236   In the trial of Timothy McVeigh, defense counsel Stephen Jones discussed the issue of time during his opening statement to the jury. He stated, "I don't apologize for the time. This is an important case. It's the only other opportunity I will have probably for several weeks, if not months, before we put on our case. I thank you for your attention."

237   Cindy Hale, "Testimony in Hart Trial to Start on Monday." *Daily Times,* March 18, 1979 at 1.

238   Cindy Hale, "Hart Jury Selected Trial to Begin Monday." *Daily Times,* March 16, 1979, at 2.

239   *See* Cindy Hale, "After Jury Selected : Trial to Begin Monday." *Daily Times,* March 16, 1979, at 1.

240   *See* "Juror Names To Remain Silent." *Daily Times,* February 4, 1979, at 1 ("District Judge William Whistler has asked the news media to not make public the names of prospective jurors in the Gene Leroy Hart murder trial. Whistler says in a January 29 letter to individual media that the publishing of these names would be a 'temptation' for anyone who might wish to contact prospective jurors").

241   Doug Hicks, "Hart Innocent, Case Won't Be Reopened." *Tulsa World,* March 31, 1979, p. A4. In his article, Doug Hicks listed the jurors by name, occupation and place of residence: George L. Kelly, foreman/plant manager, Pryor; Jack Mitchell, Jr., basketball coach, Adair; Sandra Gossett, housewife, Spavinaw; Mrs. Melvin Young, housewife, Adair; Lilly Ramsey, housewife, Pryor; Vanda Virgie Shipp,

Utility Foreman, Pryor, Lawrence Berry, Aircraft, Adair; Leota Maye Jackson, Inventory Clerk, Pryor; Wanda R. Hale, housewife, Pryor; Olce D. Shamblin, pipefitter, Pryor; Marvin Richard, electrician, Adair; John Littlefield, loader/operator, Adair.

242 David Gustafson, "Jurors Say 'Things Just Didn't Add Up.'" *The Paper,* June 10, 2002, at 8.

243 Cindy Hale, "Hart Denied Self Defense." *Daily Times,* March 20, 1979, at 1.

244 *Id.*

245 Cindy Hale, "Hart Denied Self Defense." *Daily Times,* March 20, 1979 at 1. *See also* Susan Witt, "Hart Rejected in Bid To Be Own Lawyer." *Tulsa Tribune,* March 19, 1979, at 1.

246 *See generally* Keith A. Findley & Michael S. Scott, "The Multiple Dimensions of Tunnel Vision in Criminal Cases, 2006 *Wis. L. Rev.* 291 (2006).

247 Cindy Hale, "Hart Denied Self Defense." *Daily Times,* March 29, 1997, at 2.

248 The substance of the defense opening statement is taken from a newspaper article written by Cindy Hale. *See* Cindy Hale, *Daily Times,* March, 1979, at 1.

249 Bill Curry, "Cherokee Goes on Trial in Slayings of Three Girl Scouts." *Washington Post,* March 20, 1979 (Lexus-Nexus).

250 *United States v. Timothy McVeigh,* Transcript of Opening Statement of Stephen Jones. The cited comment is from the following complete text: "I have waited two years for this moment to outline the evidence to you that the Government will produce, that I will produce, both by direct and cross-examination,

by exhibits, photographs, transcripts of telephone conversations, transcripts inside houses, videotapes, that will establish not a reasonable doubt but that my client is innocent of the crime that Mr. Hartzler has outlined to you"

251 Email from Richard "Dick" Rouse, 9/17/09. *See also* "Sheriff Weaver, Deputies Give Testimony." *Daily Times*, June 28, 1978, at 1. .

252 Cindy Hale, "Autopsy Testimony Presented." *Daily Times*, March 21, 1979, at 1.

253 Cindy Hale, *id.* at 1.

254 Doug Hicks, "Jury Learns of Photos Near Camp." *Tulsa World*, March 21, 1979, at C1.

255 *United States v. Hildago*, 229 F. Supp. 961, 966 (D. Ariz. 2002).

256 Cindy Hale, "Hair Samples Could Be Damaging." *Daily Times*, March 22, 1979, at 1. ("The State of Oklahoma introduced possibly damaging evidence against triple-murder defendant, Gene Leroy Hart, as the fourth day of testimony got underway")

257 *See generally* Bennett L. Gersham, "The Use and Misuse of Forensic Evidence—Misuse of Forensic Evidence By Prosecutors." 28 *Okla.City.U.L. Rev.* 17 (2003). McLeod expressed his factual findings in terms of statistical probability, *see* Jonathan Koehler, "The Psychology of Numbers in the Courtroom: How to Make DNA-Match Statistics Seem Impressive or Insufficient." 74 *S.Cal.L.Rev.* 1275, 1279–80 (2001) (Footnotes omitted)("A large body of research on statistical reasoning suggests that people have poor intuitions when it comes to reasoning with statistics in general and forensic statistics in particular").

See also Brian J. Foley, "Until We Fix the Labs and Fund Criminal Defense: Fighting Bad Science With Storytelling." 43 *Tulsa L. Rev.* . 397 (2007); Michael J. Saks, "Protecting Factfinders From Being Overly Misled, While Still Admitting Weakly Supported Forensic Science into Evidence." 43 *Tulsa L. Rev.* 609 (2007).

258 *Compare* Scott Roloff, "No Traces of Sperm Found on Bodies." *Daily Times,* June 9, 1978, at 1 with "Fallis Balks: New Lab Tests Reveal Sperm." *Daily Times,* June 29, 1978, at 1.

259 *See, e.g.,* Jonathan Koehler, "The Individualization Fallacy in Forensic Evidence." 61 *Vand. L. Rev.* 199 (2008).

260 Thom Shanker, "Gene Leroy Hart Summarizes His Life." *The Oklahoman,* June 5, 1979, at 10 (Internet Archive)

261 Doug Hicks, "Hart Jurors Visit Desolate Slaying Site." *Tulsa World,* March 23, 1979, at D1.

262 Doug Hicks, *id.*

263 Doug Hicks, "Prosecution Rests Case in Hart Trial." *Tulsa World,,* March 25, 1979, at A4.

264 For a summary of Ms. Buckskin's testimony, *see* Cindy Hale, "Mother Says Son 'Out of Her Sight,'" *Daily Times,* March 27, 1979, at 1.

265 Cindy Hale, "Defense Re-Opens With Surprise Witness." *Daily Times, ,* March 28, 1979, at 1.

266 Stevens was serving a fifteen to life sentence for kidnapping, robbery and rape of a Garden City, Kansas woman.

267 Robert B. Allen, "Judge Declares Mistrial in Perjury Case." *Daily Oklahoman,* May 2, 1980 (Internet Archive).

268 Robert B. Allen, "Hart Death Trial Testimony at End." *The Oklahoman,* March 29, 1979, at 23 (Internet Archive)

269 Robert B. Allen, *id.*

270 Jim Bradshaw, "Girl Scout Slaying Goes to Jury in Oklahoma." *Washington Post,* March 30, 1979, at A16.

271 Robert B. Allen, "Hart Declared Armed By Sheriff, Witness Said." *The Oklahoman,,* March 27, 1979, at 77 (Internet Archive)

272 Jim Bradshaw, *id.*

273 Robert B. Allen, "Hart Declared Armed By Sheriff, Witness Said." *The Oklahoman,* March 27, 1979, at 77 (Internet Archive)

274 Email from Mary Long to Gloyd L. McCoy, October 3, 2009.

275 For a discussion of why O. J. Simpson did not testify at his murder trial, *see* David Margolick, "Simpson Tells Why He Didn't Testify: As Two Sides Rest Case." *New York Times,* September 23, 1995, at A1.

276 Mark Curriden, "Joe Jamail: "If You Are Not Emotionally Involved, Your Client is Not Getting Your Best Effort." *ABA Journal,* March 2009 (Internet)

277 The comment "even though she can't be here today" was objectionable as an attempt to elicit sympathy for the victim. Here, no objection was made. In most trials, defense lawyers do not object to every part of the argument that might be technically improper.

278 Closing Argument Transcript, State of Oklahoma v. Gene Leroy Har, Mayes County District Court (1979).

279   Identification from hair is not accepted under the current status of the law. *See Williams v. Reynolds*, 904 F. Supp. 1529 (E.D. Okla. 1995) and Clive Stafford Smith & Patrick Goodman, "Forensic Hair Comparison Analysis: Nineteenth Century Science or Twentieth Century Snake Oil?" 27 *Colum. Hum. Rts.L. Rev.* 227 (1996).

280   Closing Argument Transcript, State of Oklahoma v. Gene Leroy Har, Mayes County District Court (1979).

281   The use of the term "smokescreen" was improper. *See Waters v. State,* 486 S0.2d 614, 616 (Fla. App. 1986) (Florida appellate court was critical of prosecutor's repeatedly characterizing defense counsel's argument as a "smokescreen.")

282   The biblical quote was an egregious example of an improper prosecutorial comment. The Oklahoma Court of Criminal Appeals has historically condemned such remarks. In *Gibson v. State,* 1972 OK CR 249, 561 P. 2d 891, 890, the court held: "[T]he extensive recitation of Mosaic law and quotation from the New Testament, were unnecessary and served only to appeal to the individual religious prejudices of the respective jurors. If this were a close case, this type of closing argument may well tip the balance, justifying a reversal." *See also* Monica Miller & Brian Burstein, "Religious Appeals in Closing Arguments: Impermissible Religious Appeals in Closing Arguments: Impermissible Impact or Benign Banter." 29 *Law & Psych. Rev.* 29 (2005); Note, "Thou Shalt Not Quote The Bible: Determining the Propriety of Attorney Religious Philosophy and Themes in Oral Argument." 33 *Ga.L. Rev.* 1113 (1999).

283 The most famous line in a closing argument in modern history is Johnny Cochran's statement in his closing argument in the O. J. Simpson case, "If the glove don't fit, you must acquit." David Margolick, "Simpson's Lawyer Tells The Jury That Evidence 'Doesn't Fit.'" *New York Times*, September 28, 1995, at A1.

284 Cindy Hale, "Closing Statements Made; Jury Deliberating." *Daily Oklahoman*, March 29, 1979, at p. 1.

285 Closing Argument Transcript, State of Oklahoma v. Gene Leroy Har, Mayes County District Court (1979).

286 This paragraph from the defense closing argument shows the strategy of playing off Mr. Fallis's anticipated bombastic oratory. Mr. Pitchlynn tells the jury to not be impressed by oratory but by EVIDENCE. When Mr. Fallis gives his later closing, he falls into the trap. Relying on emotion and criticism of Mr. Isaacs, he fails to give the jurors what they were looking for–legitimate and understandable evidence that Gene Leroy Hart was at Camp Scott. A review of the State's final closing shows that this major blunder occurred. The failure to link Hart to the camp with non-speculative or more than circumstantial evidence was the reason for the State's defeat. The prosecutors and the State of Oklahoma paid the price for their blunder in not stressing and, in fact, actually presenting non-circumstantial evidence. For similar analysis in other cases, *see* Greg Risling, "Blake Not Guilty of Wife's Murder, Prosecution 'Couldn't Put Gun in His Hand,' Foreman Says." Chicago Sun-Times, March 17, 2005, at 3 (detailing the shortcomings of

the presentation in Robert Blake's case); Scott Turow, "Prosecutors Pay For Their Behavior." *New York Times,* October 4, 1995, at A21.

287 Closing Argument Transcript, State of Oklahoma v. Gene Leroy Har, Mayes County District Court (1979).

288 This part of the defense closing argument is the beginning of the "Hart was railroaded" argument. *See* Mark Curriden, "Bobby Lee Cook: If You Can Railroad A Bad Man to Prison, You Can Railroad A God Man." *ABA Journal,* March 2009 (Internet)(Bobby Lee Cook is a great criminal defense lawyer, still trying cases at age 82. He is quoted in the cited article with a saying applicable to Mr. Pitchlynn's argument: "If you can railroad a bad man to prison, you can railroad a good man. That's why we should always vigorously fight for the constitutional rights of even those who are most despised in our community.").

289 Closing Argument Transcript, State of Oklahoma v. Gene Leroy Har, Mayes County District Court (1979).

290 Brian Barber, "Elusive Truth: Speculation Still Rampant 20 Years After Slayings." *Tulsa World,*, June 9, 1979 (Lexus-Nexus).

291 This was, of course, not the first time Garvin Isaacs had been critical of Sid Wise. *See, e.g.*"Isaacs Accuses Wise of Lying Under Oath." *Daily Times,* January 31, 1979, at 1.

292 Closing Argument Transcript, State of Oklahoma v. Gene Leroy Har, Mayes County District Court (1979).

293 Closing Argument Transcript, State of Oklahoma v. Gene Leroy Har, Mayes County District Court (1979).

294 Closing Argument Transcript, State of Oklahoma v. Gene Leroy Har, Mayes County District Court (1979).

295 Closing Argument Transcript, State of Oklahoma v. Gene Leroy Har, Mayes County District Court (1979).

296 Here, Mr. Fallis began a series of arguments complaining about what Mr. Isaacs had done. He should have been more concerned by the points raised by Mr. Isaac's with regard to the State's evidence.

297 This remark was objectionable. A lawyer cannot vouch for a witness.

298 These remarks, although not objected to, were highly prejudicial.

299 Defense counsel objected. ("That's a misstatement of the facts") The trial judge overruled the objection.

300 This objection was obviously made so that defense counsel could make his point about the evidence.

301 This was a proper ruling and proper admonition to the jury. The jury is instructed at the start of a trial and at the end of a trial that statements by counsel are not evidence.

302 Closing Argument Transcript, State of Oklahoma v. Gene Leroy Har, Mayes County District Court (1979).

303 There was an objection to these remarks. The objection was overruled.

304 These statements may not have had the intended effect. The prosecutor admits that Pete Weaver could have framed Hart. The jury was provided with an answer to the next question. Why would he do it? Defense counsel argued throughout that Weaver hated Hart because he had twice escaped from his custody.

305 Closing Argument Transcript, State of Oklahoma v. Gene Leroy Har, Mayes County District Court (1979).

306 Defense counsel objected. The objection was overruled.

307 Closing Argument Transcript, State of Oklahoma v. Gene Leroy Har, Mayes County District Court (1979).

308 Cindy Hale, "Closing Statements Made; Jury Deliberating." *Daily Times,* March 29, 1979, at p. 1.

309 "Jury's Time Out Means Little, Experts Say." *The Oklahoman*, December 23, 1997, at 37 (Internet Archive)

310 Telephone conversation with John Zelbst, July 2010

311 Cindy Hale, "Hart Not Guilty." *Daily Times*, March 30, 1979 at 1.

312 David MacKenzie, "Gene Leroy Hart's Life of Jail Cells Ends Peculiarly." *Tulsa World*, June 5, 1979, at B20 ("Hart's acquittal was like a thunderbolt. It boosted Isaac's standing, [and] put a dent in the armor of Fallis.")

313 Jim Bradshaw, "Gene Leroy Hart is Found Innocent in Sex Slayings of Three Girl Scouts." *Washington Post*, March 31, 1979, at A3.

314 Doug Hicks, "Hart Innocent; Case Won't Be Reopened." *Tulsa World*, March 31, 1979, at 1.

315 Doug Hicks, *id.* at A4.

316 D. C. Thomas was a high profile criminal defense lawyer from Oklahoma City. D.C. Thomas died in 2009. *See* "Late Lawyer D.C. Thomas 'Absolutely Lived His Work.'"Newsok.com, April 3, 2009 ("In remembering him, attorney [of Oklahoma City] Merle Gile said, 'He could talk. He didn't necessarily have to have a defense…In the '70s, he was it. He was 'the' criminal lawyer in Oklahoma."). Thomas

went by "D. C." because he did not like his full name Dolorin Carl Thomas.

317 *See* Judy Powell, "Hart Attorney Says He's Sorry." *Daily Oklahoman,* April 24, 1979, at 81 (Internet Archive)("Oklahoma City Attorney Garvin Isaacs was 'censured and reprimanded' for his conduct during the March murder trial of Gene Leroy Hart, but was neither fined or jailed by the judge who had cited him for contempt") The hearing lasted three minutes. Judge Whistler, when questioned about the matter, said, "Part of the arrangement is that I don't talk," adding his silence on the matter "wasn't his idea." "Attorneys, Judge Reportedly Work Out Agreement on Contempt Citation." *Daily Oklahoman*, April 18, 1979, at 43 (Internet Archive)

318 Jim Bradshaw, "Girl Scout Slaying Case Goes to Jury in Oklahoma." *Washington Post,* March 30, 1979, at A16 ("Hart wept quietly as his attorneys declared in closing arguments that he was railroaded and alleged that a Kansas convict, Bill Stevens, murdered the little girls").

319 "Letter Arrived Monday." *Claremore Daily Progress,* June 6, 1979, at 6A.

320 Tom Carter, "Gene Leroy Hart Collapses, Dies." *Tulsa World,* June 5, 1979, at A1 ("At the end of the ruling, one juror told a reporter that the panel had made up its mind within five minutes after beginning deliberations").

321 Thom Shanker, "Gene Leroy Hart Summarizes His Life." *Daily Oklahoma,* June 5, 1979, at 10.

322 "Hart Innocent in Girl Scout Murders." *Claremore Daily Progress,* March 30, 1979, at 1.

323 Douglas Hicks, "Hart Innocent; Case Won't Be Reopened." *Tulsa World,* March 31, 1979.

324 Jim Bradshaw, *supra* at A3.

325 Jim Bradshaw, "Girl Scout Slaying Case Goes to Jury in Oklahoma." *Washington Post,* March 30, 1979, at A16.

326 Judy Fossett, "Prosecuting Evidence Seemed 'Mixed Up' Hart Juror Says." *Daily Oklahoman,* April 1, 1979, at 14 (Internet Archive)

327 David Gustafson, "Hart Juror Says 'Things' Didn't Add Up," *The Paper,* June 10, 2002.

328 *Id.*

329 David Gustafson, "Open But Inactive." *The Paper,* July 8, 2002, at 8 ("I've tried to convince myself that Hart could have done it by himself but the facts have proven otherwise in my mind").

330 Judy Fossett, "Prosecution Evidence Seemed 'Mixed Up' Hart Juror Says," *Daily Oklahoman,* April 1, 1979 at 14.

331 Cindy Hale, "Hart Not Guilty." *Daily Times,* March 30, 1979, at 1.

332 "Gene Hart Verdict." *Tulsa World,* March 31, 1979.

333 "Sen. Keating Goads OSBI." *The Oklahoman,* April 4, 1979, at 13 (Internet Archive)

334 Email from Dick Rouse, September 17, 2009.

335 "Oklahoma Girl Scout Murders." http://en.allexperts.com.

336 David MacKenzie, "Gene Leroy Hart's Life of Jail Cells Ends." *Tulsa World,* June 5, 1979, at B1.

337 "Gene Hart Death 'Not Surprising.'" *Daily Times,* June 5, 1979, at 1.

338   Judy Fossett, "'More Hills to Climb,' Hart Faces Other Trials." *Daily Oklahoman,* March 31, 1979, at 53 (Internet Archive); "Gene Hart to Face Escape Trial." *The Oklahoman,* May 5, 1979, at 71 (Internet Archive)

339   "Hart Assigned to General Inmate Section." *Claremore Daily Progress,* April 5, 1979, at 7A.

340   Chuck Erwin, "Hart Disease Took Hart." *Tulsa World,* June 6, 1979, at 1; "Gene Leroy Hart Dies After Heart Attack in Prison." *Washington Post,* June 5, 1979(Lexus-Nexus).

341   "Hart Had Coronary History." *Washington Post,* June 6, 979, at A7 ("The medical examiner refused to speculate if Hart's month long trial added to his heart problem")

342   "Hart Fans Doubt Death Cause." *Claremore Daily Progress,* June 7, 1979, at 10A.

343   Affidavit of Jimmie Don Bunch, May 2, 2007, at 8.

344   Affidavit of Bunch, at 8.

345   Affidavit of Bunch, at 8.

346   Ed Kelley, "Inmate Claims Hart Death Makes Him A Target for Revenge." *Daily Oklahoman,* December 15, 1980, at 34.

347   Ed Edmondson was a long-time United States Congressman from Muskogee, Oklahoma. His brother, J. Howard Edmondson, was Governor of Oklahoma. One of his sons became Oklahoma Attorney General and another a Justice on the Oklahoma Supreme Court. The federal courthouse in Muskogee, Oklahoma is named for Ed Edmondson.

348 David MacKenzie, "Gene Leroy Hart's Life of Jail Cells Ends Peculiarly." *Tulsa World,* June 5, 1979, at B1.

349 "Tragedy or Divine Justice?" *Tulsa World,* June 6, 1979, at 10A.

350 *Id.*

351 "Gene Hart Death 'Not Surprising.'" *The Daily News,* June 5, 1979, at 1.

352 *Id.* Sid Wise spoke of a "higher" law. For a discussion of this concept of a "higher law, *see* Symposium, "Is There A Higher Law? Does It Matter?" 36 *Pepp. L. Rev.* 463–665 (2009). *See specifically* Dallas Willard, "Why It Matters Whether There is A Higher law or Not." 36 *Pepp.L. Rev.* 661 (2009).

353 *Id.*

354 Kim Stott, "If You Want to Tour This Museum, Don't Forget to Make An Appointment." *The Oklahoman,* February 12, 1984, at 8 (Internet Archive)

355 Doug Hicks, "Locust Grove Tired, Hopes Publicity Over." *Tulsa World,* June 6, 1979, at C1.

356 *Id.*

357 David Gustafson, *"Hart Defense Attorney Knows The Truth,"* The Paper, June 24, 2002, at 7.

358 Doug Hicks, "1,000 Mourners Pack Locust Grove Gym for Hart's Funeral." *Tulsa World,* June 9, 1979, at 1.

359 Hart's grave can be viewed on the website, www.find-agrave.com. Hart's tombstone makes no reference to his notoriety. At the Healdton, Oklahoma cemetery, executed death-row inmate Robert Brecheen's grave marker has the following statement: "Man Could Not Forgive But God Could." In Chattanooga, Tennessee,

a cemetery called Pleasant Garden contains the grave of Ed Johnson, a black man who was lynched. His granite marker besides his birth and death dates contains the following: "GOD BLESS YOU ALL, I AM A [sic] INNOCENT MAN. FAREWELL, UNTIL WE MEET AGAIN IN THE SWEET BY AND BY." The graves of Lori, Denise and Michele can also be found on the findagrave website.

360   Charles Sasser, "He Couldn't Forget: Sheriff Pete Weaver Was Haunted By Camp Scott Murders." *The Paper,* July 1, 2002, at 10 ("Gene Leroy Hart was buried within 2 miles of Camp Scott. A simple stone marker in the little Ballou Cemetery near Snake Creek claims for all eternity that Gene Leroy Hart died on June 4, 1979").

361   Brian Barber, "Ellusive Truth; Speculation Still Rampant 20 Years After Slayings." *Tulsa World,* June 9, 1997 (Lexus-Nexus).

362   In the O. J. Simpson matter, the family of murder victim Ronald Goldman filed a civil suit against Simpson. J. Michael Kennedy, "Goldman Sister, Father File Suit." *Los Angeles Times*, May 6, 1995, at A25.

363   "Teens Recall Seeing Strangers at Scout Camp." *Dallas Morning News,* March 21, 1985, p. 52A. Bettye Milner said she did not want to go through a civil suit but did so because her late husband, Walter Milner, a policeman, needed someone to pay for their daughter's death, especially after Gene Leroy Hart was acquitted. "Questions Still Linger 20 Years After Girl Scout Slayings; 3 Raped, Killed at Rural Camp." *Dallas Morning News,* June 10, 1997, at 16D.

364 Ruth Baxter, "Mother Testifies in Scout Trial." *Tulsa Tribune,* March 19, 1985, at C1.

365 Of course, the counselors were asleep at the time the girls were killed. It would not have mattered if tent number eight was visible.

366 "Teens Recall Seeing Strangers at Scout Camp." *Dallas Morning News,* March 21, 1985, at 52A.

367 Ruth Baxter, "Father Recounts Missing Slain Daughter." *Tulsa Tribune,* March 22, 1985, at F1.

368 This remark was certainly objectionable on the grounds of speculation.

369 Coincidently, the jury in the criminal case had been six man, six woman panel.

370 Unlike a criminal jury, a civil jury verdict does not have to be unanimous.

371 Pam Olson, "Shadow of Doubt." *Tulsa World,* June 9, 2002, at 1.

372 Ron Jackson, *supra* at 6A.

373 "Questions Still Linger 20 Years After Girl Scout Slayings: 3 Raped, Killed at Rural Camp." *Dallas Morning News,* June 10, 2007, at 16D.

374 Rhett Morgan, "Pieces of Pryor History Going on Sale." *Tulsa World,* January 27, 2006, 2008 WLNR 151317 ("Decades of chunks of local history will be carted away when the contents of the former Mayes County Courthouse are put on the block")

375 David Harper, "Mom Keeps Low Profile on Girls' Murder Anniversary." *Tulsa World,* June 13, 2007 p. A1. ("Fallis, now 72, said Thursday, he is still convinced of Hart's guilt. Even if the DNA points to another person, Fallis will believe that Hart was also at the scene and involved in the crime, he said").

376   Charles Sasser, "He Couldn't Forget: Sheriff Pete Weaver Was Haunted By Camp Scott Murder." *The Paper,* July 1, 2002, p. 10 (article was a reprint from the *Tulsa Tribune,* November, 1985).

377   Closing Argument Transcript, State of Oklahoma v. Gene Leroy Har, Mayes County District Court (1979).

378   Brian Barber, "Elusive Truth; Speculation Still Rampant 20 Years after Slayings." *Tulsa World,* June 9, 1997 (Lexus-Nexus)

379   Ron Jackson, *supra.*

380   Rob Jackson, "DNA Tests Bring More Questions." *The Oklahoman,* June 25, 2008 at 18A.

381   Ron Jackson, "DNA Tests Bring More Questions." *id.* at 13A.

382   Ron Jackson, *id.* at 18A.

383   *No DNA Clues, Tulsa World,* June 26, 2008, 2008 WLNR 1200, 1330.

384   Ron Jackson, *supra* at 18A.

385   Wayne J. Pitts, David Giacopassi & K. B. Turner, "The Legacy of the O.J. Simpson Trial." 10 *Loy. J.P.Int.J.* 199 (2009).

386   Cahleen Decker and Sheryl Stolberg, "Half of America Disagrees With Verdict.," Los Angeles Times, October 4, 1995, at A1.

387   Brian Barber, "Elusive Truth: Speculation Still Rampant 20 Years After Slayings." *Tulsa World,* June 9, 1997 (Lexus-Nexus)

388   *See* Greg Krikorian, "Blindsided By Fame: Sudden Prominence Was Boon to Some, A Burden to Others, But None Had A Choice." *Los Angeles Times,* October 11, 195, at 52. *See also* Norma Zamichow, "How the Case Changed the Lives It Touched." *id.* at 52.

389   Email from Dick Rouse, September 17, 2009. .

390   For an example of a civil matter handled by Isaacs, *see* Lois Romono, "Records Detail Duncan Priest's Long Trail of Abuse." *Tulsa World,* May 21, 1002, at A1.

391   Email from Creekmore Wallace II, July 26, 2009.

392   Patrick A. "Pat" Williams was a long-time Tulsa, Oklahoma defense attorney. He was a legendary figure in Oklahoma criminal defense. Before he entered private practice, he had worked as a prosecutor for Buddy Fallis.

393   Creekmore Wallace, II ,is best known for his dramatic closing argument given in the state case which charged Terry Nichols with assisting Timothy McVeigh in bombing the Murrah Building. Wallace's punishment phase closing argument is given credit for convincing the jury to impose a life without parole sentence rather than the death penalty.

394   *See* Tim Pratt, "Trooper Found Not Guilty of Fondling Teen." *The Dispatch,* February 6, 2009 ("The jury deliberated for roughly 90 minutes before returning its verdict") The case had ended in a mistrial with a hung jury the first time it was tried. That vote was 10–2 for acquittal.

395   "Former DA Inducted Into Lawyer Group." *Tulsa World,* December 13, 1994, at N11.

396   Bill Braun, "Veteran Judges Taking Their Leave." *Tulsa World,* January 4, 2007, p. A9; "End of an Era: Veteran Judges to Step Down." *Tulsa World,* June 7, 2006, 206 WLNR 9745160.

397   David Gustafson, "Controversial DA Still Has 'No Doubt' of Guilt." *The Paper,* June 17, 2002.

398 "Ex-Mayes County Sheriff 'Pete' Weaver Dies at 71." *Tulsa World,* October 13, 1991 ("Glen 'Pete' Weaver, the former Mayes County Sheriff who received national attention during the investigation of the 1977 Girl Scout Murders, has died, he was 71"). *See also Daily Times,* October 11, 1991, at 1.

399 Ron Jackson, "Murder Case's Lore Mystery Keep Growing." *The Oklahoman,* June 25, 2008 at 20A.

400 "Scout Data Reviewed." *The Oklahoman,* June 8, 1984, at 1 (Internet Archive)'

401 *Id.*

402 Robby Trammell, "Sheriff Vows to Continue Girl Scout Murder Investigation." *The Oklahoma,* June 13, 1984, at 45 (Internet Archive)

403 Griff Palmer, "Sheriff Checking 'Lead' in Girl Scout Slaying." *The Oklahoman,* March 29 1985, at 17 (Internet Archive)

404 Bruce Lambert, "Cathy E. Bennett, Who Pioneered Jury Selection Method, Dies at 41." *New York Times,* June 12, 1992 (Internet) ("Cathy E. Bennett, who pioneered new strategies for picking and persuading juries, died on Tuesday at her home in Galveston, Texas. She was 41 years old").

405 *Id.*

406 Rebecca Ellis Christy, "Cathy Bennett—A Brief Tribute." *Champion,* Dec. 2004, at 96.

407 Jimmie Don Bunch, Affidavit, May 2, 2007.

408 Bunch Affidavit at 1. In this cited portion, Bunch discusses an "association" with Hart during the past thirty-five years. Hart, of course, has been dead sine 1979.

409 Bunch Affidavit at 1.

410 Bunch Affidavit at 1.

411 Bunch Affidavit at 1.

412 Bunch's statements did not differ from the incriminating testimony that Bunch had given at Hart's preliminary hearing.

413 Bunch Affidavit at. 6.

414 Bunch Affidavit at 6.

415 "Question Still Lingers 20 Years After Girl Scout Slayings: 3 Raped, Killed at Rural Camp." *Dallas Morning News,* June 10, 1997, at 16D.

416 David Harper, "Mom Keeps Low Profile on Girls' Murder Anniversary." *Tulsa World,* June 13, 2007, at A1.

listen|imagine|view|experience

AUDIO BOOK DOWNLOAD INCLUDED WITH THIS BOOK!

In your hands you hold a complete digital entertainment package. In addition to the paper version, you receive a free download of the audio version of this book. Simply use the code listed below when visiting our website. Once downloaded to your computer, you can listen to the book through your computer's speakers, burn it to an audio CD or save the file to your portable music device (such as Apple's popular iPod) and listen on the go!

How to get your free audio book digital download:

1. Visit www.tatepublishing.com and click on the e|LIVE logo on the home page.
2. Enter the following coupon code:
   7755-fcba-95e1-5fc7-134d-4dc0-3fcb-a0de
3. Download the audio book from your e|LIVE digital locker and begin enjoying your new digital entertainment package today!